Jon Hassler –

Voice of the Heartland

Jon Hassler –

Voice of the Heartland

A Critical Appraisal
of His Work

Ed Block

NODIN PRESS

ISBN: 978-1-947237-19-3
Cover painting: Jon Hassler

ACKNOWLEDGMENTS
This book would not have been possible without the work and support of Jon Hassler's friend, Joseph Plut, on whose *Conversations with Jon Hassler* I have relied for some of the biographical information. This book also owes a good deal to the hard work of bibliographer extraordinaire, Jim Englert, whose *A Badbattle Bibliography*—which lists almost everything associated with Jon and his work that you can imagine—was a key resource in "fact-checking" many of my citations. I also acknowledge the help and support of numerous book discussion groups with whom I have shared my enthusiasm for Hassler, and, finally, the many students at Marquette University, to whom I first introduced *Staggerford*, and with whom I learned to love and appreciate that too-little known classic and its author.

I am also grateful to Norton Stillman of Nodin Press for publishing this book, and to John Toren for his help with the final form the book has taken.

Library of Congress control number: 2019941456

Nodin Press
5114 Cedar Lake Road
Minneapolis, MN 55416

www.nodinpress.com

Printed in USA

*For my wife and family, who have encouraged me
in this long labor of love.*

Contents

* *A Green Journey,* along with its sequel *Dear James,* is discussed out of chronological order.

INTRODUCTION

This book is a study of the late Minnesota novelist, Jon Hassler's life, career, and work. The opening chapters deal with Hassler's life and growth as a writer; his themes and style; his particular kind of Irish humor. They also look at his Catholicism and his treatment of Native Americans. Then, beginning with his early short stories and the early young adult novel, *Four Miles to Pinecone*, it discusses the novels from *Staggerford* through *The New Woman* and *The Staggerford Murders*.[1] These chapters will frequently refer to characters whom the reader will meet—or has already met—in the various novels. Starting in 1970, Hassler began creating memorable characters in a variety of comedic and tragic situations. A short list, covering just the first three novels, includes Agatha McGee and Miles Pruitt; Simon and Barbara Stearns Shea; Chris Mackensie, Larry and Rachel Quinn. He also introduces a host of memorable minor characters.

This book began as a series of reviews. The difference between a review and a book: the reviewer tries to tell potential readers what to expect. The purpose is to persuade the reader to read the novel. Hence, the reviewer generally does not reveal the parts that will be of greatest interest to a reader. In a book, however, an introduction to the author's work, such as this, the author assumes that the reader may have read some, though probably not all of the works under discussion. Since that may not be the case with all readers, I suggest the following.

Read the first two chapters. The first provides background on Hassler's life; the second, on his development as a writer. Then, if you have not already done so, read one, two, or more of the novels, novellas, or collections of short stories. Come back to the book and read, in any order, the individual chapter or chapters devoted to the work that you just read. In that way you won't blame the author of this book for having "spoiled the suspense" of the particular work. If you choose to read this book without having read any of the novels, a "spoiler alert" is in order. Each chapter includes a brief plot summary of the work under consideration, to provide an overview, and to make the chapter's analysis more understandable. As Jon's friend, Joseph Plut, said in an interview: "the plot is the reason for reading a novel the first time, and then the second time is for everything else about it; the subtleties and the way it's put together" (*C,* 247). This book is devoted to both the plot and "the subtleties and the way it's put together" as they occur in all of Hassler's work.

Born in 1933, Jon Hassler was not, technically, a "baby boomer." But his novels span an era (1944 to roughly 2000) with which most "boomers" will be familiar – at first hand, or through memories of their parents. He is, therefore, an author of and for the "boomer generation," but he is also an author for anyone willing to experience that particular world. He is also an author whose sense of humor—as well as a wicked sense of satire—can reawaken a sense of mirth in an era when humor seems often either superficial or downright destructive.

What, one might ask, would persuade a person to read a book about a novelist whose first novel was published in 1977, and whose last appeared only three years before his death in 2008? What might persuade a person to read a novel published over thirty years ago? One might as well ask: what persuades anyone to read (or reread) *Gone With the Wind*, Shakespeare, or that favorite Victorian novel? The easy answer is: to experience a world different than one's own. For some, raised on the internet and popular fiction, reading Hassler may be like an earlier twentieth-century generation reading that Victorian novel. Except Hassler reads more easily; almost "effortlessly" – as award-winning novelist Richard Russo once said of Hassler's novels. Without extra effort, a Hassler novel makes you slow down, savor details, take interest in character, setting, and the nuances of plot. No Jane Austen or Charles Dickens, Hassler is, nevertheless, better than some authors who have already been included in the *Library of America*. His novels are also just plain fun to read.

Reading Hassler also provides an opportunity to marvel at the insight (and prescience) of a genuinely gifted and humane writer, and to watch a craftsman develop the skills and techniques of a fiction writer, at the micro-level of changing viewpoint, changing tones, varied pace, and a host of other "writerly" tricks. Put another way: (and it is almost a truism, if not a cliché): a good book teaches you how to read it. Jon Hassler's novels teach you how to read again. No more frenetic page turning; no more painful, post-modern searching in vain to find a non-existent plot. As the critic in the *New York Times Book Review* who said *The Love Hunter* was a novel "to restore your faith in fiction," Hassler is a writer you can approach with confidence and lack of fear or anxiety. Not that his novels don't have their share of bizarre, grotesque, and sometimes genuinely tragic events. But what his novels teach us is that patient attention to the details of everyday life reveals an element of mystery that anyone can find, even in the mundane world in which we find ourselves immersed. In that way, we find *ourselves* in new ways.

Jon Hassler celebrates the (un)common woman and man. That fanfare—sometimes a satiric raspberry—nevertheless reverences all it touches. Not the sensationally marginal, odd, or deviant, but the uncommon in every one of us. Not Flannery O'Connor's redneck or fundamentalist, but the greatness of America's vast and often struggling middle classes. He does this by focusing his sustained attention on them, for more than a caricaturist's moment of fiendish glee.[2] Hassler's attention paid to detail is both a way to temper satire *and* avoid sentimentality. For instance, in his first novel, *Staggerford*, Hassler introduces a minor character whom he describes as a "giant" state patrolman. Yes, this patrolman appears, for awhile, as "larger than life." In time, however, the narrator sees him in a motel room. Suddenly, the larger than life becomes a part of our everyday world. That sustained attention can be like the attention that the French philosopher and writer, Simone Weil, said that we all should devote to one another: *caring* attention. Hassler even gives such caring attention to his villains; their vulnerabilities, their similarities to us.

Years ago the Pulitzer Prize-winning novelist, Wallace Stegner, observed that American literature is sick. He was referring to the cynicism, barbarism, and nihilism of much contemporary fiction. We need only look at a sampling of prominent novels from the 70s, 80s, 90s, and even the current decades. And while the situation may *seem* to have changed somewhat with "globalization" and the influx of fiction from around the world, a closer look will reveal that angst, unrest, and anger still remain, like a coating of grease atop our ice cream dreams. In turning to Jon Hassler the reader will find a different approach to the problems and tragedies that beset our times. That different approach involves hope and care, and close attention to the world.

According to French novelist, Gustave Flaubert, everything becomes interesting if you look at it long enough. Having looked at Jon Hassler and his work for so long (since the early 1990s), I find that almost everything in his work has proved interesting in some way. I have tried not to inflict that intense interest on readers by overanalyzing his work. But where I have, please accept this apology, and consider it an expression of admiration for Hassler and his work, and a possible inducement to the reader to "look at it long enough" and perhaps see many of the same things.

Jon Hassler –

Voice of the Heartland

1

BIOGRAPHY[1]

Jon Hassler was born on March 30, 1933 in Minneapolis, Minnesota. His father, Leo Blaise Hassler, was a grocer of Bavarian background: his mother, Helen (Callinan), was Irish and a part-time music teacher and store clerk. She was "the eldest daughter of the eldest daughter of Irish immigrants, and so had two generations of hard work, religious zeal, and a gradually improving lifestyle to model her own life on."[2] Within a year of his birth, Hassler and his family moved to Staples, a small town in central Minnesota, where Mr. Hassler managed a Red Owl grocery. In "Remembering Churches" Hassler records a memory, at the age of four, of his mother pulling him in a sled and stopping at Sacred Heart Church.[3] His cousin, Bunny Horner, who came to live with the family when Hassler was two, would take Hassler to a local movie theater for the week's feature, but he and Cousin Bunny were sometimes asked to leave because of Hassler's wailing at the sad parts in such films as *Heidi*. In *Good People* Hassler tells an anecdote of his mother and cousin Bunny repeating the word "mortified" and laughing uncontrollably. Referring to his parents and Bunny, he says, "The power of words was only one of several things I learned from these three good people who doted on me as a child. The magnetism of stories was another" (*GP*, 9-10). Another favorite relative was a great-aunt named Elizabeth. She was an unmarried school teacher who spent a number of summers with the Hasslers, and who, he says, taught Hassler table manners and other things.

Hassler jokingly says that his mother, who read to him every evening on the couch, first betrayed him by leaving him in kindergarten (three days late because he had had chickenpox). He also credits her with having trained his powers of observation. "My mother was forever pointing out things and places to me, especially funny things, eccentric people … I think I learned to pay attention to things through her eyes."[4] In his writer's memoir, *My Staggerford Journal*, Hassler says, "I can trace my desire to be a writer back to the age of five when I was being read to by my parents and cousins and uncles and aunts."[5]

He tells of having been locked in a closet at school on that first day of kindergarten, by "two boys, lying in wait for a timid newcomer … I've come to think of this event as emblematic of my schooling." A bit later he notes, "From that day through graduate school, with very few exceptions, I never entered a classroom with anything but the heavy heart of a prisoner, dreading the hour of stultifying tedium that lay ahead. Obviously I was never much of a student. Only two things kept me interested in school: football and library books."

The Hasslers lived for ten years in Staples, where Jon attended Catholic schools for four years. Hassler said, "I recall Sister Constance saying that, because playing came naturally to children, we served God by playing." Sounding a lot like the narrator in *Staggerford*, Hassler describes his belief from those days in Catholic grade school. "I was a champion believer in those days. I believed every fact, myth, and holy opinion taught me during those first years of parochial school. I believed in the Communion of Saints, the Knights of Columbus, the multiplication tables, and life everlasting."[6]

After ten years in Staples, the Hasslers returned to Minne-apolis, where Mr. Hassler took a job in a munitions plant (it was still WW II). Hassler's recollections of life on South Aldrich Avenue in Minneapolis, living with the elder Callinans, empha-size the family's piety. "Surely our household of five went to Mass every Sunday (a serious strain of religious devotion came down to me out of Bavaria on my father's side of the family, out of Ireland on my mother's side)." Referring to the summer of 1943, he recalls learning to love the old hymn, "Tantum Ergo" and lighting votive candles. "This was also the year," he says, "that my sainted grandmother, in that very church, was refused absolution and cast out of the confessional by a roaring priest whose name we never learned and whose form of insanity we speculated about for years afrter we left the city."[7]

Hassler said his paternal grandmother Elizabeth was "a pio-neer." Calling her an "angel of mercy" for her acts of charity in the community, Hassler remembered her as "large, strong, and resourceful." He believed her "unquestioning faith in God" was the kind of belief common to that generation. Grandfather Au-gust Hassler, on the other hand, appeared to Hassler as a pioneer too, but "a man who had cracked under the strain," and who was "someone who'd snuffed out his vital spark well before he died." Hassler's maternal grandfather Callinan had worked on the rail-road and spent a number of years with the family. He was an Irish storyteller and sang songs about his time on the railroad. Hassler says his grandfather's stories were "retold with such frequency that he grew tired of listening to them." Hassler would later tell how, when he was thirteen, his eighty-year old grandfather took him on a train trip to Oshkosh, Wisconsin. The train was filled with soldiers in uniform on their way to Camp McCoy, Wisconsin. "All those within earshot grew deferential toward Grandfather as he spun out his skein of railroad stories, pointing out the fact that we were traveling the very same roadbed he had traveled as a young conductor on the Milwaukee Road" (GP, 12).

When Hassler was ten, the family moved to Plainview, where his father bought and operated another Red Owl store. Hassler says that he learned about story-telling—and learned many stories—while hanging around in his father's store. "My father's grocery store was my theater." An anecdote in "Remembering Churches" (which has little to do with churches)[8] tells of the mischievous Timmy Musser who orders Jon, a fifth-grader in a new town, to join him in some mischief, and how Hassler, because he had learned obedience from the nuns, ended up obeying Timmy Musser as well, and participating in the mischief. It was Timmy's plan to derail a train, and though the plan never succeeded, the experience left an indelible imprint on Hassler's memory. It was in Plainview, as well, that Hassler became an altar boy and, from watching various parish priests, acquired a number of the memories about priests that he would use in his fiction. He briefly considered becoming a priest, but he thought he was "too dumb." He also built model airplanes and lit them on fire before setting them off flying, something he has a character in *Grand Opening* do. He played center on the Plainview High School football team in the year it won the Whitewater League championship, defeating St. Charles high school forty-nine to nothing, an event that he compared to the excitement he felt when his agent sold his first two novels.

Another insight into his character at about this time comes in an interview about his memoir, *Good People: from an Author's Life*. Referring to some of his childhood adventures in Plainview, Hassler's comment says a lot about what made him a writer. "With my proclivity for patient watchfulness, I would always play the role of the idle bystander. I could thrill to tales of derring-do, and I could admire sainthood, but I'd never come close to either end of the morality scale." In high school, he says,

I secretly read a lot of poetry. Secretly, because poetry, like all artistic pursuits in that little town, in that day and age, was considered entirely feminine and I didn't want to be known

as a sissy. My friends let me get by with playing the piano, because I was on the football team, and because men were occasionally shown playing the piano in the movies.[9]

He speaks of loving poets with three names, like Edwin Arlington Robinson and Henry Wadsworth Longfellow. He says he memorized a lot of poetry and even recited it, for instance, while doing the job he held in his high school years; mowing the grass in a local cemetery.

In 1951 he matriculated at St. John's University in Collegeville, Minnesota, north of St. Cloud. He took business classes in college but couldn't grasp accounting. He tells of taking world literature from a Fr. Dunstan Tucker, O.S.B. Fr. Tucker criticized the didacticism, mawkishness and sentimentality of one of Hassler's favorites, Henry Wadsworth Longfellow. Hassler also tells of reading lots of Graham Greene, Flannery O'Connor, and Evelyn Waugh; and of having learned to write from everybody from Shakespeare to J.D. Salinger. In chapter six of *Good People*, Hassler also refers to another St. John's faculty member, Steven B. Humphrey, who further nurtured his love for literature, and in whom he found a model for his teaching. "It was in his fiction class that I gained an immediate fondness for Hemingway, Fitzgerald, and Greene and developed a lifelong hunger to know what the latest of my contemporaries is writing." Summarizing Humphrey's influence, Hassler says, "He topped off my education as a reader, taking my interest in literature, which dated back to my early childhood, and shaping it into a vital and lasting companionship" (*GP*, 53).

After graduation, in August, 1955, he began teaching high school English in Melrose, Minnesota, living at home with his parents. He hated the pressure, and the discord in the school sometimes drove him to vomit in the alley before school began. After a year he took a job in Fosston, Minnesota, where he taught from 1956-1959. Of this predominantly Lutheran community, he says, "It was like moving from Rome to Oslo."

Hassler married Marie Schmitt on August 18, 1956. They had three children, Michael, Elizabeth and David. While at Fosston he met and became friends with Bob Nielsen, another teacher, who later died of multiple sclerosis and who became one model for Larry Quinn, a central character in Hassler's third novel, *The Love Hunter*. In Fosston, Jon also became friends with Dennis Nelson, who taught him to hunt ducks, and who—with his wife—are also models for the Quinns.

It was also while in Fosston that Hassler heard the story of a band teacher in nearby Clearbrook, Minnesota, who was secretly married to one of his students, but who continued to live at home with her mentally unstable mother. One day, when the band teacher was returning his wife to her home, the deranged mother shot and wounded him. The band teacher got to his car and tried to drive home but crashed and died on the way (*MSJ*, 10). This event became the kernel for Hassler's first novel, *Staggerford*. In 1959 Hassler went to teach in Park Rapids, where he stayed until 1965. Later he would say, "I made Park Rapids the setting for *Staggerford*." During those years he also ran the local drive-in theater during the summer, which was an experience that might account for the number of movie allusions in his novels. Minnesota had around eighty drive-in theaters at its peak in the 1950's.

Hassler earned his Master's degree from the University of North Dakota in 1960, where he wrote a thesis on moral decision-making in Hemingway's novels. Hassler said he had read all of Hemingway's novels numerous times, and in *My Staggerford Journal* he refers to imitating Hemingway's objective style of narrative, before editors and the examples of fiction in *The New Yorker* and other prominent literary magazines showed a preference for "editorializing" narrators who commented on and told the reader how to interpret various elements in the stories (*MSJ*, 17-18).

In the 1960s he also wrote a number of poems, even publishing a chapbook titled *The Red Oak*.[10] A favorite poet was Theodore Roethke. Other favorites included Richard Hugo, Ted Kooser, and Philip Larkin. Friend and former colleague, Dan Lange, said, "Jon loved poetry. It might be Shakespeare, Emily Dickinson, Dylan Thomas, or Billy Collins; whenever people got together with Jon, he would almost always read poetry. Sometimes at the beginning of the night, sometimes at the end, or in the car on the way to wherever the group were going, he would read a poem from memory or from a printed copy. Robert Frost's, 'Nothing Gold Can Stay' was one of his favorites; so much so, that it was recited at his funeral."

Hassler left high school teaching and taught from 1965 to 1968 at Bemidji State University. In the "Whimsical Roots," chapter of *Good People*, he tells of six colleagues at Bemidji State as they faced the uncertainty of keeping their jobs, but because he was not interested in getting a doctorate, his future there was limited. As a result, in 1968, he took a job at Brainerd Community College, where he taught until 1980. During this period Marie worked at a hospital pharmacy in Brainerd. It was while at Brainerd that Hassler determined to become a writer. In a story repeated many times, he describes how on September 10, 1970, at age thirty-seven, he took a notebook to school and "after my eight o'clock class, I began to write a story called 'A Story Worth Hearing'." Thereafter, he wrote whenever he could. "I wrote on weekends, nights, mornings before school, summers —whenever I could fit it in."

On a dare with a fellow teacher, he determined to write a short story every two weeks. At the end of twenty-eight weeks he had fourteen stories. At the end of five years he had eighty-five rejection slips, and six published stories, including "The Undistinguished Poet," in *South Dakota Review* (C, 24).[11] This short story introduced Agatha McGee, one of Mr. Hassler's most beloved characters. Hassler describes some of his early writing failures and successes in "Agatha McGee, John Milton, and I," an article he published in *South Dakota Review* in 1995.

Another story he told a number of times involved his admiration for John Cheever. He says he loved Cheever's sentences and sought to imitate them. He would copy out Cheever's sentences longhand, "hoping that his skill with the sentence would go up my arm and into my brain."[12] He was still reading Cheever as he began his second novel, *Simon's Night*, and his journal of the time comments on Cheever's last novel, *Falconer*, the story of a murderer who escapes from prison. Other favorite fiction writers were Flannery O'Connor, Evelyn Waugh, Kingsley Amis, Alice Munro, and William Trevor. He speaks of admiring Hemingway's descriptions of nature. He also saw and liked the work of Irish playwright Brian Friel. In the classroom Hassler taught courses in composition, grammar, and literature. From allusions in his novels it would appear that he taught a traditional syllabus of authors and works in fiction, poetry, and drama.

Before he began writing seriously, he took up oil painting as a way to make extra money. In his August 3, 1975 entry of *My Staggerford Journal* he records, "It was ten years ago this month that I began painting…" The journal tells about his passion for painting, and how he would go to malls and craft fairs to sell oil paintings and water color miniatures. He also compares painting and writing (*MSJ*, 24). In 1968 he met Joseph Plut, a colleague at Brainerd Community College. In 1971 Plut agreed to speak at an art appreciation class that Jon was teaching in Wadena, Minnesota.

In the 1970s, Hassler began visiting the Blue Cloud Benedictine Abbey in Marvin, South Dakota. Brother Benet Tvedten, O.S. B. tells the following anecdote about Hassler and the Abbey. "Jon Hassler visited Blue Cloud Abbey for the first time in 1973. He returned every year to spend a week working on whichever manuscript was occupying him at the moment. On an evening near the end of the week, he would read for the monks and guests what he had accomplished during his time at the abbey. An excerpt from a journal Hassler kept while visiting Blue Cloud exhibits his characteristic perceptiveness and insight.

> *I ate breakfast this morning with a charming redhead named Rachel, a junior social studies major from Pasadena. She wants to be a farmer-writer. And now, Brother Gene is lecturing the students [from Gustavus Adolphus, a Lutheran college in St. Peter, MN] on the monastic life. They are gathered in the lobby down the hall from my room, and I hear his husky voice as he describes the Rule of St. Benedict and the ordered day of the monk. It occurs to me that the Benedictines have survived for 1500 years by paying attention to form. Lots of form in their lives. Lots of ordered routine. More than necessary, it might seem to an outsider. But maybe that's why they've endured. Maybe if they'd grown careless about form, the substance would have disintegrated and there would be no abbeys for people like me and the Gustavians to visit."*

At Brainerd Hassler became acquainted with Mark Bunsness, the real-life model for Fred Vandergar, the *Staggerford* teacher who dies of cancer. Hassler acknowledges that some of the journal entries included in *Staggerford* are his own, from when he taught at Brainerd (*C*, 8). He speaks of filling thirty-four notebooks; with "not one abstract thought" among them, but only "concrete observations." The notebooks started as carbon copies of letters sent to a long-time writer and artist, a St. John's classmate, Dick Brook, who at the time lived and worked in New Hampshire. At Brainerd Jon also made the acquaintance of Lavina and Ray Erickson. Lavina worked with the local theatrical group, and she became another model for Rachel Quinn in *The Love Hunter*.

In *My Staggerford Journal* Hassler tells of his apprehensions as he determined to apply for a sabbatical in 1975. Peg Meier describes the decision: "He took a sabbatical in 1975-76, moved into his nonwinterized [sic] cabin seventy-five miles northwest of Brainerd that October and started what became *Staggerford*. It was based on diaries he had kept of his real-life teaching experiences." Meier also notes the downside of this decision. "Hassler had no idea at the time that he was putting his teaching and his family behind him. His first marriage, to the mother of his three children, didn't survive many years beyond *Stagggerford*. As he put it, 'I did nothing to help it by closing myself up in the garage all evening during the school year and retreating to the cabin most of the summers.'"

In spring, 1976, Hassler mailed the completed manuscript of *Staggerford* to his agent, Harriet Wasserman, and left for a vacation in England and Ireland with Joe Plut. He learned that both *Staggerford* and *Four Miles to Pinecone* had been accepted for publication within ten days of each other (*LCJM*, 2002, 40). Hassler says he took five years to write *Four Miles to Pinecone*, rewriting it each summer until he got it right. But it appeared after *Staggerford* because the publisher reviewing *Four Miles to Pinecone* temporized until it was learned that *Staggerford* had been bought. *Staggerford* won a number of awards, and, in time, earned him two invitations to the White House, at the request of Hillary Rodham Clinton.

Following the publication of *Staggerford*, Hassler went to work on his second novel, *Simon's Night*, the story of a retired English professor named Simon Shea, which appeared in 1979. Thereafter, Hassler would publish a novel approximately every two years for the next two decades. In 1980 he published *Jemmy*, about a mixed Ojibwe and Caucasian teenage girl, a novel of some 150 pages, which the publisher listed as "young adult fiction" but which, except possibly for length, deserves to be included among his serious adult fiction. In 1980 Hassler was also awarded a Guggenheim Fellowship. Robert Spaeth, the dean of St. John's University, was responsible for inviting Hassler to spend his fellowship year at St. John's. They soon became friends, Hassler calling him "the wittiest man I ever knew." Spaeth visited Hassler's cabin, and together they would spend hours on their typewriters, Spaeth "churning out articles and book reviews while [Hassler] proceeded with my fiction."

At home, however, Hassler's marriage was dissolving. Readers who care to can find suggestions of marital difficulties, children's problems with drugs, and the like, throughout his fiction. In *Good People*, he refers to this time; how his wife, Marie, had "sieges of depression" and was hospitalized; how their three children were often cared for by his parents, his oldest son, Mike, spending ten years with them. He later received an annulment from Marie. He also speaks of visiting both his father and his mother in the hospital as they lay dying, in each case sitting with them as he revised a work of fiction, "my device for warding off grief" (*GP*, 20). *The Love Hunter*, about the friendship of two teachers, one of whom has multiple sclerosis, was published in 1981. Among its many incidents, the satiric account of duck-hunting in Canada, was taken from a real duck hunt that Hassler had treated his son David to, after David's high school graduation. Hassler says he wrote thirty pages in one of his journals following the trip, and then lifted them from the journal when he came to write the novel. (*C*, 67, 73).

Of Hassler's time at St. John's, Rebecca Hill says, "When I met him, he was living in a dormitory at the college. He thrived among the academic and monastic Benedictines, since women and children were, for him, two of the traps writers faced. He had obtained an annulment from his long marriage, and saw raising kids as burdensome." Hassler taught at St. John's for another seventeen years, before retiring as Emeritus Professor of literature and creative writing, and where he had been "writer in residence" for several years. Hill tells an interesting story about Hassler at St. John's. For some misbehavior on a young fellow-teacher's part, Hassler sent him a note with a "black spot," a pirate sign of ostracism, suggesting Hassler's familiarity with

Robert Louis Stevenson's classic boy's tale, *Treasure Island*. In those years at St. John's he published three more novels, *A Green Journey* (1985), *Grand Opening* (1987), and *North of Hope* (1990). His experiences, and many of the stories he heard at St. John's, became material to be used in many of those novels. Another story about Dean Robert Spaeth relates to those years. "I remember so well the time I spent touring Italy and England with Bob and his wife, Betty, and being constantly buoyed by his witty observations virtually every time we turned a corner" (*GP*, 80). One of the trips to Italy became the inspiration for Hassler's *Dear James*.

In 1986 Hassler entered into a brief marriage with Elizabeth Anderson. Rebecca Hill tells it like this. "In 1986, he got married—having twice cancelled within 24 hours of the wedding day—to the writer Elizabeth Anderson, 23 years his junior. The marriage lasted less than a year, and ended in agony for both." Hassler later told Joseph Plut that he had dedicated *Grand Opening* to Elizabeth "because she deserved it" (*C*, 118).

In July, 1986, Ballantine re-issued, in paperback, all of Jon's novels to date. In 1987 he published *Grand Opening*, the only novel placed in the historical past—the last year of WWII. He received the Best Fiction of 1987 award from the Society of Midland Authors, for *Grand Opening*. The novel is based on his family's experience owning the grocery store in Plainview. Hill tells an interesting story about *Grand Opening*.

> *When his novel* Grand Opening *was twice rejected by Harvey Ginsberg, his editor at William Morrow, Jon buried it—here we're talking a shovel and brogans—in his yard. He found his own impulses as amusing as any of his characters, but he unswervingly did what peace of mind required. He said if the novel could sprout a few shoots on its own, it might be worth rescuing. It must have done so. He dug up the novel a year later, pruned it, and Harvey published it ("Remembering Jon Hassler").*

In 1990 Hassler published *North of Hope*. It was, he says, the culmination of years of "priest-watching." It was also the first novel he wrote using a word processor. That fact, he said, might account for its substantially greater length. While at St. John's, Hassler became acquainted with the renowned Catholic writer, J. F. Powers, and his wife, Betty Wahl. Powers and he would sometimes see each other at afternoon mass, and they talked occasionally, though rarely about each other's work. Hassler later wrote an appreciative memoir of their acquaintanceship in chapter eight of *Good People*. Hassler also gave the eulogy at Powers' funeral at St. John's in 1999. An article in *America* magazine by Fr. Andrew Greeley[13] made a review of *North of Hope* the occasion to introduce Hassler's work to a wider Catholic audience.

Hassler met special education teacher and widow, Gretchen Kresl, and married her in 1993. Gretchen had raised three children after the death of her husband. She valued individuality, beautiful cities, the arts, and politics. She took notice of effort and talent whether in a garden, a musical performance, or a child's painting. Calling her a soulmate, Hassler and she enjoyed fifteen happy years together. It was in 1993 as well, according to Minnesota author Mark Vinz, that the Blue Cloud Literary began. The first festival was held at Blue Cloud Abbey that autumn. The annual festival lasted ten years, and Hassler attended all of them, accompanied by Gretchen. He was unable to read at the last festival; so Brother Benet Tvedten read his story for him.

In May of 1993 Hassler made a first visit to the White House at the invitation of Hillary Rodham Clinton. He was invited back two years later following the publication of *Rookery Blues* (C, 203). In 1993 Hassler received an honorary doctorate from Assumption College in Massachusetts. It was also in 1993 that Hassler was diagnosed with what he would at first describe as rigid-muscle Parkinson's Disease. In time his

condition was specified as a Parkinson-like disease called supranuclear palsy. In 1994 Hassler received a second honorary
doctorate, from the University of North Dakota, where he had
done his master's degree.

Hassler published the first of two "campus" novels, *Rookery
Blues* in 1995. In 1996 he went public with the news of his
disease, at least in part to support Struther's Parkinson's Center
of Minneapolis, where he was under treatment for the disease.
It was in the same year that he received an honorary doctorate from Notre Dame University. He and Joe Plut discuss the
honorary degree in connection with Hassler's having included
in *Dear James* a character, Fr. Gene deSmet, who is described
wearing a "Fighting Irish" t-shirt. Plut asks Hassler whether the
mention of Notre Dame in the novel accounted for the honorary degree. Hassler said, "I hope not. I don't think it had anything to do with it, Joe" (*C*, 178). He then tells how Fr. Edward
Malloy, then president of Notre Dame, had been teaching Hassler's books in class, and that it was Fr. Malloy who had recommended him for the honorary degree (*C*, 179).

Also in 1996, as part of a series of book signings, Hassler gave
a reading from his works at Marquette University, in Milwaukee,
Wisconsin. There I interviewed him for a piece that later appeared in *Image* magazine. In 1998 he published *The Dean's List*,
a sequel to *Rookery Blues*, and contributed an autobiographical
chapter to a collection titled *Why I am Still A Catholic*. In 1999
he published *My Staggerford Journal*, a writer's journal-memoir
of the year's sabbatical during which he wrote his first novel. In
the late nineties Hassler and his wife began spending a number
of weeks each winter in their townhouse in Melbourne Beach,
Florida. Before the supranuclear palsy restricted his mobility,
he also led a number of European literary tours, and taught a
number of writing workshops. These included trips to Antigua,
Guatemala, and a writing tour of Tuscany in 1997. In 1999 and
2000, Afton Press, a small Minnesota publisher, brought out

Underground Christmas and two collections of Hassler's early stories, *Keepsakes* and *Rufus at the Door and Other Stories*.

Sally Childs, an English teacher with an MFA in theater, and founder of the Lyric Theater in Minneapolis, adapted and directed a number of plays based on Hassler's novels. Her first production was *Simon's Night* at the Lyric Theater in 1991. Chris Samuelson began and Hassler himself completed an adaptation of *Grand Opening* that was produced at the Lyric in 1996, the same year that an adaptation of *Jemmy* was produced. *Dear James* followed in 1997, and in 1999 Dwight Callaway directed an adaptation of *The Staggerford Murders*. The John Hassler Theater opened in Plainview, MN in 2000. *Grand Opening, Simon's Night, Dear James*, and a rewrite of *The Staggerford Murders* all played at the theater, as well as Childs' adaptation of *Rookery Blues*, which was produced with funding from the National Endowment for the Arts. *Theater in the Round* of Minneapolis brought *Grand Opening* back to the stage in October, 2018.

In 2003 Hassler donated a portion of his papers to Saint John's University. That same year Saint John's presented Hassler with the 10th annual Colman Barry Award for Distinguished Contributions to Religion and Society. In 2004 Penguin Plume published *The Staggerford Murders*, a collection of two novellas, *The Staggerford Murders* and *The Life and Death of Nancy Clancy's Nephew*, both adapted from earlier short stories. Together, Hassler and his wife published *Stories Teachers Tell* in 2004. Hassler was interviewed and spotlighted in Minneapolis and St. Paul publications and on TV shows. Hassler also intended to publish a memoir, *Days Like Smoke*, but that project was never completed. In his last years, Hassler was unable to travel, give readings, or conduct tours. He spent much of each day in a motorized wheel chair, but he continued a regular schedule of writing insofar as he was able. He completed the manuscript of an autobiographical novel, *Jay O'Malley*, shortly before his death on March 20, 2008 in Minneapolis. He was buried from the

Basilica of St. Mary's in Minneapolis on March 27. Joseph Plut delivered the eulogy.

In 2010 Joseph Plut published *Conversations with Jon Hassler*, a series of interviews that covers the first nine of Hassler's novels. I am indebted to Joe's book for some of the background to specific novels. In July, 2015 Joe organized the Jon Hassler Festival in Brainerd, Minnesota to celebrate the author's life. I gave the keynote address. Due to illness, Jon's wife Gretchen could not attend the festival. She died in Minneapolis in September of that year. At the festival, the Central Lakes Community College Library in Brainerd was designated a National Literary Landmark, and the library was renamed The Jon Hassler Library in his honor. The room contains additional Hassler papers.

2

HASSLER'S GROWTH AS A WRITER

My *Staggerford Journal,* Hassler's journal of the year when he wrote that first novel, is full of humor, detail, and insights into the writing process that will interest beginning writers and reward anyone interested in Hassler and his work. In the first sentence of the "Introduction" he says, "I can trace my desire to be a writer back to the age of five when I was being read to by my parents and cousins and uncles and aunts" (*MSJ*, 3). When, years later, Hassler was asked whether anyone had suggested that he become a writer, he said, "Nobody ever recommended I write. I don't think a teacher ever did. I wanted to write all my life, I'm sure, but I never told anybody." Hassler says he learned to write without the help of teacher or mentor, though he does credit a former St. John's classmate, Dick Brook, and a younger colleague, Jim Casper, with whom he shared much of his early writing (*MSJ*, 11).

Hassler says he read and wrote poetry in high school. Otherwise, he wrote very little until the year 1970, when he determined to do what he had always wanted to do: try to be a writer. But before that day, and for more than fifteen years, he had taught English in high school and community college.

19

He taught grammar, composition, and all genres of literature. Before beginning *Staggerford* during his sabbatical year from teaching at Brainerd Community College, he took a trip to New England, where he visited literary sites connected with Nathaniel Hawthorne, Ralph Waldo Emerson, Henry David Thoreau, and Emily Dickinson. He also read a number of authors: Flannery O'Connor, John Cheever, and, as noted, all the novels of Ernest Hemingway for his Master's degree. As the previous chapter notes, he loved Cheever's sentences. As will become clear, he also learned other lessons, including the way to write "domestic satire," from Cheever's short stories. As late as 1997 he admitted he still read Cheever. "Just yesterday I picked up his journals and I began to read again. Just for the sake of wallowing in the lovely prose he writes. Not that I liked his subjects or his people so much but it was his sentence structure. I think of him as my mentor, although I never met him. I just kept imitating him" ("Colleges," p. 35). He also mentions reading Evelyn Waugh, Kinglsey Amis, William Trevor, and Alice Munro in almost the same breath as Cheever. Asked what he got from each of them, he told his friend, Joseph Plut, "With William Trevor it's the story. William Trevor gets to the heart of the character faster than anybody I ever read … Alice Munro—it's the same thing—it's the story with her. She puts so much into her stories it's like she's saying to you, 'When you write, don't hold anything back'" ("Colleges," p. 35).

A perceptive review of William Trevor's *Last Stories* by Cynthia Ozick is informative.[1] Ozick notes, "His [Trevor's] stories are uncontaminated by principles of composition or even by respectable generalities touching on how sentences ought to be made." About Trevor's use of detail, she says, "If there are flowers in pots on a windowsill or in someone's small garden, he will patiently identify each one," then adds, "He records the names of streets and neighborhoods, of restaurants and pubs. He tells minutely how women and men are dressed, the color, the cloth, the fit." About the relationship of structure and detail, she says, "Most notably, his stories open with comments so blandly informational, so plain and unnoticeable, that they arouse no expectation and appear to promise little." Hassler may have adapted these techniques as he sought to render the everyday feel, the everyday details of life in northern Minnesota in the 70s, 80s, and 90s. One could argue that for each writer detail is a key component of style.

With reference to one Trevor story, "Making Conversation," Ozick observes something else about Trevor's style that also connects with Hassler. In the story a woman, "besotted with her sister's bridegroom," touches his cap, which makes her wish that she could die. Ozick observes that "This odd and fleeting fragment slips in from nowhere, to drip with poison; such subtle intrusions are Trevor's way." This intrusion suggests a form of digression, and digression, we shall see, is a key component of almost everything Hassler wrote.

Hassler is unlike Trevor in one important respect. Of Trevor's stories Ozick says, "Here you will experience no flashes of culminating revelation, none of those so-called epiphanies that decorate the endings of so many workshop products." In the coming chapters we shall see that Hassler, too, is careful about sentimental or unearned consolation. But a sense of revelation and consolation is one of the rare features that distinguishes Hassler's writing from that of not only William Trevor, but many another American author of the late twentieth and early twenty-first centuries.

Late in his life Hassler was still crediting authors like Cheever, Waugh, Trevor, Munro, and Carol Shields (C, 246). He also read and praised the work of another formidable Catholic writer of the mid-twentieth century, Graham Greene. Some might claim that Hassler got his taste for paradox, irony, betrayal, and a view of the world's squalor from Greene, but he makes each of these traits or themes his own. Hassler's betrayals, for instance,

are always betrayals of persons, not necessarily or primarily betrayals of principles. The irony is more obvious, and the paradox more carefully structured—as contrasts of situation, tone,
or theme. But Hassler read these authors as an aspiring writer.
From Cheever, as he said, he learned to construct sentences.
In his mature writing, Hassler's sentences rarely exceed twenty-four words in length. This gives his style a lean and supple
quality. Hassler also learned a lot about authorial "intrusions."
In *My Staggerford Journal* he talks about how he tried to write
like Hemingway; the narrator as "fly on the wall." But then he
learned that readers—and, even more, editors—wanted to hear
the narrator's view.

The Beginning

As noted above, it was in September, 1970 that Hassler began
his career as a writer. After an eight a.m. class at Brainerd Community College, he took a notebook to the campus library and
began "A Story Worth Hearing." Thereafter, he determined to
write a story every two weeks. After five years he had six published stories and eighty-five rejection slips. But of the stories
published, one caught the attention of an agent, Harriet Wasserman, who said she would be interested if he ever wrote a
novel. Hassler tells the story of *Staggerford*'s beginning in *My
Staggerford Journal*. Having laid aside a 174 page manuscript
tentatively titled "The Willowby Uprising," he went back to it
at the start of his sabbatical and found it more promising (*MSJ*,
16). During that sabbatical year (1975-76) he worked on the
manuscript, completing it on April 3, 1976.

About the time he began writing in earnest, Hassler also
took up painting. *My Staggerford Journal* relates how he would
paint Minnesota landscapes and sell them at local malls and craft
fairs. It was his interest in art that brought him together with
fellow St. John's graduate, Joseph Plut, who became a lifelong
friend. For awhile Hassler was torn between pursuing an artistic

or a writing career, but in time he turned his full attention to writing. His artistic eye, however, never left him, and a number of his novels use art or allusions to art in significant ways.

Work Habits

My Staggerford Journal describes his work habits, writing daily, taking few breaks; resenting interruptions like family life and obligations. Like novelist Marilynne Robinson, he couldn't wait to get back to his characters. A passage from *My Staggerford Journal* for April 13, 1975 reads:

> *Up again at five yesterday. Showered and shaved, I was at my writing table by 5:30 and finished story Number 22 by 8:00 A.M. It's a zany tale called "Christopher, Moony and the Birds," ...(MSJ 15).*

Besides writing in the garage he had remodeled as a writing studio, he wrote at the family cabin, seventy-five miles northwest of his home in Brainerd, near the town of Park Rapids.[2] He also occasionally went to Blue Cloud Monastery in Marvin, South Dakota, perhaps out of something like habit, having experienced monks and monastic life at St. John's University. His friend, Joe Plut, knew Brother Benet Tvedten, a member of the Blue Cloud community. Brother Benet organized the Blue Cloud Writing Festivals, which Hassler attended and read at during the 90s.

Academic Criticism

It is a curiosity—and perhaps a blessing—that Hassler came in for little "academic" criticism during his lifetime. But in 1994 two very different writers did comment at length on Hassler in mid-career. Anthony Low[3] gives credit to a review of *Dear James* by Philip Zaleski[4] for inspiring his essay. In the same year, C. W. Truesdale, founding editor of New Rivers Press, published a long survey essay.[5] Both studies praise Hassler for different things, and the current book acknowledges a general debt to both authors, even as it differs in emphasis and exceeds both of the earlier works in comprehensiveness—since, in 1994, neither had the advantage of seeing Hassler's career as a whole.[6]

Low begins by referring to the review of *Dear James*, in which Zaleski quotes an unnamed librarian who, upon seeing that Zaleski was checking out a stack of Hassler's novels says, "Isn't he great? I wish there were more like him. A writer that makes you glad to be alive." In one sense, this anonymous statement says more about Hassler's significance than a dozen critical articles or even a book. But Low sums up that quotation with one of his own, confirming the first: "not only are his books powerfully and beautifully written, they are a pleasure to read and to remember. They are often funny, and they end in joy." A bit later he accurately claims, "Great writers must have penetrating moral vision," which Hassler most certainly does. And, when addressing Hassler's regionalism, Low makes the standard—and true—response: "A certain kind of realism, fidelity to truth, material and moral, is precisely what makes great art universal."

Referring to Hassler's relative obscurity in 1994, Low cites a *Washington Post* review of Hassler's *North of Hope*, "Hassler now seems on his way to achieving the sort of breakthrough that Baltimore's Anne Tyler achieved in *The Accidental Tourist*." Low notes that "Hassler is indisputably as brilliant a stylist as Tyler, as fine a portrayer of eccentric characters, as powerful a teller of stories. And much more besides." Then he points points out a contemporary problem. "But movies and reputations are made from novels with quirky moral visions these days, which the reviewers promptly name 'wise.'" He says movies are made from Anne Tyler and John Irving, but not Jon Hassler. Contrasting such tastes to an older literary tradition, Low says, "Like [Jane] Austen, Hassler can give readers endless pleasure by the acute observation of petty, predictable people ... This talent is the very opposite of the one exhibited in countless postmodern novels, which desperately seek for novelty in perverse and eccentric variations, but predictably find instead that life is meaningless."

Comparing the 1950s Catholic writer, Flannery O'Connor, and Hassler, Low says,

> *They are, indeed, much alike. Each has a strong sense of the comic and the grotesque. Each has a strong Catholic moral vision that must find itself in a secular American culture, although Hassler does not, like O'Connor, avoid using Catholic protagonists. Each is an unsparing realist; each succeeds in that hardest of tasks in a materialist age, making religion an essential, an integral, part of their worlds and not just a pious veneer or an artificial incrustation (62).*

The conclusion of his comparison is critically apt. "Why, then, should we read Hassler if we may read O'Connor? As well ask, why read *The Great Gatsby* if one may read Faulkner? Despite their similarities, O'Connor and Hassler have very different things to say." But both, he concludes, are important in part "because they understand that life, despite its manifold sufferings, doubts, and evils—even despite death—has purpose and meaning."

Truesdale's essay is another matter. Long on quotations and flawed by factual inaccuracies, the New Rivers editor was nevertheless an astute reader of Hassler's work to that point in the novelist's career. Speaking of narrative technique, Truesdale highlights Hassler's "in and out" way of using point of view, often allowing "double vision" while maintaining the narrator's "detachment" from his characters. In a telling quotation, he says, the detachment "is at the very heart of his approach to the novel, an approach similar, I think, to what E. Talbot Donaldson once wrote about Chaucer—something to the effect that Chaucer had the capacity for delighted involvement in a world from which he remains philosophically detached."

Referring to the many digressions and flashbacks in Hassler's first several novels, Truesdale notes that "he [Hassler] dubbed himself Mr. Flashback." Truesdale also notes the "introspectiveness" that he finds in Miles Pruitt and Simon Shea—especially as related to attractive young women. He correctly draws attention to the place of the past and memory, as Hassler's characters are frequently "sorting out ... memories." Sounding a bit like Low on Hassler and Jane Austen, Truesdale uses the term "social comedy" to describe Hassler's treatment of the Catholic Church. But "social comedy" is a term that readily applies to <u>much</u> of the detail from everyday life that Hassler uses to contrast with moments of more "transcendent" significance—and beauty.

In one of his more curious insights, Truesdale argues that Hassler's work is "psychological realism" and not "archetypical [sic]." This suggests that the alternatives are either/or. In fact, juxtaposing psychological realism (with its emphasis on the everyday and the mundane) and the archetypal is just another way that Hassler creates contrast. Truesdale bases part of his argument on Hassler's skillful involvement of the reader with a variety of flawed but ultimately valuable—and deeply valued—characters. His final claims, that Hassler will "outlast all or almost all of his flashier contemporaries" and that "he will come to be recognized as a major twentieth-century novelist" corroborates Low's view. Such claims are yet to be proven true, which is another reason for this book.

Hassler and Cheever
Other than the references to Austen, O'Connor, and Chaucer, neither Low nor Truesdale says much about other, comparable authors; so before turning to the specifics of Hassler's narrative techniques and style, it is worthwhile to address briefly some of the most obvious comparisons. Besides an eye for everyday social situations, Hassler shares with Cheever an interest in the incongruous mystery that "opens up" in everyday life. The angel who saves the narrator in Cheever's "Angel of the Bridge" is an

everyday mystery if not a miracle. A late Cheever story like "The World of Apple" is more numinous, including repeated ritual bathings, though it is there, too, in the early "Goodbye, My Brother." Cheever is more consciously allusive; he also includes more melodrama. The repeated "blood-letting" in the latter might also be one possible literary source for Hassler's including such incidents in so many of his novels. Hassler is also more sensitive and less chauvinistic than Cheever. Hassler adds a laconic Midwestern (Irish) tone to his satire. Perhaps Hassler includes more of a different kind of moralism because of his Catholicism and his Midwestern characters.

Hassler and O'Connor

It is probably dangerous to compare Hassler and O'Connor, but—following Low's example—some further comparisons can be made. Both show an awareness of social class and direct their satire at pretentious individuals. They both introduce varying degrees of the grotesque and the bizarre, and both use natural description to create tone and symbolic resonance. But O'Connor's narrative style is relatively straightforward. Because she writes primarily short stories, there is little space, time, or opportunity for digression, episodic development, flashback, and similar techniques that Hassler uses.

O'Connor is unquestionably a major Catholic writer of the 40s and 50s. Short stories like "A Good Man Is Hard To Find," "The Lame Shall Enter First," "Parker's Back," "Displaced Person," and "Judgment Day" touch a nerve and expose a fundamental blindness to the transcendent in mid-twentieth century America. But despite her personally almost vehement Catholicism, O'Connor's focus is primarily on fundamentalist Protestants in the South with—some may argue—exaggerative presentation of their beliefs and practices. Compared to the way O'Connor satirizes Southern rednecks, Evangelicals, and liberal do-gooders, Hassler's satire and parody might appear rather tame. Hassler's satire of Catholic attitudes is gentler, more humorous, and for the most part less "scathing." But Hassler's novels, from *Staggerford* and *Simon's Night* to *Grand Opening*, *A Green Journey*, and *North of Hope* have a currency not only to the late 60s, and early 70s but can still "hold a mirror up to nature" in the twenty-first century. But in exchange for O'Connor's often violent critiques—almost condemnations—of her characters and their choices, Hassler is more understanding of human failings.

Given his careful depictions of nature—Hassler *sees* the birds, the trees, and the rivers of northern Minnesota—he may be more of a Romantic Incarnationalist than O'Connor, who, it seems, has a hard time seeing the trees for the forest conflagration.[7] Yes, she values concrete details, but as critics like Robert Fitzgerald point out, for O'Connor, every single thing seems to be viewed *sub specie aeternitatis*, whereas Hassler is more a follower of poet Theodore Roethke who says, "Things throw light on things / And all the stones have wings." That is a key difference between O'Connor's Catholicism of the 40's, 50's and early 60's, and Hassler's, who is writing in and about the end of the 60s to the early 2000s. It is as if Hassler has taken Roethke and the late Jesuit poet, Gerard Manley Hopkins, more seriously, and—to take one of Hassler's favorite bird images—he sees, first, the grosbeak *as* grosbeak. Then, he may suggest, imply a mystery, a transcendence that, somehow, "permeates" or otherwise shines through (or "flashes out," to use Hopkins's terms) the bird, the tree, the character, the incident. Following Pierre Teilhard de Chardin, O'Connor believes in seeing spirit in the material world, but for her, matter sometimes doesn't really seem to matter. Yes, everything that rises must converge, but in the present world, Hassler's seeing the glimmer of "godlight" in his teacup or a child's eyes may be truer than the Teilhardian vision.

Hassler's imagination and style come closest to Flannery O'Connor's in his use of "grotesques." In *Staggerford* these include not only Corrine Bingham, the bonewoman, but some of the seniors in the Staggerford Community Center; like the "humpbacked woman" or the "simpleton" who turns out to be Ozzie Lutz, the center's director. In the same book, a "giant" state patrolman begins as something of a "sideshow" grotesque, but he quickly assumes almost archetypal dimensions as he makes the protagonist and other characters seem "diminished," and everyone at one of the novel's major confrontations with Native Americans "drew back a step," startled by his size." Miles later reflects on how the giant would "go through life astonishing people" by his very existence (227), suggesting that he is at least an ominous, if not a numinous presence. Even the casual reader will find grotesques in almost all of Hassler's novels.

Hassler and Powers

Hassler and J. F. Powers would seem to be more comparable. Charlotte Hays says as much. "A comparison of Hassler and Powers is inevitable. For one thing, they both write about the same German/Scandanavian culture—everybody in their books seems to be either Catholic or Lutheran in religion—of the remote reaches of Minnesota and Illinois."[8] In another insight, Hays puts her finger on the Catholic connection that Hassler and Powers share.

> *Powers was a master of portraying preconciliar American Catholicism during what the nostalgic regard as the American Church's halcyon 1950s. Powers had a somewhat more jaundiced view of that self-satisfied era ("Hope on Ice").*

Though she doesn't make the connection, she even refers to Powers's priests as "men committed to the eternal ... relaxing in the Barcalounger," forgetting that Hassler's Fr. Frank Healy and Monsignor Adrian Lawrence both adjourn to their Barcaloungers at various points in *North of Hope.*

Both Hassler and Powers satirize Catholic mores in an ironic mode. Both focus on the details of everyday life. But, once again, because Powers wrote primarily long short stories, there is little use of episode, digression, or flashback. Powers *is* more adventurous in plotting, but he is also more plodding. He seems to write deliberately for the *New Yorker* reader, who prides him or herself on meticulous care for style and nuance. If Powers uses style to create tone, that style is like molasses, slow-flowing, sticky, and sometimes over-rich. His focus primarily on priest-protagonists is also, in the long view, a limitation and a narrowing feature.

Noting that in Powers's work "there are rarely any happy endings," Hays concludes her comparison of Hassler and Powers in much the same way Low concludes his comparison of Hassler and O'Connor.

> *Who is the better novelist, Powers or Hassler? I suppose that in the way that Shakespeare's tragedies are of a higher order than his romantic comedies, Father Urban's bleak redemption is probably higher art than James and Agatha's transforming but ultimately cozy love, or Frank Healy's perhaps too easy rediscovery of his vocation. But it's hard to say ("Hope on Ice").*

Powers can appear as a malicious writer (not unlike James Joyce). He won't give the reader any pleasure but the kind *he* wants the reader to have. Self-centered and exhibitionistic, his stories seem to say, "See what I can do?" "See what I can make *you* do!" His is the only way to tell a story, and—God help them!—readers had better enjoy his performance. This is Joyce with a hangover; O'Connor catatonic. Can the reader really sympathize with the character named Didymus in Powers's "Lions, Harts, Leaping Does"? Irish satire, yes, but with what I would guess Powers considered a cynical East Coast spin. Powers is writing within and for a group that Hassler might have sought to emulate: the "show don't tell" crowd, among whom Hassler numbered

Hemingway. Powers's style does not wear well. Far better that of Marilynne Robinson, or Hassler himself.

Mode of Composition

What neither Low's nor Truesdale's essays address in any sustained way is Hassler's mode of composition. Now, a decade after the author's death, it is important to stress that Hassler was a "natural," unconscious Irish storyteller, and that this fact shapes the novels profoundly and affects the way readers respond to his work. Hassler's mode of composing was to start "by imagining two or three central characters in a dramatic situation—usually an unhappy and volatile one," and see where it took him. Because of this process, he was given to the associative digressions that Truesdale notes, and which can produce sometimes surprisingly "natural," even uncanny effects. But they can also backfire, fizzle, or at least dissipate focus and reader interest. This mode of composition is the "open-ended" approach to fiction adopted by many of the best recent authors, including Marilynne Robinson.[9] To describe Hassler's gift for the short sketch or scene, one might also resort to what critic Denis Donoghue[10] calls a writer's "native breath." Hassler's native breath is the anecdote or episode; hence the construction of many of his novels out of interlocking scenes, punctuated by digressive flashbacks, anecdotes, and repetitions. This is also a characteristic Irish storytelling form. It is also native to Mark Twain and other American authors with whom Hassler would have been familiar from teaching English in the high schools and community colleges of Minnesota during the 60s the 70s.

The longer I spend with Hassler and his work, the more I am convinced of the Irish element in Hassler's work. The irony, the almost Swiftian humor, and the near obsession with death are among the other obvious traits. Hassler is not a philosopher but an Irish ironist. But like Jonathan Swift (in a much less scatological way), he is an ironist whose serious satire nevertheless points to and implies a philosophical outlook, as does Swift's. He also indulges the Irish tendency to spin out a story—particularly a humorous one—at length, waiting to drop the "punch line." Many of his characters have Irish names, allowing the author—and the reader—to imagine them with Irish characteristics: Simon Shea, Chris Mackensie and Larry Quinn; Brendan Foster, James O'Hannon, Frank Healy, the artist Connor, and, in his final novella, Aunt Nancy Clancy. The most obvious instance is Agatha McGee, and in two late novels, Hassler makes Agatha's reflections on her Irish forebears an important part of the novel's reflective texture.

Themes

For many readers, it is the kind of human experiences, their density and texture, in short, their themes, that will be most important in evaluating an author. Hassler gives readers the everyday "feel" of life in the rural and small-town Midwest (specifically, Minnesota) of the 1940s through the early twenty-first century, many complete with accurate historical details. Though Hassler claimed, "I never have an abstract thought," readers and reviewers are quick, accurate, and almost unanimous in identifying a number of abiding themes. They are community and the loss of community, faith and the loss of faith; depression, loneliness, and the need for love. As an only child, he often writes about only children, children or young people in straitened circumstances, or young people betrayed by or betraying those whom they have trusted or loved. He also once told his friend, Joseph Plut, that "one of the things that interests me about writing; portraying the endurance of the human spirit in my characters" ("Colleges," p. 36). At the end of *Good People* Hassler describes the source of his happiness in life. "I believe I can trace my happy attitude back to my earliest years, when, as a little boy, I looked out and saw the world from the security of that all-important cocoon of goodness, my parents' love" (*Good*

People, p. 120). It is out of this core experience of security that Hassler is able to write about not only joy and happiness, but tragedy, misfortune, and betrayal as well. The loss or absence of such a "cocoon of goodness"—and the security that it entails— becomes a central source of tension and conflict in his work.

Hassler's Humor

A stress on the Irish element in Hassler's style of humor would distort the picture, without a look at other possible sources for his humor. Though Hassler does not mention it, there is also, as noted, a strain of Mark Twain's humor; especially the deadpan absurdity, like some of his outlandish characters and situations. It may also relate to Hassler's particular brand of the grotesque shading into the macabre. Burying a limb is not a typically O'Connor twist. Nor will a reader find it in Cheever, but it is something Twain might have thought up.

Turning to another kind of comedy: Dante's medieval work, the *Divine Comedy* is satiric, if not humorous, at the same time it is mystical and concrete. The evil are punished, the good rewarded, and the three-part work moves from damnation through repentance and purgation to beatitude. Dante judges and judges severely. He imaginatively punishes and even "tortures" those whom he has found guilty of various personal or political crimes, and religious sins. He also presents scenes of sublime beauty and revelation. Geoffrey Chaucer's incomplete masterpiece, *The Canterbury Tales*, depicts a group of medieval citizens on pilgrimage. The characters and the tales they tell include the comedic, the ribald, and the edifying. But, unlike Dante, Chaucer largely refrains from judging. More like a modern "realist," he presents characters concretely but more or less impartially, leaving it for the reader to "judge" them. There are few mystical flights. Hassler mixes the Dantean and Chaucerian modes. He satirizes superficiality, foolishness, ineptitude, arrogance, and venality. But he does not "judge" even his most depraved characters. He leaves them for the reader to evaluate for themselves, but, like Dante, along with scenes of the sordid and the squalid, Hassler presents scenes of almost transcendent beauty and awe.

Point of View

In *My Staggerford Journal* Hassler spoke about the narrator's viewpoint. His favorite viewpoint is the third-person, selectively omniscient narrator, able to "enter" any character's perspective, revealing as much—or as little—of that character's "inner self" as will be useful to the story. Though some of his early short stories are in first person, Hassler wrote only two first-person novels, the young adult *Four Miles to Pinecone* at the start of his career, and *The Dean's List* near the end. In most of his novels the narrator preferentially "occupies" one character's—usually the protagonist's—point of view for most of the novel. But, at different times, the narrator will more or less briefly occupy another character's point of view, in order to provide other perspectives, or to achieve "dramatic irony," where the reader enjoys greater knowledge than the protagonist (or other characters) because the narrator has shared those inner views with the reader.

In a 2008 *New York Times Book Review* review of Marilynne Robinson's novel, *Home*, A. O. Scott has a clever—but I think accurate—way to refer to a subtlety in point of view that Hassler employs regularly. Scott speaks about a character "allowing his creator to speak through him." Whether they all "allow" their creator to speak through them, many of Hassler's characters <u>do</u> find him speaking through them, from Miles Pruitt, to Brendan Foster, to Leland Edwards near the end of his career. When the reader is aware that the narrator *is not* exclusively in one character, it can create uncertainty and a degree of insecurity. In all these cases, therefore, the author's "tone," or attitude toward the character, and the events narrated, becomes of key importance to the reader. This is precisely the point about Hassler's involvement with his characters that Truesdale made.

Other Techniques of Style

While a high school teacher, Hassler worked summers at a drive-in movie theater and developed his taste for movies, while in the process he absorbed some cinematic techniques that he would adapt to novel-writing. He also alludes to movies throughout his career. Though he disliked television and most television shows, he knew them well enough to use some of their techniques to vary the pace of his novels, [11] and to satirize, as he alluded to, some of the most popular shows of the 70s, 80s, and 90s. One of the most obvious television techniques is the quick shift, between chapters and even sometimes within chapters, from scene to scene, particularly to create contrasting tones. He also juxtaposes for effect the comedic and the seriously dramatic. And, from the beginning, he was fond of introducing sub-plots to complicate the action. Another technique that may owe as much to literary conventions, but which gains emphasis by its similarity to television, is the "snappy" or "dramatic" ending to an episode, a segment, or a chapter. From early on Hassler developed the habit of ending his chapters with surprising, striking, or dramatic moments.

Nature, Place, and Gesture

From the time of his first short stories, the role of season, setting, and natural environment is important in Hassler's work. Seasonal changes and even the behavior of various birds can be "clues" to tone and theme. Places and gestures are also frequently important. The geography of Staggerford and the Badbattle River figure prominently in his first novel. Thereafter, like Norman Maclean's Blackfoot River, the Badbattle runs through Hassler's fiction like a thread of personal association and significant value. It is there right up to the final Agatha McGee novel, *The*

New Woman. When a character like Miles Pruitt wades into the Badbattle, or when a character like Chris Mackensie (*The Love Hunter*) descends into the valley of the Badbattle, those moves are significant. Despite such significant "descents," Hassler the narrator and his characters prefer the heights to the plains, and an elevated vantage point is frequently the place a character retires to reflect, or to make an important decision. And though gestures are common in other authors as well, for Hassler gestures like embraces, stumbles, kisses, and chance meetings at crucial junctures in a story convey the nuance and depth of emotional involvement, and psychological insight. Betrayal is a common theme or sub-theme in many of the novels. In his earliest fictions: *Staggerford, Jemmy*, and *Four Miles to Pinecone*, it is linked to the season. If *Simon's Night* and *The Love Hunter* are included, that makes *five* early works that employ autumnal imagery to highlight betrayal and create mood, but also to prepare for restoration, reconciliation, and rejuvenation.

Hassler, the Elderly, Young People, and the Hardscrabble Girl

Two of Hassler's earliest stories, "Small-Eye's Last Hunt" and "Willowby's Indian," portray elderly characters: two retirees in the first and an old hotel desk clerk named Grover in the second. From that time Hassler will continue to depict the aged and their particular concerns and foibles with generosity and sensitivity—but not without satiric insights as well. Agatha McGee is in her sixties when she appears in *Staggerford*, and Hassler follows her into her eighties as she enters the Sunset Senior Apartments in *The New Woman*.

Besides introducing Agatha McGee, *Staggerford* presents the first appearance of one of Hassler's most pervasive character-types, the "hardscrabble girl." Miles Pruitt's student, high school junior Beverly Bingham, is the first of several such characters; young women from unpromising, deprived, or dysfunctional backgrounds, who have to struggle to cope with life and the disasters life sends their way. Each will be treated individually in the novels, but a brief listing will suggest their prevalence: Beverly Bingham is followed closely by Jemmy Stott, the title character of his young adult novel *Jemmy*. Janet Raft (later Janet Meers) makes her first appearance in *A Green Journey* and then returns in *Dear James*, *The Staggerford Flood*, and *The New Woman*. Libby Girard Pearsall from *North of Hope* is perhaps—next to Janet Meers—the most fully developed version of the type.

Young Children, and the Intergenerational Theme

Like his affinity for the elderly and the hardscrabble girl, Hassler in his fiction has a special interest in very young children. Two early short stories ("Keepsakes" and "Chief Larson") feature instances of the interaction between youth and age. Then there are the students in *Staggerford*, and Jemmy Stott, Brendan Foster, Dodger Hicks in the other early novels, down to Kevin Luuya and the "small boy who spoke clearly for his age" in Hassler's final novella, *The Life and Death of Nancy Clancy's Nephew*. Along the way Hassler introduces variants of the intergenerational theme. One of the most interesting late instances is that of Agatha McGee and five year old Jennie Beezer in *The New Woman*. Agatha's tenderness for neglected children and their innocence is like the narrator's feelings for Jemmy Stott, Brendan Foster, and even—to a degree—a character like Dodger Hicks and the little boy in *The Life and Death*. When, as is frequent, the young person encounters one or more adults, an intergenerational relationship develops with revelations to both the children and the adults who pay them attention. But Agatha—and, with her, Hassler—can also be critical of children. The narrator acknowledges that Dodger Hicks is an incorrigible thief. Jennie Beezer is addicted to TV, and Agatha tries to do something about it, encouraging the child's *good* taste (*Mr. Rogers* and *Sesame Street*) while trying to eliminate the bad—Jennie's watching *Law and Order*.

Love Triangles

As he sometimes stoops to TV melodrama, Hassler also makes fairly frequent use of the conventional love-triangle. It starts with Miles and Dale Pruitt in *Staggerford*—who fall for the same girl, Carla Carpenter. Later it is Miles, Anna Thea Workman, and Imogene Kite; then, in *Simon's Night,* his second novel, it is Simon, Barbara Stearns Shea, and Linda Mayo, and, in *The Love Hunter*, Chris Mackensie, Larry Quinn, and Rachel Quinn. The pattern recurs with Connor, Peggy Benoit, and Connor's wife in *Rookery Blues,* and Leland and Sally Edwards, and Mary Sue Bloom in *The Dean's List*.

Shock and the Grotesque

There is little shock or use of the grotesque in Hassler's short stories. It is only in *Staggerford* that Hassler begins to include the shocking and the grotesque. Nothing is quite as shocking as the story that a student, Roxie Booth, tells early in *Staggerford,* about a young corporal who swallows glass shavings on a dare and then bleeds to death. With the sudden death of Donald Stearns in *Simon's Night* and later Mrs. Kibbikoski's "bleeding out" after a leg amputation, sudden death and more and less violent blood-letting become—albeit often minor—features of almost every novel.

On the Archetypal

As noted earlier, Hassler said he didn't plan his novels beyond imagining a dramatic situation and a few characters. Like Marilynne Robinson (who says the same), he lets the characters and who they are determine the direction of the story. In an interview with Dick Dowd for *The Critic*,[12] Dowd asked Hassler about his various novels. The author said: "I think of myself more deeply involved with them. Sort of pulled along or pulled down into that mood" (23). He adds: "You know, I'm the last one you should be asking about my novels. I really don't understand a lot of what goes into these books." With his mode of composition, and his unwillingness to "interpret" his own work (not uncommon in other authors), Sigmund Freud, Jacques Maritain, and a wide range of other "psychological" critics would suggest: the unconscious likely played a part in such a writer's creative activity. Despite Truesdale's demur, the degree of autobiographical detail in many of Hassler's stories and novels, and the recurrence of familiar "family" issues (drug and alcohol addiction, divorce, infidelity) might also imply the intrusion of the unconscious.

One way to understand the place of the unconscious in literature is to invoke the concept of the archetypal. Parry Lord, Joseph Campbell, and Northrop Frye have identified characters, situations, and major life events that they call "archetypal," in that they recur across cultures and literatures throughout history. The most prevalent—and perhaps most familiar—is "the journey of the hero." In *The Morphology of the Folk Tale*, Russian formalist critic Vladimir Propp identified thirty-one "features" or components of the hero's journey in the folk tale and explains how stories combine, modify, and relate these various features. Even in literate cultures Propp and others argue that authors observe—even as they modify—similar "rules" and use the same features.

C. G. Jung, Mircea Eliade, Erich Neumann, and—again—Northrop Frye have also identified constellations of objects, images, locations, etc. that imply the presence or the operation of the unconscious and therefore the archetypal. [13] Frye and Propp have shown how various elements can be combined, modulated, transformed, and transferred. Among the objects that recur in stories of the hero's quest are animals and birds, omens, curses, spells, grotesque and ominous characters (including giants), messages (letters), various forms of transformation, false accusations, impersonations, secrets, ordeals, tests, gifts, rituals, bloodletting, "recognition" scenes, moments of revelation, and patterns of debility, illness, and infertility that end in rejuvenation, re-vitalization, or even resurrection.[14] All of these, readers will discover, occur, to varying degrees, in Hassler's novels. Of course, a critic's awareness can make such features seem more prominent in a work than the casual reader might otherwise acknowledge. What a critic "unconsciously" looks for is likely to turn up. But if a work—or the body of a writer's work—contains so many archetypal characters, situations, or other features, it seems reasonable to take note of them in reading, understanding, and appreciating the individual work, and the overall achievement. At the very least, the prevalence of such "universal" features can lend an almost "numinous"[15] quality to a character, an object, or an entire scene or novel. When the scene or the character or the object is also connected to or associated with a specific religious belief or practice, such numinousness can also work to create a "transcendent" dimension in the entire work.

Discernible from as early as *Staggerford*, Hassler knowingly or not employs many features of the hero's quest in his novels. Recognizing that group of features I am calling "archetypal," the reader gets a helpful guide for understanding aspects of many of the novels. To take *Staggerford* as an example: the seemingly quotidian events of Miles Pruitt's week take on special significance when characters, events, and images occur that recapitulate many of the typical stages of the hero's journey or quest. Like T. S. Eliot's *The Waste Land*, *Staggerford* includes a sick "king," in this case, Superintendent Stevenson. It is fall and therefore a time of death, and debility. Illness is also prominent (Fred Vandergar and Miles's toothache). Like the Greek king, Oedipus, Miles, effectively an orphan, is called upon to give aid and thus begin his quest. Because he responds to his student, Beverly Bingham's request for help, suspicions are aroused. There are disguises, omens, tests—or ordeals—and scenes of recognition and revelation. In the end the hero dies, and his death brings about a rejuvenation—in this case, of Superintendent Stevenson. Viewed from the broadest perspective, not only *Staggerford* but a surprising number of Hassler's other novels take the classic (archetypal) form found in Shakespeare's late comedies—and innumerable other works of literature—a journey from disorder, isolation, depression, and alienation to relative order, reconciliation, and re-integration of the characters into their community.

Hassler's Catholic World View

Reference to the numinous or the transcendent makes an appropriate segue to discussion of Hassler's Catholic world view, as it can be read from his work. In an interview for *Image* magazine in 1996, Hassler said that his early Catholic education gave him a sense "that everything in life is connected. Everything in life has its consequences. This life is attached to the next life, and so forth" (58).[16] This succinct statement has a number of corollaries.

Besides an (often implicit) belief in Catholic "doctrines" like "The Fall" in the Garden of Eden, the Incarnation, the Resurrection, and values like charity and forgiveness, a writer with a Catholic world view will distinguish good and evil. A Catholic world view acknowledges mitigating circumstances and the effect of people's backgrounds and individual weaknesses. But it does not—as many *do* in what they see as an increasingly deterministic world—exonerate everyone of individual responsibility for their actions. "Hate the sin but love the sinner" is still a possibility for a writer like Hassler with a Catholic world view. The gospels record only one outburst of anger on Jesus's part. But he uses strong language against hypocrisy, heartlessness, and the narrow outlook.

Because of this distinction, Hassler shows an almost uncommon compassion and love for his characters. But he can also criticize, even satirize the evil, narrowness, and bigotry of individuals and groups. A Catholic world view accepts human responsibility, but it does not, gnostically, expect that human beings alone can solve all problems. A Catholic world view opposes evil and works to alleviate suffering. But it does not expect results from its own efforts alone. It believes in grace and lives in *hope*. Even when "bad things happen to good people," as the old cliché goes, Hassler's Catholic world view seeks to discover meaning and significance in suffering. He also shows this attitude in the way he celebrates uniqueness, in the way he values the detail, the particular. Like Jesuit poet Gerard Manley Hopkins, Hassler says, in every novel, "Glory be to God for dappled things."[17] And these dappled things can include not only the unique and variegated characters who appear; but also events and phenomenal details that are—in Hopkins's words—"counter, original, spare, strange." And, often, the way in which they are unique and variegated is in the way they mix the evil and the good.

Finally, Hassler's Catholic world view sees life whole. He often finds this wholeness, paradoxically, by attending to the little-noticed detail. Though Hassler says that the poets referred to in his work are ones he is reading at the time (*Image* interview), it seems clear that the work of Theodore Roethke has had a more than usually pervasive impact on Hassler's life and work. Even before he used a passage from Roethke's short lyric, "The Small," as the epigraph to *A Green Journey*, his work was imbued with something of the "awed" sensibility manifested there. The poem begins:

> *The small birds swirl around;*
> *The high cicadas chirr;*
> *A towhee pecks the ground;*
> *I look at the first star:*
> *My heart held to its joy,*
> *This whole September day.*

I won't argue that Hassler imitates Roethke's style, though he may, in places. Nor will I point to the significance of the particular images: of birds or insects, moon and wind, and sodden ground. These too may be part of Roethke's attraction for

Hassler; part of that "attunement" to the seasons referred to earlier. Rather, it is the spirit of Roethke's poem, which goes on to record another half-dozen impressions of a day in September, with an almost breathless awe; an awe simply at their "being." To recognize such "Being" in the things of this world, without immediate, particularly self-interested judgment; this is how Hassler's Catholic world view acknowledges the wholeness, the connectedness of all creation. The couplet that concludes Roethke's poem, with its almost Biblical metaphor, is perhaps as much "metaphysics" as Roethke, or Hassler, will allow to creep in: "Things throw light on things,/ And all the stones have wings." Such juxtapositions—one might say of light and dark —also lead to contrasts that can affect atmosphere, tone, and even the degree of humor. At almost every turn—though not in as concentrated a way as in Roethke's poem—Hassler's fictions show how "things throw light on things," yielding "visions" of a world that is loved by God.

Hassler and Native Americans

Hassler included Native American characters from the very beginning of his career. His first published short story, "Smalleye's Last Hunt" makes Smalleye, an off-reservation retiree, the chief character. In "Willowby's Indian," Hassler introduces Frederick "French" Lopat, who is of mixed Native American and white blood. Another early story, "Chief Larson," makes a small off-reservation adoptee the protagonist. Then, starting with *Staggerford*, Hassler included Native American characters in no fewer than five novels. Except in the case of Jemmy Stott (in *Jemmy*), Hassler does not make a Native American a protagonist in any of the novels, but they are important characters in the other four. Hassler freely enters the viewpoint of Native Americans like Roger Upward and Billy Annunciation (in *North of Hope*), and part Native Americans like Beverly Bingham (in *Staggerford*). In the current climate of identity politics, some critics have suggested that a writer cannot accurately—or sympatheti-cally—portray an ethnicity that s/he does not share. Though there might be demurs, Hassler seems to have achieved such accurate and sympathetic depiction.[18]

From such mundane issues as Native American children leaving school at sixteen, to details of reservation life (*Stagger-ford, Jemmy*) to the tension between assimilation and asserting identity, and Native Americans' confrontations with the domi-nant white culture (*Staggerford, Jemmy, North of Hope*), Has-sler is not shy of dealing directly with Native American culture. His most extensive treatment of Native American life, *North of Hope*, includes plot elements that address many specific issues of Native Americans: drugs, alcohol, and violence. In all the stories and novels, Hassler treats Native American characters with sen-sitivity, humor, and accuracy of depiction.[19]

Literary Placement

To complete this introduction, it will be useful to place Has-sler in a larger literary context. Hassler belongs in the tradition of Midwest writing that goes back at least to the nineteenth century and the early twentieth century, with Hamlin Garland, Sinclair Lewis, and Sherwood Anderson. Hassler's portrayal of small-town Midwestern life is more modern than Garland's, less acerbic than Lewis's, and (only slightly) less grotesque or maca-bre than some of Anderson. A native of central Minnesota, it is little wonder that Hassler—who traveled very little until later in life—has a sensitivity for the sights, sounds, and events of central and northern Minnesota. His novels and stories are full of descriptions of familiar plants, animals, birds and weather, and his descriptions are replete with the topography of his part of Minnesota. The reader experiences the feel of everyday occu-pations as well as ordinary pleasures. And, as noted, in each of several novels "a river runs through it," most often the fictional "Badbattle," which links the equally fictional towns of Staggerford, Rookery, Ithaca Mills, and Berrington. As a graduate of the Benedictine St. John's University in Collegeville, MN, it is little wonder that Hassler's sensibility is Benedictine, where hospitality is the central value, because every stranger or guest is seen as Christ; and where the monk shows sensitivity to nature and the seasons and tries to live in harmony with nature and its rhythms.

Hassler's Relevance

In part because of such structures and elements—but also because of his storytelling skills—as long as teachers grow weary of teaching, *Staggerford* will speak to them. As long as the elderly struggle with self-esteem and a sense of aimlessness in life, *Simon's Night* will speak to them. As long as friends have to watch friends die from terminal illnesses, *The Love Hunter* will be relevant. As long as the white race struggles to understand Native Americans, *North of Hope* will be of value. One could make a similar claim for the relevance of each of Hassler's other novels, right up to the final novella: as long as the elderly struggle with loss and the diminishments that accompany aging, *The Life and Death of Nancy Clancy's Nephew* will provide a monitory lesson. Despite changes in literary fashion, such varied, but ultimately universal themes suggest why Jon Hassler's work will continue to appeal.

Having looked at Hassler's life and growth as a writer, the next chapter will try to show how a number of early short stories and his young adult novel, *Four Miles to Pinecone* point in various ways to the writer who would compose twelve moving and unforgettable novels. If the reader prefers, however, s/he can skip this further "introduction" and go directly to the individual chapters on his or her favorite novels.

3

THE SHORT STORIES AND
FOUR MILES TO PINECONE

The reader of chapter one has already heard the story of how Hassler began his writing career on September 10, 1970. Without a writing class or an MFA and only one or two confidants, Hassler learned to write from writing—and reading. As he worked on his young adult novel, *Four Miles to Pinecone* every year, he also concentrated on the short story form. In 1975 he was still writing short stories, even as he was about to return to work on the manuscript of a first novel. It is worth quoting again from *My Staggerford Journal* where Hassler describes his work habits, writing daily, taking few breaks. The entry refers specifically to a story that will later appear in the short story collection titled *Keepsakes*.

> *Up again at five yesterday. Showered and shaved, I was at my writing table by 5:30 and finished story Number 22 by 8:00 A.M. It's a zany tale called "Christopher Moony and the Birds," . . . (p. 15).*

With this energy and discipline, Hassler carried forward his career as a short story writer.

"Smalleye's Last Hunt" and "Willowby's Indian"

It is not hard to see why "Smalleye's Last Hunt" and "Willow-by's Indian" became two of Hassler's earliest published stories.[1] Skillfully plotted and full of comic action, they also deal with Native Americans, a topic which was becoming popular in the early 1970s.[2] But looked at more closely, the stories manifest both strengths and weaknesses within the short story genre. Small touches of—sometimes satiric—humor look forward to the novels. Smalleye, the protagonist in the first, is an anomalous Native American. Living in a retirement home, off reservation, he has few features that identify him as Native American. "French," in the second story "is not, in fact, certain of his Indian ancestry" (284). The first story is really more about aging and the aged than it is about Native Americans. The second is about an unemployed Korean War veteran who, in a moment of unaccountable honesty, forfeits his unemployment check, and a Christmas dinner.

The minor characters in the first story are Nelson, who is Smalleye's companion; a forgetful retired farmer who ends up betraying Smalleye. Alice Ahman is a hysterical old woman who repeatedly imagines people dying. Hattie Norman is the authoritarian proprietor of the retirement home whose constant worry is lawsuits and lawless residents. In the second story, French interacts with an equally memorable cast of slightly unusual characters: Grover, the aged WW I veteran and desk clerk at the Morgan Hotel, "a man so stooped and hollow-chested that his suspenders stand away from the front of his shirt" (285); an unnamed ten year-old who steals a pack of gum at the Morgan (thus preparing for a later twist in the plot); Steffanson, the unemployment officer, Ulm, French's summer employer from the Chamber of Commerce, and the unnamed manager of the Rialto Theater.

In "Smalleye's Last Hunt" an improbable premise is made believable by the careful selection of detail. As fall approaches,

Smalleye wants to shoot a goose, reliving earlier years on the reservation. He and Nelson sit on aluminum lawn chairs in the middle of a gravel road that runs past the retirement home where they both live. Smalleye describes how, in years past, he shot geese from the top of a "high pile of hay" (133). The story details Smalleye's elaborate plans to shoot a goose from the roof of the Norman Home. The plans include tossing a rug out the window of his room. He later uses the rug to conceal a shotgun that he takes from his niece. That evening, the narrator gives the reader access to Smalleye's fears as he climbs a ladder to the roof and then passes up two shots at low-flying geese, fearful that he might miss. Then the reader shares Smalleye's tension as night comes on and he fears he'll have to use his one shotgun shell to signal for help.

The climax comes with great vividness and action, and (with a bit of exaggeration) a hint of the kind of the quasi-mysterious that will make many of the later novels memorable. As Smalleye is about to fire that signal shot, "he heard geese. Hundreds of geese in patterns as wide as the town skimmed chimneys and power poles." Smalleye sees them "as wildly flapping forms surrounding [him] in a dizzy dance" (140). Then, when he shoots into the flock, the chimney he has been leaning on collapses, and he falls to the Norman Home balcony. The policeman called to investigate the ruckus pronounces him dead. But a doctor and ambulance driver find that he is not dead after all. The understated denouement occurs the next afternoon when Nelson "found near the street a dead snow goose. On the white down were small rusty spots of dried blood where shotgun pellets had penetrated its throat" (142).

"Willowby's Indian"

With carefully selected and perceptually rendered details, "Willowby's Indian" begins by creating a vivid sense of a cold, late December Saturday in Minnesota. Then careful plotting takes over as, first, the unemployed French anticipates an "extravagant" Christmas dinner in Duluth, and an evening with a couple of cigars and a half-pint of Schnapps back at the Morgan Hotel, after which he would exist "on soup and sardines for a week" (285). When French goes downstairs, he meets the desk clerk, who complains of all the children in town for two free Saturday movies at the Rialto. Then "a lanky ten-year-old"—who with a friend comes into the Morgan Hotel to get out of the cold—steals a pack of gum from the counter of the Morgan Hotel and French tries, but fails to stop him.

Later on that Saturday morning, as French stands in line for his unemployment check, he notices a fat woman's corsage "so large and spiny she seemed to be standing behind a hedge" (287). This type of exaggeration will become a familiar form of humor in his novels. Their mundane conversation about "kids today" is followed by French's unaccountable "No," when the unemployment officer asks if French has looked for work. When Steffanson refuses to give him his check, French rushes next door to the Chamber of Commerce where he shouts a question, "Any work for me here?" (288), then intends to head back to the unemployment office where he can say he has looked for work. But his offhand inquiry leads to a surprise offer of employment: step in as a substitute Santa Claus, to hand out candy after the free movies at the Rialto. The exaggerated description of French's anomalous appearance in the Santa Claus costume is another typical exaggeration. Then, after the movie, when French tries to refuse candy to the teenager who stole the pack of gum, the chaotic climax is assured. The denouement comes as French discovers that he is too late to collect his unemployment check after all, and returns resigned to the Morgan Hotel where he opens a can of sardines and heats a can of soup "with the reassurance that he deserves more than he's getting" (293). The subtly ironic conclusion will become a Hassler trademark.

Both stories exhibit somewhat greater concentration but

only marginally greater craftsmanship in character and plot than the reader will find in the two collections of short stories that were published in 1999 and 2000. The remainder of this chapter will examine in greater detail how some of those previously unpublished stories show in greater detail how Hassler learned and honed the skills that produced not only "Smalleye's Last Hunt" and "Willowby's Indian," but the eleven novels and two young adult works that have assured his lasting reputation as a comic Catholic novelist.

Keepsakes and *Rufus at the Door and Other Stories*

In 1999, the Afton Historical Society published *Keepsakes*,[3] a collection of seven of Hassler's early stories. In 2000 the society published *Rufus at the Door and Other Stories*, another seven stories.[4] From these two collections, a reader can learn much about Hassler's growth as a writer: his characters, his themes, his experiments with style. From these stories the reader also learns how Hassler imitated other authors, how he experimented with point of view, with exaggerated characters and situations, truncated summaries, and practiced different kinds of humor and satire. The exaggerative, almost Twainian humor and satire that will mark his novels are not as much in evidence in these early stories as they will become, for instance, in *Staggerford*. Even the stories written later show, by contrast, what makes the novels so much more successful works. As introduction to each collection, editor Patricia Condon Johnston provides background by quoting Hassler's comments on the various stories. While these comments are helpful, a closer look at the stories themselves tells the reader more about Hassler the writer.

Taken together, these two collections are a mixed bag. As a short story writer, Hassler's mentors are John Cheever and perhaps Ernest Hemingway, rather than older writers like Ring Lardner or John O'Hara, or younger contemporaries like Raymond Carver or Tobias Wolff. These stories class as realistic portraits of small-town life; character vignettes, and anecdotes, raised to the level of art by craftsmanship and attention to detail.

In the first collection, *Keepsakes*, the reader will find the most poignant and elegiac stories are "Keepsakes" and "Resident Priest." The central character in each is a seventy-four year old priest, Fr. Fogarty (based on one of the many priests Hassler knew and watched[5] as a boy). Pastor in a rural Minnesota town, Fr. Fogarty[6] is preparing to retire. The narrator, a young altar boy named Roger Rudy, has a grudge against the priest, but his father tells him to help the priest clean out a rectory full of junk and keepsakes. In the course of the story Fr. Fogarty reveals a good deal about his life and disappointments, and Roger's feelings toward the priest change. The priest's self-deprecatory tone and the selection of details make this fragmented look into the priest's past both haunting and compelling. The conclusion exhibits an early example of Hassler's unsentimental "shock-value" ending.

In "Resident Priest" the viewpoint is that of Ernie Booker, the caretaker of a convent on an island in the Mississippi River between Minnesota and Wisconsin, where Fr. Fogarty is to take up his retirement assignment as "resident priest." The opening develops the late summer atmosphere of the convent before Fr. Fogarty's arrival. Then an early September cold snap and rainstorm make the causeway to the convent nearly impassable. The sound of a car horn one morning alerts the convent; the priest's car is stuck on the causeway. Ernie Booker accompanies Fr. Fogarty from the car, back through the mud, and into a brief meeting with Sr. Simon, the convent's mother superior. Again, the story ends on a surprising and melancholy note.

Both stories make copious use of seasonal descriptions. Both are rich in the selection of precise, everyday detail that will become a trademark of Hassler's fiction. "Keepsakes" exhibits the intergenerational interest that will also become an important part of many Hassler novels. Both "Keepsakes" and

"Resident Priest" offer views of pre-Vatican II Catholicism and the relationship of priests and religious to the lay community. In "Keepsakes," Fr. Fogarty's self-irony as he looks at remnants of his past is a satiric highlight. In "Resident Priest" it is Ernie Booker's delicately ironic view of nuns and priests that maintains interest until the arrival of the priest.

Three of the stories in *Keepsakes*, "Chase," "Chief Larson," and "Christopher, Moony, and the Birds" involve familiar themes and look forward to specific novels. The first of these, "Chase," is definitely a journeyman effort. The first person narrator describes an early teenage game of "tag" that he and his friends engage in around their rural Minnesota hometown. The narrator never gets caught, and he never reveals his special hiding place. He revels in the feeling of isolation and his own "unfindability" (22). When, as grown-ups, the friends gather in Minneapolis and try to replicate the game, they find it is nothing like their youthful, small-town version. Recalling his early hiding place, the narrator ends by observing, "I have come down from the oil drums along the railroad tracks and stolen into the unsearchable refuge of fiction" (22).

Besides the "meta-fictional" nature of this final comment, the reader looking for the connection to Hassler's later work will find that the narrator and the initial small-town setting and certain details anticipate *Grand Opening*.

"Chief Larson," about a young Native American boy adopted by a family in a small, rural town, has elements that will recur throughout Hassler's career. An interest in the contrast between reservation culture and dominant white culture; the perspective of the young boy, and the humorous conclusion are all on display. The adoptive family—and Chief Larson's relationship with his garrulous adoptive grandfather—look forward to the *mise en scène* of *Grand Opening*.

"Christopher, Moony, and the Birds" – the story whose completion Hassler noted in *My Staggerford Journal* -- is told from the perspective of a recently divorced fifty-ish college teacher who takes a walk through his neighborhood, accompanied by Christopher and Moony, Christopher's four-year-old-stepdaughter. On the walk the narrator recounts his meetings with various more and less unusual neighbors, and at the end the reader discovers that Christopher is the narrator's twenty-year old son, who has married a woman ten years older than he is, whose lifestyle and attitudes border on the bizarre. The depressed narrator, the unusual neighbors, and the fraught familial and interpersonal relationships anticipate situations and themes in Hassler's later novels. The non-judgmental—but subtly satiric—perspective on different attitudes and values in contemporary culture will become a regular part of Hassler's later fiction.

Of the two remaining stories in the collection, "Good News in Culver Bend" is another journeyman effort about a young newspaper reporter who makes a bet with an older, jaded colleague, that he can find an unusual Christmas story for their Fargo, North Dakota paper. Traveling east from Fargo to rural Culver Bend, Minnesota, the first person narrator happens upon and saves a young female school teacher from embarrassment when her fiancée fails to arrive to be introduced at the rural school's Christmas celebration. "Good News in Culver Bend" employs a familiar self-deprecatory narrator and satiric outlook. It also exhibits the careful plotting—and management of the surprise ending—that Hassler will use to great effect in many of his later novels.

"Yesterday's Garbage" is a more bizarre story that anticipates many of Hassler's mature techniques and themes. The narrator is a garbage collector whose wife is a busybody and a hoarder. When the garbage man turns up a letter that sheds light on a mysterious murder, he and his wife become sleuths. But when the narrator tries to offer advice to one of those involved, a Mrs. Nichols, she attacks him, and he ends up giving her a blow to the head that—almost unaccountably—kills her. The conclusion focuses on how the couple disposes of the body in the municipal dump. Unusual characters, an outlandish plot, and grotesque details all anticipate aspects of Hassler's mature fiction. The nearly total absence of a moral perspective suggests that what Hassler might have learned from Flannery O'Connor had less to do with her invariably Catholic moral outlook than it did with point of view and more careful deployment and manipulation of bizarre and unusual details. Because "Yesterday's Garbage" becomes the basis for the later novella, *The Staggerford Murders*, it will be referenced again in a later chapter.

Rufus at the Door and Other Stories

The second collection, *Rufus at the Door and Other Stories,* is even more of a mixed bag." According to the introduction, Hassler wrote the title story of the collection *after* he had written *Grand Opening*. "That book only covered one year, and I wanted to know more about Rufus ... so I extended the story into the future" (iii). A number of things make that explanation peculiar. First, the title character's last name, Alexander, is different than it is in *Grand Opening*. Second, the story's first-person narrator —beyond some external details—bears only faint resemblance to Brendan Foster, the character who has the most to do with Rufus Ottman in *Grand Opening*.

A third reason that "Rufus at the Door" is a less well-formed piece of fiction occurs in the first two pages. In what has to be one of the most "politically incorrect" pages in Hassler's *oeuvre*, the narrator describes a ninth-grade bus trip to Rochester, Minnesota to visit "what was then called the insane asylum" (21). There, the teacher, Miss Sylvestri, points out what were then the different categories of developmental challenge: morons, imbeciles, and the insane. Following the visit, but before letting the students off the bus, Miss Sylvestri asks "if any of us realized that we had a moron living in Plum."

Some interesting connections with *Grand Opening* do appear, as students guess different people. As the story further develops Rufus and his history, other similarities to *Grand Opening* occur, while other details differ. The narrator describes Rufus, his "straight spine" and "ledge-like eyebrows" and his vacant stare, "his eyes directed to a point slightly above the passing people, his face locked in its customary grin" (24). When Mrs. Alexander comes to town to shop on Saturdays, she leaves Rufus in the pool hall with an older brother, Lester, or at the grocery store that the narrator's father owns. At the store Rufus stands in front of the "full-length window of the front door, looking out" for hours at a time, grinning all the while. Explaining the town's not paying him much attention, the narrator explains:

> *We became, as villagers, so accustomed to each other's presence, so familiar with each other's peculiarities, that even the most eccentric among us – were considered institutions rather than curiosities (25).*

After Rufus flies into a rage when cousins at an Alexander family picnic tease him, the possibility of Rufus being sent to the "insane asylum" becomes a point of tension.

When Mrs. Alexander dies, and the narrator describes how Rufus realized she was dead, Hassler struggles to justify the one-page account. The narrator says, "judging later by the evidence and what we knew of his habits, the village imagined this" (28). The narration ends with one of the longest and most awkward sentences in Hassler's entire *oeuvre*.

> *His great blue eyes were rolling, Mrs. Underdahl later told my father in the store, as though he sensed that this day marked the end of his childhood and now, in his late thirties, he would have to face the world alone – far off from his mother's house, which had been arranged to fit so well his simple needs, far off from his mother's love (29).*

This sentence shows none of the skill or concision Hassler said he learned from imitating the sentences of John Cheever. The final phrase, however, does recall Hassler's own observation in *Good People*—quoted earlier—about his own sense of security as a child.

"Rufus at the Door" concludes with a second trip to the "asylum." Then, as the bus is ready to leave, the narrator sees "two men on the doorstep with their backs to us. One was an orderly, the other was a tall, white-haired man with a straight spine and his hands clasped behind his back" (31). Before the bus pulls away, the narrator looks back at Rufus, who is now looking out the door at the departing bus.

> *The broad front door was now locked and he was standing behind the glass … He didn't look as healthy as he used to … His face, without a grin, was that of a much older man, the jaw hanging slack, the cheeks hollow. In his round blue eyes, without a grin, there was something obviously very deep, like yearning.*

Seeing that Rufus is looking directly at him, the narrator concludes that Rufus recognizes him, and that the eyes "told me that he had indeed tried to follow me out to the bus; moreover, they told me that mine was the face that reminded him of Plum."

With the exception of the jarring first pages, the story is competently constructed. There are connecting details like the "ledge-like brows," minor leitmotifs, a reference to religion, and a stunning natural description, of the rain in the cemetery. The story maintains a measure of suspense, tension, and climax, and even a moment of recognition.[7] Overall, however, "Rufus at the Door" is a less satisfying work of fiction—in whole and in parts—than almost anything else Hassler wrote. Though it seeks to create a sense of empathy for Rufus Alexander, the effort is incomplete.

"Anniversary" tries unsuccessfully to imitate John Cheever's technique in his much-anthologized story, "The Swimmer." The reader accompanies a first-person teacher-narrator who misses event after event in his family's life as he concentrates single-mindedly on the obligations of his teaching career. The story ends without the mysterious poignancy and ironic heartache of the Cheever story. Scarcely more than a writing exercise, "Anniversary" presents the first-person narrator, a high school teacher, going to his upstairs den to correct papers on a Sunday in June. He carries a dozen red pens bought at the drugstore. When he remembers it is the tenth anniversary of his and his wife Donna's graduation, he pours two glasses of sherry and toasts "a number of things" with her as she works on a rosebush in the yard. He sees his eight-year-old son Robbie practicing his golf shot. Donna gives the narrator a Flaming Peace rose and says, "Promise you won't be up there for the rest of the day" (35).

Going to the den, he admits that he has "an appetite for solitude" (35) and that his wife is "jealous of this room where I find it." Setting the bottle of sherry on his windowsill and hanging the rose from the burlap curtains, he first dips into his briefcase "full of quizzes, exams, themes, term papers, and office mail," and comes up with a paper by a girl, Becky Burke, about her father who is dying. After grading that paper (leniently)—and seeing a flock of geese flying, unaccountably, south in June—he reads a memo from the teachers' union president, asking that he serve as grievance officer. When the narrator tries to print "O.K. One year only" in red in the margin of the letter, he discovers that this—and the other pens he had bought—all seem to be dry. Donna calls from downstairs to say she is taking Robbie for his driving lesson. The narrator expresses puzzlement at this apparently anomalous truncation of time. After a number of similarly anomalous events leading up to a climactic revelation, the last short paragraph describes rose petals on the floor, and the rain on the window turning to sleet.

"Anniversary" strains to re-create the effect of "The Swimmer," but the story does successfully reveal a number of themes that fill Hassler's early novels: the over-worked high school teacher, failed personal relationships, students' personal woes, and the occasional satiric comment. The "cues" for time passing: dried out pens, a fading rose, an aging bottle of sherry, and the telescoping of seasons passing—are competently handled, but what is clear is that Hassler is teaching himself to write, in this case by imitating a favorite author.

Like "Chase" and "Anniversary," "The Life and Death of Delano Klein" is more of an "exercise" or—to use a musical analogy—another "*étude*,"[8] but it *does* cast light on the way Hassler constructed his stories and, by inference, his novels. The third-person narrator records the details of Delano's life, without editorial comment, trying to make interesting the condensed life story of an apathetic and self-centered boor. In time, this viewpoint yields an ironic tone that scarcely suggests the author's view of the protagonist, hence the story's tone. The story runs only nine pages and, uncharacteristically, it has no "breaks," no flashbacks, no truncated time. It is "straight narrative." The opening, one-sentence paragraph might be a "thesis." "As Delano Klein was growing up, his parents and acquaintances (he had no friends) learned to expect the unexpected" (58). The narrator follows this with two brief anecdotes, one from kindergarten, the other from second grade.

At a kindergarten birthday party, he "refused to give up the present he had brought." In second grade Delano helped build a cardboard post office in the classroom. "On the day it was Mary O'Reilly's turn to be postmistress (Mary got nothing but A's), he [Delano] put a hard dog turd in the mailbox." Accurately reflecting aspects of childhood, both anecdotes nevertheless suggest the character's early self-absorption. The remainder of the story chronicles—in summary fashion—Delano's unusual early development: "a reading binge that lasted three years," his fascination with things mechanical, his invention, production, and sale of an icemaker "in much demand by bartenders," which he calls the "Havana Cuber." In his thirties Delano quits drinking, falls in love with a dental assistant and gets married. The final sentence of this brief narrative is pure Hemingway. "She was small and calm, and her name was Ernestine." Her only flaw is "an earnest faith in God." When Delano turns his icemaker business over to a distributor, the narrator notes: "I[i]n a short time, without doing anything, he was making three times as much money as his father."

Delano buys "a farm near Ashby, New Hampshire, because Ernestine had always dreamed of living in the country." He and Ernestine have two daughters, and, in an almost aloof tone, the narrator notes that he "came to be what is known as a good family man." The narrator notes that "Ernestine often spoke about God—a little too often to suit Delano—but he bore her faith patiently." Becoming bored with unoccupied affluence, Delano conceives the plan to build a "a three story stone house with a sundeck" overlooking a sloping pasture on his land. He and a stonemason spend six years building the house themselves. When admiring the house is not enough, "Delano, at forty-two, was bored again" (64). Finding one of his wife's college textbooks ("she had spent three semesters in college") and a religious poem titled "The Voices of God" that she had written—and then four more in another notebook—Delano decides to go to college. He even thinks he might try his hand at writing poetry. In an American literature course he turns in a poem to the instructor, who "thought, but did not say, that the poem revealed a depth of soul he had overlooked in Delano" (65).

Without indicating that the story is reaching a climax, the next—one-sentence—paragraph reports: "By the end of the term Delano had handed in a total of five poems. One afternoon in May, the instructor wrote a page of comments, clipped it to the five poems, and gave them back to Delano" (66). In the very next paragraph Delano dies in a one-car roll-over accident. After two paragraphs that impassively recount the funeral and the highway patrolman delivering Delano's "effects" to Ernestine (which include the five poems with the page of comments), "Ernestine went out on the sundeck overlooking the sloping pasture and sat down to read the poems. A pair of blackbirds pecked in the grass beneath her, clucking like hens. The sky was blue-white, the color of thin milk." Here, Hassler's tendency to link emotional scenes with natural description is again in evidence. The second-last paragraph records Ernestine's response to the instructor's comments. "So it had come to pass, after all, thought Ernestine. Delano had finally put his trust in the Lord" (67). But in the last paragraph she reads the first line of "The Voices of God." The story's final, one-line paragraph reads, "The rest of the poems, too, were hers."

In overview, "The Life and Death of Delano Klein" reads like another attempt to adapt some of Cheever's themes and New England details, but compared to Cheever's complex ironic tone, Hassler's impassive narrator is less effective. Skillful in description, and quick sketching of character, situation, and plot, the story and its satire on the small-minded, narrowly focused businessman and the sketchy critique of affluence will become sharper and more specific in later novels.

"Winning Sarah Spooner" exhibits some of Hassler's trademark skill in understanding and conveying empathy for the elderly. It might appear *too* "simple-seeming" to warrant serious attention, much like the characters themselves. But it is precisely the way the narrator pays thoughtful, empathetic (but scarcely sentimental) attention to both characters that makes this story a major stage on the way to Hassler's mature style. By paying even brief attention to the everyday details (for example, Emmett's "rusted lawn chair"), the narrator values the things, and, in time, the people who use those things.

The story explores the feelings of loss and boredom, and the efforts the aged make to maintain and nurture relationships as they kindle warmth and affection. The narrator's tone toward the widow Sarah Spooner and her retired neighbor, Emmett Heed, is tactful, unsentimental, yet empathetic. Religion appears in a number of brief exchanges between Sarah and Emmett (talking about prayer), but this early in his career Hassler seems to use religion as just one facet of everyday life that helps to create and enliven character, situation, and tone. Though somewhat precious in the initial description of Sarah Spooner's garden, the confidence in composition is an advance over many of the other stories. As the reader learns of Sarah's widowhood, the mixture of "life goes on" ("a new generation of birds") and permanence ("sparrows and chickadees were the steadfast visitors") create a strong initial impression. He adds an undertone of loss and grief with references to her husband Byron's death, and to the plywood of the "homemade birdfeeder" that is "curled and the paint faded" (42).

This story, like "Christopher, Moony, and the Birds," is an early *terminus a quo* for the emotional valence that birds will have in Hassler's fiction. One could fairly call birds an "objective correlative" for various psychological and emotional states—from depression to ecstasy—in Hassler's work. When the narrator compares Sarah's gardening to caring for birds, however, the narrator has Sarah make an important distinction: "But feeding a bird was not like raising a pumpkin. Gardening was a calling, watching birds merely a diversion" (43). Here the narrator anticipates the story's subtly surprising conclusion. Underlining the theme of boredom and grief, the next sentence smoothly introduces another key feature of the narrative: Sarah Spooner's reading. "So, in an attempt to fill up the blank white hours of her first lonely winter, Sarah borrowed her first book from the municipal library, a novel by Thomas Hardy." Sarah's first audible conversations with a Hardy novel are somewhat awkward, but talking out loud *is* both a realistic insight into the loneliness of widowhood, and a preparation for much that comes later. Here it is not a "running gag" but a technique of connection. Reading Hardy's novels becomes a leitmotif.

A single paragraph describing Sarah's house creates the impression of straitened conditions. It also provides a transition to an anecdote about the young neighbors (44-45) in the house next door. One could argue that the transition from February to "the Fourth of July"—and the abrupt introduction of retired farmer, Emmett Heed, who is the new neighbor next door—is abrupt, but the design is clear. The end of the paragraph moves by means of clear descriptive markers—Emmett sits on his porch step "until the morning sun grew hot"—to the unexpected: "then he moved to the shade of his back yard, where through his overgrown lilac bushes he heard a conversation Sarah Spooner was having with a bird." Emmett's hearing Sarah talking to the oriole introduces an almost uncanny quality to the story. The deft detail of the "rusty lawn chair" makes the scene.

The first, awkward meeting is skillfully handled as the narrator slips briefly into Emmett's viewpoint. The reader then gets a quick description of Emmett and the first "commonplace" conversation, about corn and rain. Sarah offers Emmett "lemonade and six buttered buns," and they talk of mutual acquaintances. The "homely" conversation about a pair of sisters, the Waylanders, and Sarah's seeing them in terms of a Hardy novel, becomes somewhat curious. But the technique is part of Hassler's valuing the everyday. As Emmett leaves, Sarah notes "[S]she had never seen a shirt so dirty." The next temporal transition, to mid-August, is handled in a sentence, when Sarah offers to do Emmett's laundry, ostensibly in order to pay for her garden supplies (50). This detail further emphasizes the straitened circumstances but also suggests her not so subtle efforts to initiate a closer relationship. When Emmett brings his (newly purchased) clothes for Sarah to wash, Sarah introduces Emmett to *Jude the Obscure*, about which she says, "I declare it's the Herman Waylander story all over again." Sarah offers

Emmett the book, and he leaves, thanking her for it.

A major break, a typical strategy in the novels, occurs as the narrator introduces the end of summer, and Emmett Heed's friend, Old John Olson. This four-paragraph "anecdote" in Emmett's viewpoint develops (with a measure of satire) an impression of two "grumpy old men" sharing their views of the world. "Emmett and Old John were confident they were correctly going about the business of growing old." When Old John dies of an asthma attack (somewhat awkwardly handled), Emmett is unsure about striking up any new friendship. "It wasn't easy building a new set of mutual prejudices, enthusiasms, and jokes. His last set was broken up when Old John took his half with him to the grave." Emmett heating his old house with a gas oven, then a space heater—and reading in bed "under three blankets and an overcoat"—anticipates French Lopat in the Morgan Hotel in *Dear James*.

Through the winter, the closest to "intimacy" that the pair achieves is the way Sarah doesn't hear Emmett's reading aloud as she bakes and mends and sews. "Sometimes he read whole chapters without her hearing a word, for she was concentrating on the starched collar and cuffs of the shirt he was wearing, the patch on the sleeve of his sweater, the part in his white hair" (55). And while this is, perhaps, not as skillful or subtle, or as deeply felt, as he will become in his later work, it is in rather strong contrast to, for instance, "Anniversary" or "The Life and Death of Delano Klein." Another detail adds to the effect as the narrator notes that Emmett takes dinner, then lunch and breakfast at Sarah's (55-56). The final short paragraph, describing the birds' despair at finding no food in the feeder provides an only seemingly surprising conclusion. In one sense the reader might see the narrator somewhat callously jettisoning an earlier symbol—as Sarah is abandoning the birds. In another sense it is an appropriate sign of Sarah letting go of a tangible symbol of her relationship with her dead husband, Byron.

The introduction to *Rufus at the Door and Other Stories* suggests that "Dodger's Return" was an early attempt Hassler made to deal with a character from his real life who "nagged at him since childhood" (vi), and who received full development in *Grand Opening*. Hassler tells this version from the viewpoint of Ross, a fortyish businessman who returns to the town of Willowby with his wife Martha for his twentieth high school reunion. Comic and satiric comments prepare for the introduction of Dodger Hicks, whose story begins as fellow classmate, Charles Bohannon recalls Dodger. Ross's own memory of Dodger's appearance: "sallow face," "wide cheekbones," and a habit of "nodding his head when he spoke, and his manner, when spoken to, of squinting and showing his teeth" (72) exhibits Hassler's powers of observation. Add to this Ross's recollection of Dodger's "lying in wait" to make Ross his friend and Dodger's reputation for theft but having a "heart like Robin Hood's" complete the sketch of the character who is central in *Grand Opening*. A highpoint of the story are the scenes in which Ross shows Dodger his boomerang, and Dodger shows Ross how to throw it (73). Ross's betrayal of Dodger occurs when he lies, telling Dodger that his parents did not want him to play with Dodger anymore.

After a long expository anecdote and a break in chronology, the narrative takes the reader to "Three A.M. at the Willowby Motel" (82) where Ross confesses to his wife his feeling of guilt for having abandoned Dodger. He adds, "I have this vivid memory of Dodger trying to follow me home on that third day, and my telling him he was anathema" (82-83). As Ross continues to reflect on his guilt and the changes that have occurred in his life since his childhood, his mind returns to the boomerang — and its popularity in 1943. Reflecting on its possibly symbolic meaning, he asks himself:

> *what made it so suddenly popular? Was it simply the magic of flight, or was there something in the boomerang's trajectory that appealed to the instincts of ten-year-olds? . . . Having*

been graspers for a decade, ten-year-olds were learning to give, but they gave only with a reward in view. They loved, but only with the promise of love in return. (85-86).

This reflection is integral to the story's conclusion but will appear only in truncated form in *Grand Opening*. Its relative awkwardness shows Hassler still learning the skill of subtle editorializing. As Ross and his wife discuss Dodger's return to Willowby,[9] Ross recalls a final memory that becomes another brief, but vividly realized anecdote. In spring, 1944, Dodger had appeared on the school playground after several days' absence and had poured a bag of marbles into Ross's pocket. At the end Ross reflects: "What do they mean? Are they life-signs in a friendship Ross assumed was dead? (89). The story never answers the question nor explains the meaning of the gift.

One of the previously unpublished stories about the title character, "Agatha McGee and the St. Isidore Seven"[10] begins with a characteristic element of mystery as Sr. Rose, the principal of St. Isidore's Elementary School announces an unusual Saturday morning faculty meeting and will not say what the meeting with the teachers from the public school will be about. The story then moves economically among three settings: the St. Isidore lunch table, the back room and barroom at Axel's Tavern, and the school board meeting room, ending back at St. Isidore's on Monday morning.

The Saturday meeting reveals that the public school teachers are preparing to strike because the school board rescinded a 5 percent pay raise that they had promised. The reason given: "unforeseen expenses" (95). The public school teachers have voted for the strike and ask that the teachers from St. Isidore's strike in sympathy. When the vote is three to three, Agatha McGee is asked to cast the deciding vote. Instead, she says she will talk to the board members.

That evening Agatha attends "a special meeting" of the board (five men "at a long, polished table … and two white telephones"), where she confronts the president, Jerry Logan, owner of "an ice cream drive-in at the edge of town" (98). She learns that the "unforeseen expenses" are travel costs and new uniforms for the high school band, which has just been invited to march at the Rose Bowl Parade. Almost half of the teachers' 5% raise will also go to pay for new sod and a new sprinkler system for the football field. Jerry Logan argues the importance to the community of the band's appearance at the Rose Bowl. Agatha calls the board's decision "reprehensible." Before she is asked to leave, she learns that the board is preparing to call a list of sixty unemployed teachers as substitutes. Announcing that she will cast her vote for a strike by the St. Isidore's teachers, she tells Logan she "never cared for the soft ice cream that comes out of your machines" and leaves the room.

When she discovers it is raining outside, she steps back inside and overhears a disparaging personal remark made by Logan. With that, she storms back into the meeting, surprising the president, whose cigar "erupted in a shower of sparks" (102). While he is trying to put out the sparks and recover himself, Agatha grabs one of the white phones and calls Herbert Greeley, president of the Public School Faculty Association, to ask for a ride, and to prepare to have his teachers call the unemployed teachers the school board plans to call, a list "graciously" supplied by one of the wavering board members. Other wavering board members second a motion to reconsider the faculty salary decision. When Herbert Greeley arrives, Agatha tells him that the board has already voted four to zero to restore the pay raise. On Monday, in the St. Isidore lunch room, all the talk is of the strike averted. Agatha McGee resolves to run for the school board.

"Agatha McGee and the St. Isidore Seven" is a model of Hassler's mature comic/satiric style. Vividly realized and full of dramatic moments (Agatha's leaving then returning to the school board meeting), the satire too is wide-ranging, beginning with the Catholic practice of abstinence on Fridays and the modernization of nuns' garb. It then works up to an indictment of small-minded, small-town businessmen and their skewed values, complete with clichés, especially viz à viz education and educators ("Like it or not, Miss McGee, in this day and age all educators are expendable"). Sr. Raphael's concern with her food is a running joke that provides bookends to the story. If one were to point to weaknesses, they would be the portrayal of Agatha's indecisiveness (95). The description of the school board meeting room misses opportunities for clarity, and, finally, the title of the story is somewhat inept, since it is "Agatha," not "the St. Isidore Seven," who is the real focus.

The final story in *Rufus at the Door and Other Stories*, which is titled "Nancy Clancy's Nephew," is another story that looks forward to Hassler's later career. Inasmuch as it is a shorter version of the novella, *The Life and Death of Nancy Clancy's Nephew*, a discussion of the short story will be part of the final chapter in this book.

From these two collections, then, the reader learns much about Hassler's development as a writer; about his characters, his themes, his experiments with style. The reader also learns how Hassler imitated other authors, how he experimented with point of view, with exaggerated characters and situations, truncated summaries, and practiced different kinds of humor and satire. In the short stories, however, with rare exceptions, the exaggerative, almost Twainian humor and satire are not as much in evidence as they will become, beginning with *Staggerford*.

Four Miles to Pinecone

A consideration of *Four Miles to Pinecone* will now show how Hassler taught himself the techniques of the longer narrative. While writing short stories in the early mornings and on weekends, Hassler had already begun trying his hand at longer forms of fiction. In *Conversations*, Hassler tells Joseph Plut that "*Four*

Miles to Pinecone was the first novel I wrote; I wrote it over five years; I wrote it once a year for five years until I got it right" (5). Published in hardback in 1977, the young adult novel was republished in paperback in 1989. *Four Miles to Pinecone*[11] is a tale of multiple betrayals and the protagonist's moral growth, and for the latter reason it belongs to another familiar genre, the "coming of age" story. In the novel's second half, it also becomes a boy's adventure story.[12] Framed as an English assignment—a forty-seven page story—that Thomas Barry must write over the summer after his sophomore year in high school, in order to clear an "F" grade in English, one might even see a "meta-fictional" dimension to the story. It is a story about writing a story.

At 116 pages and sixteen mostly short chapters, *FMP* is still apprentice, perhaps journeyman work. But it begins to show Hassler employing techniques from his short stories to construct a larger work of fiction. The reader will note a few differences from the short stories and the novels. A first difference is the first-person point of view. *FMP* is only one of two longer fictions in which Hassler used first person. Second, there is no temporal or historical context to speak of. Third, while it does employ anecdotes and digressions—as in some of his short stories—except for the opening paragraphs, the novel is straight, chronological narration; no flashbacks, no compression of time.

The story begins in June, on the last day of school. It ends with the Labor Day weekend, and a look ahead to October. But other than these basic references, the seasons play less of a role than they do in any other Hassler novel. The opening reads like the young adult novel it is.

> *Summer is over.*
> *I hope I never have to live through another one like it.*
> *First, I flunked English. Then there was the break-in at the grocery store that put Mr. Kerr in the hospital and me out of work. And finally, a three-hundred-pound goon tried to run me over with a truck.*

This opening foreshadows three of the key plot elements, though the paratactic recital of these unconnected events does little more than build an indeterminate sense of suspense. The novel then quickly introduces a number of more and less interesting characters. Besides the narrator, Tom Barry, a sophomore at Donnelly High School in St. Paul, Minnesota, the reader meets Morris (Mouse) Brown. Mouse is another sixteen year old. Tom is a well-realized young adult character. Mouse Brown's characterization is more superficial. Mr. Singleton, the boys' English teacher, has bad teeth, a frightening smile and is given to exaggeration. When the boys learn of their grades, Mouse says he'll leave school at sixteen anyway and brags about a night job he has taken. Mr. Singleton offers Tom an opportunity to clear the failure: write a forty-seven page story by the end of summer (the number of assignments he had missed).

In the second chapter, Tom goes off to work at Kerr's grocery store—his summer job where the narrator introduces Mr. Kerr and his store. Mr. Kerr is short, fat, and given to irony, if not exaggeration. In place of natural descriptions, the narrator offers gritty descriptions of the grocery store—like the front window "full of dead flies" (7). Other everyday details (such as a meal of "sardines and crackers") are or will become familiar in Hassler's work.

When Tom goes home for dinner with his parents, they confront him about his failing grade (Mouse betrayed him). Tom's parents border on stereotypes: the off-work factory worker in his undershirt; a quiet mother worried about her son's grades. As Tom is about to head back to the store, his mother reminds Tom to leave half of his pay in the refrigerator. As the first part of the novel proceeds, digressive (sometimes humorous) anecdotes and vignettes slow the forward movement of the plot. From the first foreshadowing when Mouse talks about a night job, to Mouse watching Mr. Kerr count the grocery proceeds on Friday night—then asking Tom where Mr. Kerr keeps his money—the narrator keeps moving toward the robbery plot. Chapter five ends as Mouse goes off with Bob Peabody, a former student who has served time for robbery.

On Saturday morning (the beginning of chapter six) the Barrys' rooftop breakfast introduces Uncle Chad, Aunt Gert, the northern Minnesota resort near Pinecone, and a city-country contrast. An anecdotal digression about Mr. Kerr catching and butchering a large pike caught in the Mississippi River anticipates the robbery of the store that night, in which Tom saves the week's cash and hears Mouse's name spoken by a second robber. Tom withholds from Mr. Afton, the investigating detective, the fact that he had heard Mouse's name. With Mr. Kerr hospitalized, Tom thinks he is out of a summer job, but Tom's father gives him a savings account containing everything Tom had given his father every Friday for a year, and for the rest of the summer Tom helps Mr. Kerr close the store.

Chapter eleven provides a smooth transition to the second half of the novel and the secondary plot line—the boy's adventure story. It is one of the strongest chapters, beginning with a subtle descriptive element. Summer has passed, and Tom rides a bus north to house-sit for his aunt and uncle, who are driving to North Dakota for a Labor Day wedding. Picked up from the bus by Uncle Chad and Aunt Gert, Tom describes the ride through the woods.

After we had gone about four miles on the highway, we came to a sign that said CHAD'S CABINS, and we turned onto a dirt road that dipped and rose through a thick pine forest. The sun hadn't set yet, but the trees were so thick and close to the road it was like driving through a tunnel, and Uncle Chad had to turn on his headlights (65).

A stop at the cabin of Lester Flett introduces the former newspaper man and occasional fishing guide. Tom's uncle excusing Flett's "poaching" serves to lower the ethical standards in the north country and prepares for Tom's almost grotesque description of Lester Flett. "He was smaller than I remembered him. He came up to my shoulder. His face was dark and wrinkled like an old leather glove" (67). Later, while the adults share a glass of Lester's homemade chokecherry wine, the description of the cabin contributes to the slightly grotesque description of the man.

> *I looked around at the cabin. I saw a window on each of the four walls and realized that the small room we sat in was Lester's entire house ... Besides the table and icebox, he had an old cast-iron stove with a flat top for cooking, two cupboards made out of wooden boxes, a kerosene lamp, and a cot. On one wall was a gun rack containing a rifle and a shotgun (70).*

The description increases the sense of enclosure, even confinement that the trip through the woods had established. Suspense builds as Uncle Chad and Flett talk about a string of outboard motor thefts around the lake. The supreme irony, and an almost *noir* element to the story, comes as Tom's uncle talks about catching the outboard motor thief, in the presence of the man the reader will soon discover is the thief. The chapter ends with Lester offering to take Tom walleye fishing the next morning. Hints of a coming storm prepare for the next night and the climax of the boy's "adventure" story.

The seemingly digressive morning fishing with Flett (preceded by a surprise visit from a great blue heron and highlighted by a discussion of morality) anticipates the storm, Tom's catching sight of the outboard motor thief, and soon thereafter learning that the thief is Flett. The adventure story concludes with Tom's four-mile drive to Pinecone in the thieves' truck, Flett's accomplice, Bruno Rock, clinging to the running board and then the roof.

With one thief in jail and Flett lit out to Canada, chapter

sixteen finds Tom back in St. Paul. After meeting Mouse for a Coke and finding his friend unrepentant—and in fact prospering in crime—Tom finally goes to Mr. Afton, and Brown is arrested. Mouse confesses, implicates Bob Peabody and others, and receives a one-year sentence in the State Training School in Red Wing.[13] At the end of the chapter, Tom—completing his writing assignment in the public library—reports that the forty-seven page writing assignment has grown to sixteen chapters, and that summer is at an end. Mr. Kerr will move into Lester's cabin, and Tom will go to Pinecone in October to duck hunt and to testify at Bruno Rock's trial. The coming of age adventure story ends with Mouse Brown suffering the consequences of his misdeeds, and Tom Barry having learned, through multiple betrayals and his experiences at Leaf Lake, the greater wisdom of doing what is right.

4

Early Successes

Staggerford

Jon Hassler's first novel, the tragic-comic satire, *Staggerford* (1977), presents a week in the life of a burnt-out high school teacher, Miles Pruitt, who has lost his belief. As the ironic narrator (who sees intimately into his protagonist) puts it:

> *ten years ago, at the age of twenty-five, he had lost his faith in the Father, the Son, the Holy Spirit, the Holy Catholic Church, the Day of Judgment, and Life Everlasting. He had lost the whole works (22).*

Struggling to live a meaningful life in the face of this loss, and multiple personal disappointments, Miles cares for his students—particularly a troubled young woman named Beverly Bingham—his colleagues, and his community. In the end he meets a tragic, almost random, fate, due at least in part to his existential commitment to others. Before beginning an analysis of Hassler's venture into adult fiction and the last week in Miles Pruitt's life, it is useful to consider some of the autobiographical and compositional issues that were not already covered in the biographical chapter, or the chapter on Hassler's growth as a writer.

Returning to a manuscript he had abandoned a year earlier, Hassler found new promise in a story that relies heavily on the author's own ten years' experience as a high school teacher. Going to work during a year's sabbatical from teaching at the local community college, he says that the original title, "The Willowby Uprising," changed to *Staggerford* when he woke up one day with the word "Staggerford" on his lips. He imagined characters in the book "staggering" through the week in school (*C*, 6). Describing the actual process of composition, he says it was the fastest book he ever wrote; five months, with a month to revise. "It just came pouring out" (*C*, 7, *MSJ*, 7). Readers will marvel at the picture of a high school teacher's drudgery and the sheer exuberance of the satire and the humor. Characters pour forth from Hassler's imagination like the images painted by Fra Lippo Lippi in Robert Browning's famous monologue.

Discussing some of those characters, Hassler says that (as was noted in the biographical section) Fred Vandergar is based on a teacher at Brainerd, Mark Bunsness, who had cancer. Hassler says, "He's the man whom Miles hugged because I didn't" (*C*, 8). The story of Jeff Norquist pulling a knife on a Native American student and precipitating an "uprising" was based on an incident when Hassler was teaching high school in Park Rapids. The name of the Staggerford High School principal's wife, Anna Thea Workman, derived from a student of Hassler's, Theanna Winkeleman, at Brainerd Community College (*C*, 9). The story of Mrs. Hawk, who gives her husband a black eye for coming home drunk the night before his daughter's wedding, is based on a story Hassler heard in Park Rapids (*C*, 10).

The interview with Plut anticipates a number of issues that this chapter's analysis will consider. Plut, for instance, notes that Hassler often describes characters "in non-human terms." His examples are Coach Gibbon looking at Miles "the way a woodpecker examines the bark for grubs," calling Agatha McGee "quick as a bird," and comparing Imogene Kite to a horse and Carla Carpenter to "a Kodiak with a fresh wound" (*C*, 11, 12). As astute as Plut's comments are, they ignore the fact that a variation of this technique is found in almost all of Hassler's novels. Animals, and particularly birds, are favorite sources of analogy.

Plut is also insightful in other ways, getting the author to admit that "most of my protagonists are the same man" and that if Hassler hadn't "killed off" Miles Pruitt, he might have ended up writing several other books about Miles (*C*, 16-17). Focusing on a passage in the novel that is taken from Hassler's personal journals and incorporated in the novel, Plut asks about Miles's observation that life is a mixture of "Light and Dark" (*C*, 13). But he does not point out—perhaps is unaware—that this is a first articulation of the "things throw light on things" technique discussed in the chapter on Hassler's growth as a writer.

Addressing larger themes, Plut and Hassler reflect on teaching as a "sacrificial" profession and the consequences of Miles's death. Plut acknowledges the "rebirth" of Superintendent Stevenson (C, 17) and even an "ascension or resurrection" (C, 19), though not in connection with Miles or the superintendent, but "displaced" to Mrs. Stevenson. Plut does not see the potential irony of such displacement, or its place as part of the novel's archetypal pattern, which was discussed in the chapter on Hassler's growth as a writer.

Set in northern Minnesota, against a realistic background in the first decade of post-Vatican II Catholicism, the novel anticipates in its themes many twenty-first century issues. These include dysfunctional families, public immorality, parochial rivalries and animosities, and racial tensions that adumbrate the "multi-cultural" emphasis of two decades later. Decades before more celebrated authors like Ian McEwan, Salman Rushdie, or Martin Amis, Hassler was using the cautionary, satiric tale to depict the consequences when individuals and communities suffer the loss of active, deeply felt religious faith. A drifting, thoughtless secularism may not cause the tumult of an aggressive "new atheism," but it will often lead to confusion, sadness, and a loss of vitality. Those caught up, or mindlessly drifting, will lack direction, purpose, and any sense of joy.

Except for Miss McGee's—and Miles's former—Catholicism, and the references to Miss McGee's parish, St. Isidore's, the novel's world is more thoughtlessly rather than aggressively secular. But the consequences of this secularism constitute a potential cause of the novel's sadder and more tragic events. Even those who believe, or once believed, will suffer these effects. Miles is one such former believer. Betrayed by his brother in high school, and robbed of his first love, Miles from that time forward no longer had "the ability to see life as simple and cohesive" (129). Going forward with the realization "that everything in life was subject to change without notice," it is little wonder that Miles loses his Faith.

How does a novelist portray this state of affairs? Conflicted by the secularism, but empathic toward his characters, the artist who continues to believe that life can still have meaning will try to understand the pain, criticize its unique causes, and endeavor to see the humor, and the hope. How can a story, set in what Miss McGee calls "a new Dark Age" (15), about a burnt-out teacher, who had lost his faith half a decade before, inspire not only admiration but a sense of mystery? How can a novel that may appear to devolve—as Joyce Carol Oates put it in her *New York Times* review—into "a series of unexceptional comic scenes reminiscent of television" (C, 21) still leave the strong impression of grace operative in an increasingly unbelieving world? The explanations are numerous and complex.

Autumnal, elegiac, and exaggerative, the seemingly quotidian events of Miles's week take on special significance when seen (as suggested in the chapter on the author's growth as writer) to recapitulate some of the classic features of the hero's quest. These stages, as well as specific events, images, and characters, provide a helpful key to reading *Staggerford* as a hopeful, but knowing and nuanced response to a world of belief and unbelief.

Perhaps obscuring the universal pattern of the hero's quest are many of the issues and events that have persisted from the late twentieth century into the first decades of the twenty-first century. As examples, the town's newspaper editor, Albert Fremling exhibits compulsive drunken driving. The increasingly open (and often inebriated) infidelity of the town dentist, Dr. Oppegaard and his married assistant, Stella Gibbon, are further persistent symptoms. This infidelity causes additional pain and heartache, manifested in the couple's children, Nadine Oppegaard and Peter Gibbon.

At the start, the novel focuses on the parochial and high school rivalries and animosities that illustrate the self-centered lives of many of the characters: the principal, Wayne Workman's insecurity and ambition; Coach Gibbon's ambition and obsession with competition. The superintendent, Ansel Stevenson's weakness, abetted by his fear of death, further undermines the social fabric. Though treated in humorous and satiric fashion, student misbehavior and a Native American "uprising" that it precipitates suggest an undercurrent of suspicion, violence, hate, and anarchy that Miles's bumbling efforts avert almost by accident.

The most painful instance of confusion, sadness, and lack of purpose manifests itself in the dysfunctional Bingham family and their long-hidden secret. The father was wrongfully jailed for a murder committed by his unstable wife, Corinne. The murder sends one daughter fleeing and the other daughter, Beverly, to live with the secret of her mother's violence. The father dies in prison, and Beverly's depression and indecision result from her conflicted sense of responsibility for her mother and her own sadness and guilt. She is disgusted with her life on their rundown chicken farm in a gulch outside of town, and guilty at having hidden her mother's crime. The novel's tragic climax follows directly from Beverly's silence and Miles's attempts to resolve both the Native Americans' grievances and give Beverly's life a sense of direction. These painful events, treated in realistic detail, may incline one to overlook the story's universal dimension. The novel, with its omniscient narrator, thus presents a struggle between the quotidian and an archetypal, even transcendent perspective.

The end of Miles's week begins mundanely enough. The reader follows him through his Friday classes and a Friday night football game with Imogene, the librarian daughter of his landlady's neighbor. After that they go to the superintendent's house for bridge and raspberry sundaes. On Saturday Miles takes a walk, meets by chance both Beverly and her mother, and returns home to prepare for a Halloween party for the high school staff.

Despite a hangover following the party,[1] Miles unaccountably goes to All Saints' Day Mass the next morning, and later that day he and his landlady, Agatha McGee, discuss the relation of good and evil. Starting on Monday, Miles struggles with student misbehavior, requests for help, and an impugning of his reputation. Called from his sickbed (after a bad Tuesday at the dentist), Miles arrives to take his study hall as one of the Native American students, Hank Bird, pulls a knife on Jeff Norquist, and Jeff Norquist breaks Hank's nose and knocks out one of his teeth. Thus immersed in his students'—and later his community's—lives, he ends up trying to deal with the uprising of Native Americans who want retribution for what Jeff Norquist did to Hank Bird.

The autumnal setting and connection to the liturgical year (All Saints' Day) establishes an archetypal dimension that is somber yet somehow reassuring. The seemingly quotidian events of a high school teacher's week take on special significance as they recapitulate a number of conventional stages in the hero's quest. The narrator of the novel enters the perspectives of a full range of characters, from the slightest to the most central; from the mean and petty to the unconsciously selfless protagonist. This provides an almost "olympian" view of events. The narrator's drily realistic observations result in a pervasive tone of humor, gentle irony, and sympathy that is both tragic and comedic. In short, the novel reads like a small-scale "divine comedy" whose surprising and tragic ending does not dispel a sense that, in one character's words, the story, for all its sadness, death and loss, makes the reader aware of "some kind of life [we are] unaware of."

To pick up the archetypal dimension from the very start: The novel begins in the dry futility (pp. 9, 10) and loss of autumn. The Badbattle River is low. Two images of death occur in the first two pages. It is also Friday, a day on which Agatha McGee commemorates "the barrenness of a world bereft of its Savior" (25), a reference to Christ's death on Good Friday. The reader soon learns of other deaths. In second hour of Friday's class, Miles's student, Roxie Booth, tells about a corporal who swallowed crushed glass and died (6). That evening, after the football game, the reader meets Superintendent Ansel Stevenson, who has a heart condition, and whose "passionate clinging to life had fixed his attention squarely on death" (42).

During Miles's regular Saturday "hike," the reader learns of fellow-teacher, Fred Vandergar's death from cancer (pp. 63-68), and just before the Halloween Party, the narrator includes an anecdote describing Lyle Kite's death (72). At the party Anna Thea Workman learns that a close friend's mother has died (90, 135-36), and later in the novel the reader hears the story of Beverly's father's death three years before, and Jeff Norquist's father's drowning, eight years before. And, of course, there is the constant reminder of death in the paradoxical "nickname" Miles has given to the principal's wife, Anna Thea. He calls her "Thanatopsis," whose meaning, Miss McGee points out, is "view of death" (48), adding, "there's nothing fitting about it. Anna Thea Workman is young, and she has a lot of vitality."

The most clearly archetypal figure of death in the novel is "the bonewoman." The reader first meets her while Miles and Miss McGee are at dinner on Friday. There is a knock at the back door, and when Miles opens it, "the shadowy form standing below him on the bottom step" (27) asks a one-word question, "Bones?" It is Beverly Bingham's mother, who sells chickens to the citizens of Staggerford and then returns to ask for their bones. As she leaves through Miss McGee's garden, Miles registers the following complex observation:

In the darkness, the fragrance of Miss McGee's old garden, turned up and tired, seemed to be rising in faint whiffs from the Bonewoman's deep footprints – the tuberous smell of roots freshly exposed and the sour smell of tomatoes spoiled by frost and left with a few blighted potatoes to blacken and nourish the spent, gray soil" (28).

The contradictory images of death and future fertility imply both apprehensions and hope. Later, at the Superintendent's house, the Bonewoman appears again, and Superintendent Stevenson reacts violently, telling Mrs. Stevenson, "Viola, don't open the door to that woman again" (42). Here a character associated with both death and mystery evokes a powerful reaction from the person in the book who most obviously fears death.

Connected to the images of barrenness, futility, and death are the suggestions of mental instability. These first surface in a flashback. Miles spends an evening filling his journal with memories of his first love, Carla Carpenter. This includes the overtly "grotesque" picture of Carla Carpenter's mother, whose "illness" appears mental. A few pages later, as Miles narrates the tale of his betrayal by Carla and his brother Dale, we learn of a cop "driven mad by traffic and teenagers and dreary weather." Then, when Carla comes to Dale's hotel room and upsets Miles's simple view of life, he sees *her* action as "like the ravings of her [Carla's] mother and the traffic cop, it was nonsense."

Of course, the most striking instance of mental instability is Corinne Bingham. The "Bonewoman," in one of Miles's first meetings with her, is compared to a bear, an archetypal symbol of the feminine. "It was the Bonewoman. She was striding forward like a bear, heedless of the spongy wetness of the creek that covered her shoes" (71).

Like classic heroes, Miles, effectively an orphan, is called upon to give aid and thus begin his quest. Because he responds to his student, Beverly Bingham's request for help, suspicions are aroused. As in the hero's quest, there is also a curse, as well as omens, tests, ordeals, and secrets. Near the end of Miles's quest, he also receives a kind of "acknowledgment of his followers," as Jesus did from his disciples (Luke 16:16). One form that the omens take are the various birds, in flocks or singly, that Miles sees at various junctures in the plot. One of the first occurs when Miles goes for a walk along the river and just before he meets, first Beverly and then her mother.

> *Before leaving the cemetery, Miles again studied the sky. Now a heavy cloudbank was moving over the prairie like a sheet of slate. When its forward edge put out the sun, the wind doubled its force, blowing a flock of blackbirds out of a cedar tree and causing Miles to shiver in his tweed jacket (68).*

This scene has "omen" written all over it.

The first reference to a curse occurs after Jeff Norquist jumps out of Miles's second hour classroom window on Monday morning. When Miles goes to explain the event to Superintendent Stevenson, Stevenson refers to the "Staggerford Curse" (144). "I recognized the curse I've been fighting for twenty years—the desire of a certain percentage of our students to run away from school, to stay away, to reject what we offer them. I call it the Staggerford Curse." Repeating the phrase twice more before Miles leaves the room, the character in the novel most associated with death also underlines the centrality of the "curse" to the novel's sense of fate and futility.

The first test Miles endures is associated with his visit to Fred Vandergar. All the staff know that Vandergar is dying of cancer, but they hold a retirement party anyway. "Miles dreaded it" (65), but he is also the only staff member who visited Fred before his death and, being unable to speak, gives the dying man a hug. Among the most ironically humorous tests is that administered by Wayne Workman at the Halloween Party on Saturday night. Wayne is wearing a suit and tie. His explanation: "'It's a test.'...' I decided to wear one of my everyday suits and see if people notice that I'm not in costume. This is one of the suits I wear as principal, and it's possible that some people will subconsciously assume that I'm in costume ... deep down inside they probably don't think of me as a real principal. They think of me as an imposter" (79-80).

A first, kind of double crisis in the novel occurs on Sunday afternoon. Miles meets Beverly Bingham in Pike's Park, where teenagers meet to neck. At the end of the meeting, Beverly declares her love. "'Mr. Pruitt, is there any chance you'll fall in love with me?' She opened her door as she said this, and before she stepped out into the rain she leaned over and kissed him quickly on the cheek" (105). When Miles returns home, Miss McGee has been watching the rain fall on the dying ferns, reading the Sunday paper, and pondering good and evil in the world. "Could it be, she wondered, that the vice and barbarism abroad in the world served, like the rain, some purpose? Did the abominations in the Sunday paper mingle somehow with the goodness in the world and together, like the rain and sun feeding the ferns, did they nourish some kind of life she was unaware of?" When Miles returns from Pike Park, Miss McGee shares with Miles her insight about ferns and the relationship of sin and goodness. Miles expresses skepticism in an ambiguous metaphor: "'Well, it's an arresting thought, a fern of goodness and sin,' he said absently." Their talk then turns to Miles's relationship with Beverly Bingham, and Miles admits to being confused. Later that night he spends hours typing out recollections of his first love, Carla Carpenter.

The hero also undergoes a number of struggles and ordeals with various "villains." The most comical is, once again, Wayne Workman. Miles struggles with Wayne over his wife's request for a day off to attend a friend's mother's funeral; they struggle over the faculty handbook, and they struggle over Miles's relationship with Beverly Bingham. A particularly grotesque—almost surreal—ordeal is Miles's encounter with the dentist, Karstenburg. Miles travels to Duluth on Tuesday in order to have a wisdom tooth removed. Karstenburg makes such a mess of Miles's mouth that he has to "eat aspirin" all the way home, and the only thing he can tell people about his experience is that "Karstenburg did me wrong" (164). There is sufficient blood in the narration for the incident to qualify as part of the hero's quest. Of course the most serious struggle is with Corinne Bingham, the bonewoman. The various times that Miles meets the bonewoman become "mysterious meetings." Whether Miles is actually "reconnoitering" the enemy—as Propp's list of heroic struggles might label them—these meetings belong to the heroic quest, even as they add to the aura of heroic mystery and help build narrative suspense.

One overt allusion to a famous version of the hero's quest comes Thursday afternoon. Miles has just been reading some of his students' "What I Wish" papers. When he opens his briefcase to take out a paper, he muses, "No wonder the briefcase was so heavy, thought Miles … The wrongs and losses and near misses of 114 people, when packed together in one briefcase, took on the heaviness and solidity of rock" (229). Miles realizes that it is not the poor quality of the papers that oppresses him, "It was the way these papers teased him off the road of hope into the gulch of despair."

Like Christian, the hero of Bunyan's *Pilgrim's Progress*, Miles carries a heavy burden through his week's journey, and, like Christian, he is tempted to fall into his own version of Christian's "slough of Despond." Combined with the numerous references to the "gulch" in which the Bingham's chicken farm is located, this "gulch of despair" adds further resonance to Miles's week as a recapitulation of the hero's journey. Likewise, there is a sinister forest (surrounding the Bingham farm). Miles traverses real and figurative valleys of death.

The central secret of the novel relates to the past and Beverly's mother, "the Bonewoman." First alluded to when Beverly and Miles meet in Pike Park (104), it returns in Miles's journal entry for Thursday (226), and is finally revealed on Friday afternoon (237-241). It is Miles's involvement with Beverly's secret that precipitates Miles's final, fatal meeting with the Bonewoman.

A final, archetypal feature of the hero's quest occurs in conjunction with the revelation of Beverly's secret. It is book report day, and, reporting on *John Brown's Body*, Nadine Oppegaard marvels at Stonewall Jackson; "what I mean is that here was Stonewall Jackson in his thirties with the respect of all his troops ... How many of us will be able to claim that much respect for ourselves by the time we're thirty-nine?" (235). In response, Peter Gibbon says, "Mr. Pruitt has the respect of his troops ... We're his troops." While always tinged with irony, this affirmation or acknowledgment makes Miles a kind of representative of his people. As the students pursue the analogy, Nadine reminds the class that a hero like Stonewall Jackson has to have someone "he lives for and is ready to die for." As the students argue about who is Miles's equivalent for Jackson's Robert E. Lee, the narrative returns to the mundane, but the seed is planted that will ripen in the kenotic nature of Miles's death. Despite ambiguity and irony, Miles does die for his community.

The narrator's role in the novel contributes significantly to both the satire and the sense of higher powers at work in the lives of Miles Pruitt and the other characters. The narrator's satiric side comes through particularly well with exaggeratedly one-dimensional characters, like Coach Gibbon. After complaining about Superintendent Stevenson, "Coach" gets exasperated.

> *Coach Gibbon crumpled his paper napkin and threw it at the wall. He was full of the smoldering anger that always burned hot and clouded his vision for several days after a lost game. Beyond that, he was said to be losing his wife. (57-58).*

In another instance, the narrator subtly enters Beverly Bingham's consciousness in order to reveal her multiple intentions. When Beverly asks Miles about her future, her words are, "'Don't talk to me about college,'" but then the narrator adds, "hoping he would" (54).

The narrator also provides a sometimes "sweeping," almost "universal" view of things that contributes to a larger view of events. The first description of the Badbattle River and its history takes the reader back to 1806 and Zebulon Pike, the Sioux and Chippewa wars, and finally contemporary "birdwatchers and families on picnics" (59, 60). But then the narrator extends the "universal" view a little later, when Miles and Beverly meet beside the river.

> *They watched the surface of the Badbbattle sliding west toward Pike Park, toward the reservation, toward its confluence with the Red River of the North. Mingling with the Red, this water would then flow through Fargo and up to Winnipeg and from there it would angle northeast and divide itself into dozens of channels across Ontario and come together once more before emptying itself into Hudson Bay. (70)*

Of course this could be a high school teacher's ordinary view, but the "sweep" of the description, and the distances suggested, provide a more universal backdrop for the quotidian events with which the novel is concerned.

An omen before the climax of the novel occurs at the time of the "uprising." The governor sends the state patrol, headed by a giant of a man. Miles's amazement at "the governor's Giant," who arrives to deal with the Native Americans, highlights his larger than life significance. Miles records that amazement in his journal:

> What's it like to go through life astonishing people by your mere existence? I am thinking of the governor's Giant. When the Giant stepped out the front door of the school this noon, it wasn't only Bennie Bird who recoiled in amazement. I saw a thousand people take a step backward, Indians and students alike. (227)

Miles's reflections give voice to an awareness that comes close to being the "vision of being" that philosophers point to. "The governor's Giant" is an almost otherworldly "apparition" in the small town, hinting, however ironically, at some greater significance for the events taking place.

Of course, the hero's quest frequently ends in an, at least seeming, failure. Miles had done his part in negotiations with the Sandhill tribe, but he discovers, on Friday afternoon, that the National Guard have camped in the front yard of the Bingham's farm. He is worried about both Beverly and her mother. Scheduled to meet with tribal representatives on Saturday afternoon, Miles drives Wayne Workman's Mustang and the Staggerford negotiators to Pike Park. When the tribal representatives fail to appear, the state patrol and the Giant, as well as the National Guard leave, and a car from the reservation pulls out of the woods where it has been waiting. After a brief meeting that resolves the tribe's grievances, Miles drives the school negotiators back toward Staggerford. But when he sees Anna Thea driving his own car into the Bingham farm, he follows. Now worried about both Beverly and Mrs. Bingham, and wondering why Anna Thea was driving his car, Miles pulls up to the farm house and steps out of Wayne Workman's Mustang.

The Bonewoman, insane with fear, and resting her rat gun on the sill of the upstairs window, took aim and fired a .22 bullet that entered his skull an inch above the left eye (275).

Like many a hero's death, Miles's is at once both random and destined. The bonewoman had vowed to murder "the next man who set foot in her yard." That man turns out to be the one whom she had encountered on three separate occasions earlier in the novel.

In a significant moment, the narrator enters Beverly's consciousness, immediately following Miles's death. Beginning as description, the narration flows into her consciousness:

Beverly leaped off the porch and ran to Miles and dropped to her knees beside him in the mud ... She put her arms behind his head and shoulders and struggled to draw him up to a sitting position. But there was no life in him ... Then she stood up and gripped her hair with both hands and made a noise she herself had never heard before, a faint, high warble from the bottom of her soul, from somewhere further back than her birth – the anthem of the crushed spirit, the keen of the widow. (276).

Even as her trying to lift him to a sitting position suggests the *Piéta*, the somewhat exaggerative reference to "the bottom of her soul" and "further back than her birth" are of a piece with the novel's more "universal," archetypal perspectives examined earlier.

When Agatha McGee arrives, everyone is cowering in fear. But Agatha transforms the Bonewoman from mythic figure back into an everyday reality. "She stood and lifted her face to the upstairs window and said in a strong voice that echoed through the woods, 'Corinne Kaiser, you remember me. I am Miss McGee'" (278). When the Bonewoman finally comes down, she says, referring to Miles's death, "My daughter did it." Then the narrator adds a telling archetypal detail: "Somewhere geese called."

After Miles's death, Miss McGee struggles to make sense of what has happened. Her physician, Dr. Maitland, gives her "a large, befuddling capsule," and struggling under its influence, she recalls her conversation with Miles the previous Sunday. She says, "I am growing like the fern of goodness and sin," and a bit later, "I *am* the fern of goodness and sin" (280). Agatha's pastor, Father Finn, tries to console her with a superficial "he meant a lot to everybody," to which Agatha responds, "No one means a lot to everybody, Father. To whom, I ask you – besides to Beverly and myself – did Miles mean a lot? A deep abiding lot?" (280). In the mouth of this staunch believer, such a statement sounds starkly negative. It also somewhat undercuts the mysterious image of the "fern of goodness and sin." For some, Agatha's question might undermine any attempt to find a positive meaning in Miles's death.

Elsewhere in Staggerford, everything goes on as usual. Albert Fremling continues to drink and drive; Doc Oppegard and Stella Gibbon continue their infidelity. Even the believer may be tempted to think, like Miss McGee, that "the Dark Ages" have, indeed, returned. Is the only hopeful lesson to be drawn from the novel's ending the fact that life goes on, following the immemorial cycles of death and life, or, if you choose, life out of death? Is the superintendent's sudden "rejuvenation" the "natural" response of the living after someone close has died? The superintendent's "gesture" (to hug his wife) is ambiguous in content if not intent. Is it left to the reader to infer a providential meaning in the superintendent's renewed life, signified by his robust embrace of his wife?

In the 1996 *Image* interview, Hassler spoke about how Catholic school had taught him "to see life whole." One way to understand Miles's death is to see his life "as a whole." Viewed from its "end," and in the perspective of the all-knowing narrator, Miles's life is, as suggested earlier, kenotic. Having been betrayed and lost his faith, Miles (as his name implies) nevertheless "soldiers" through life, wondering about his place and purpose, but trying as best he can—though often ineffectually—to help others and to do good.

Jemmy

In his *Simon's Night Journal* for March 20, 1977, Hassler notes: "The short novel I'm finishing is not strong on imagination. It may be that teaching takes imagination and doesn't leave much for writing."[2] On May 20th of that year he comments: "The novel I finished a month ago is brief and anemic. Too much of my creativity was drained off into the classroom" (274). It should be remembered that these comments are made within a year of Hassler's having finished *Staggerford*. Despite these disparaging remarks about "the short novel," which would be published in 1980, *Jemmy* possesses many of the best qualities of Hassler's storytelling. Unlike *Staggerford*, *Jemmy* does not include any obvious autobiographical elements. An older man's relationship to a Native American teenage girl in a northern Minnesota setting would be the only similar connections to Hassler and *Staggeford*. The introduction of an artist would be the only other connection to the author's life.

Distributed and marketed as a work of young adult fiction, *Jemmy* is, in theme and tone, every bit as serious and lyrical as any of Hassler's other novels. It also develops the paradigm for many of Hassler's abiding concerns: the young woman marginalized by ethnicity and a dysfunctional family, who is "saved" by a relationship with a surrogate family. And though marketed as a young adult novel, *Jemmy* is something more than a genre specimen. Yes, it is relatively brief—149 pages in paperback—and, yes, the protagonist is a teenage girl. It also includes some incidents and dialogue that fit the genre stereotype, but plotting and thematic development, as well as a number of stunning scenes, make it comparable to the best of Hassler's other early novels. While the novel's concluding affirmation takes a familiar, somewhat melodramatic genre form, it is satisfying and completely plausible for the title character.

Set in the fall, winter, and early spring of a fictional Northern Minnesota, the plot is relatively simple, but the parts are artfully arranged, creating a contrastive episodic rhythm that adds variety and aids development of theme. Each chapter contains a link to a future chapter, creating a series of echoes. As in *Staggerford,* chapter length is significant, and chapter endings are often emphatic punctuation marks. Without *Staggerford's* religious dimension, the themes that drive *Jemmy* are nevertheless more universal than usually found in young adult fiction. Besides friendship and betrayal, the desire for independence, perseverance, individual (artistic) vision, and truth to one's own identity makes this an uncommon coming of age story.

Characters

Gemstone Opal Stott—known as Jemmy—is the oldest child of an alcoholic former house painter. Stott's wife, a full-blooded Chippewa, died in childbirth when Jemmy was eleven, and her little brother, Marty, was five. Stott has not had regular work since his wife died. Like Beverly Bingham, she is half-Indian, and, also like Beverly, one of her parents is dead. Unlike most of Hassler's other "hardscrabble girls," Jemmy has artistic talent and desire. The youngest Stott, Candy, her father's favorite, is six years old when the novel starts. The Stotts live in a dilapidated house two miles from an Indian reservation, on the edge of a pine forest. Candy and Marty attend the Reservation School, and Jemmy is starting her senior year at Eagleton High School.

Some of the novel's other characters are types, and many of them are "flat" (that is, identified by one or two specific traits). And, yes, in this only his second novel, Hassler might be re-using details from characters from the earlier novel. Mr. Olson is like Miles Pruitt, caring about particular students, especially

Jemmy. His defining trait is standing on tiptoe when he talks (98). The principal is like Wayne Workman. His singular trait is bargaining with everyone except Indians (19-20). Jemmy's classmate, Morrie Benjamin, is like Jeff Norquist in *Staggerford*. Like Norquist, Morrie has an Indian girlfriend, to show that his picking on Jemmy is not prejudice against Indians. Marty Stott and Rollie Rooster are the young mischievous kids, the younger looking up to and imitating the older. Stott is an alcoholic like a number of Hassler's minor characters.

Otis Chapman is the mysterious (perhaps haunted) artist; his beard and his love for children are among his defining traits. According to his wife, when he was drinking, Chapman, like Albert Fremling in *Staggerford*, would drive drunk and reckless through the night (89). His wife, Ann, is a former teacher, and (like Barbara Stearns Shea) a former student of the man she ultimately marries.

Roxanne Rooster and Frieda Frost are two minor characters who carry a good deal of the novel's satire. Roxanne is Jemmy's exploitive friend. It is her "betrayal" of Jemmy—telling the principal, and then Miss Frost, that Chapman has chosen Jemmy as model for the Maiden of the Rock—that triggers two of the most humorous and satiric episodes in the novel. Miss Frost, the Zuni Indian who teaches at the Reservation school and drives a sports car, is a supporter of Native American causes,[3] in this case Roxanne Rooster's greater qualifications as model because Roxanne is full-blooded Indian, whereas Jemmy is a "half-breed." Like other Hassler novels, *Jemmy* also includes a number of bit parts: the "Future Teacher," the school nurse, and Stan Rooster, the owner of the reservation store. These additional characters "animate" the scene and focus, as they amplify, the satire.

Plot

The novel's opening is deftly crafted to exhibit the setting, characters and social situation in a single page. "Out of the orange

October sun rising over the reservation came an orange school bus heading for Eagleton." When the bus stops at "the Stott place," the reader gets a quick view of "a four-room house and a small shed huddled at the edge of the pine forest. The house and shed, bleached a pale blue by years of harsh weather, were tipped slightly toward each other, drawn together, it seemed, by the tight clothesline stretched between them." Here, Hassler's artistic eye has already painted an evocative picture that forms the background of the novel. In the next few chapters Hassler deftly sketches the Stotts' home life and the father's behavior. It is a life of small meannesses and deprivations, motivating Stott's decision that Jemmy quit school. On the day she quits, Jemmy runs a gauntlet of bureaucracy and abuse, providing further occasion to satirize the educational system and attitudes toward Native Americans.

Jemmy's decision to take another route home in a snow-storm, because she remembered the way from childhood berry-picking with her mother, smoothly transitions to one of the most complex and enchanting scenes in the novel. After a stop at the Heap Big Discount Store in Eagleton, where she uses her lunch money refund to buy her sister a pair of jeans from "a pile of two-dollar jeans on a sale table" (22) and a pack of cigarettes, Jemmy steps out into a surprise October snowstorm.

Jemmy's trip home becomes a literal odyssey. There is irony in her thinking, "She would mark this special day—the end of her education—by taking a different route home" because rather than an end, this will be the beginning of a new kind of education. Even her next thought, "Today, with the car, she was free to choose," becomes ironic in that, by choosing the different route, she will become, temporarily, lost. The route first leads through a forest, up to Eagle Rock. When she stops in order to walk to the edge of the cliff, she felt "suspended in the sky, beyond sight of earth." But unlike the characters in other novels, Jemmy has no distinct view as "veils of slanting snow concealed it." Suddenly, however, she sees an eagle fly by, close enough to touch. With minute detail, the narrator re-creates this experience in a way that is almost numinous, culminating with: "She had seen the black pupil of its eye." Unexpected, unsought, this "apparition" is the first of three.

Then, however, the odyssey turns sinister. When the Dodge runs out of gas and Jemmy can't flag down a car for help, she starts down the road through the forest, choosing to go forward rather than back the "miles of wilderness" (25) to Eagleton. Despite being lost, "she wasn't frightened," but as the snow and the narrator's sentences fall softly on the scene, the reader's apprehension grows. Jemmy's hands and feet grow numb, the wind picks up, and when she finally emerges from the forest, it is not to safety, for nature appears to become an enemy as she follows the fenceposts at the side of the road and "the ground and sky—everything but the fence line—blended into a white oneness." It is almost like a miracle when the fence makes a right-angle turn and leads Jemmy to a barn where she takes shelter and meets an old horse, who, unlike the eagle earlier, stands immobile, so that Jemmy can warm her fingers and her hands.

Jemmy's overnight stay with the Chapmans prepares for the contrast of the Chapmans' and the Stotts' everyday life when chapter four switches into Marty's viewpoint, as he follows seventh-grader, Rollie Rooster, to vandalize the Reservation School. Though this episode's chronicle of mischief sounds like young adult fiction, it does prepare for Marty's later solo prank on New Year's Eve. In chapter five the reader is back with Jemmy as she wakes up at the Chapmans' on the morning after the snowstorm. The reader learns that Jemmy's snowstorm odyssey led her to the home of a couple, the Chapmans, who will take her in. Here Jemmy finds shelter, comfort, and the beginnings of friendship in the warm, well-ordered kitchen of the artist and his wife, where her new education in art and life will begin.

Chapman is an artist and recovering alcoholic who bought the farm as a base from which to do preliminary sketches and paintings for a mural that will cover one wall of the Tower Courtyard in Minneapolis. The mural will celebrate Minnesota's Native American heritage. Otis is fifty, and Ann, a former third-grade teacher, is thirty. Over breakfast Chapman discovers in Jemmy the face he wants to be "the Maiden" of his mural. Jemmy's apprehension about becoming friends with the Chapmans (56) anticipates the novel's ending, as does Jemmy's imagining herself in Minneapolis.

The next few chapters provide contrasting views of the Chapmans' farm and the Stott home. Chapman takes six days to paint Jemmy's portrait as "the Maiden." He also nurtures Jemmy's artistic talent. In time Otis's beard—a focus of interest since chapter three—becomes a link in chapter eight (90), when Ann shows Jemmy a picture of Otis without his beard. That picture then becomes a link to the final chapter. A further link (particularly between chapters seven and eleven) is Frieda Frost, who is enlisted by Roxanne Rooster to persuade Chapman that Roxanne should be the model for the Maiden. Miss Frost appears again after the completion of the portrait, offering to take Jemmy to Minneapolis for the dedication of the mural.

Then, on an extremely cold New Year's Eve, when Stott, Marty, and Candy are at Rooster's New Year's Eve party and Jemmy is at the Chapmans', Marty—embarrassed by his father's drunkenness at the party—leaves the store and breaks into the school alone. When he cannot get out of the school because the windows had been covered with wire mesh, he is found unconscious with two fingers frozen. When he is released from the hospital with parts of two fingers amputated, he refuses to return to school, sitting at home in front of the television, becoming increasingly depressed. After the new year, the Chapmans begin spending much of every week in Minneapolis as Otis begins the mural. It is not until they offer to board their horse with the Stotts, and let Marty care for the horse, that Marty breaks out of his depression. While the Chapmans are away in Minneapolis, Jemmy calls them and asks Ann if they will ever live on the farm again. Ann's answer is evasive, and Jemmy's concerns about the friendship deepen.

When spring arrives, Chapman hires Stott to paint the barn (in part an attempt to get Stott back to work), but when, after a week, Stott has accomplished little, Chapman berates him for being "a drunken bum" and challenges him to change his life. Stott renews his efforts, but when a "For Sale" sign goes up at the farm, he gives up the painting job. The Chapmans want Jemmy to meet them in Minneapolis for the dedication of the mural, but she decides not to go. A week later she drives Marty and Candy to Minneapolis, where she discovers that Otis had painted a younger version of himself into the mural as a Sioux brave looking back at the maiden. She struggles on the trip home with conflicted feelings about the six months friendship with the artist and his wife, but early the next morning Jemmy drives to the top of Eagle Rock, where she sees a golden eagle and experiences a feeling of oneness and self-confidence.

Imagery

Besides Hassler's characteristic interest in characters looking down from heights, *Jemmy* is replete with images of cold and snow and loneliness. Besides the central image of the golden eagle, the novel makes plentiful use of other birds to suggest—besides the change of seasons—the different moods of different chapters. Of course Eagle Rock is the central image of height. But Jemmy's staring from the rock is repeated in her looking down from the Chapmans' bedroom, Marty looking down into the schoolroom, and perhaps even Stott looking down from his ladder when he is painting the Chapman barn. The view is reversed when Jemmy, in Minneapolis, stares *up* at the picture of the maiden in Chapman's mural. The novel ends with her again looking down from Eagle Rock.

The snowstorm in chapter three provides the central experience of snow and cold, which is as beautiful as it is threatening. Jemmy's frostbit cheeks (which recalls her having first gotten frostbite in the third grade) are anticipated by Stott's cold hands in chapter one, and they look ahead to Marty's cold hands in chapter four. The cold of November and December anticipate the New Year's cold. The -28° cold of New Year's Eve, during which Marty receives his "wound," is a kind of climax of the snow and cold imagery, and is exclusively threatening. It is only the early coming of spring that "modulates" the emphasis on cold and snow.

Jemmy's loneliness is apparent from the very first page, and it is re-emphasized in almost every chapter. The Stotts' house— by itself at the edge of the forest—the Stotts having few visitors, and Jemmy having only one "friend" all underline the loneliness. Ann Chapman's loneliness, augmented by two allusions to O. E. Rolvaag's *Giants in the Earth*, is another leitmotif that carries through from chapter four through chapter ten.

The first significant reference to birds comes in chapter three, when Jemmy is surprised by the eagle as she tries to look down from Eagle Rock in the snowstorm. The second sighting of an eagle comes in chapter six, when Jemmy and the Chapmans stop below Eagle Rock where Chapman shows Jemmy how to draw. Jays and sparrows open the cold November and December of chapter eight, while crows, ducks, and a lawn "carpeted with robins" herald the early spring in chapter ten. An ominous apparition occurs at the end of chapter ten, when Jemmy sees a hawk or an eagle floating over the forest (135) before it is lost from sight. The final apparition occurs when a golden eagle again bursts from the face of Eagle Rock in the final pages of the novel. Here it is a sign of the freedom, and "lightness" that Chapman has associated with Jemmy's way through life.

Jemmy and Native Americans

With Otis Chapman's commission to paint a mural of "The Maiden of the Rock" as one of the central events of the novel, it is little wonder that *Jemmy* has so much to do with Native Americans. How well does Hassler handle this material?[4] The theme of isolation forms the background for the treatment of Native Americans. The Stotts live two miles from the reservation and have only the most tenuous relation to it. Candy and Marty attend Reservation School (as Jemmy had), and Stott frequents Rooster's Store, which is on the reservation, across from the school. But as a non-Indian, Stott would likely have been isolated after his wife's death. Chapter 2 focuses on Jemmy at school, and there are many references to the way the principal —and the school—treat Native Americans differently. The narrator notes the Native Americans' apparent desire *not* to upset or disappoint the whites, and this is also typical. Jemmy's caring for her siblings would be characteristic of Native American culture, though here it is as much Stott's irresponsibility and his alcoholism that account for Jemmy's role. In chapter 5 Jemmy tells Ann Chapman a good deal about her Native American background.

Onc of the most powerful, and also most accurate, depictions of Native American culture comes when Jemmy describes

> *harvesting wild rice on the Turtle Egg River, her mother paddling and holding the canoe out of the current while Jemmy bent the stems of rice over the side of the canoe and flailed at them—the rice building up around her knees until, after a time, the canoe was heavy with rice and rode low in the water (49).*

It is true that the Native American dimension of the novel is less in evidence after the fifth chapter, but having established the context, that dimension remains an important part of the novel. In later chapters it is Jemmy's recollections of her mother, and her mother's advice, that provide a further glimpse into Native American consciousness.

Neither here in *Jemmy*, nor in his other novels, does Hassler spare the Native Americans from his satire and humor. The reservation store keeper, Stan Rooster, does not judge Stott, but neither does he refuse him the orange-flavored vodka that is Stott's undoing. Frieda Frost, the Zuni teacher, comes in for at least implicit criticism for the way she makes canned speeches about Indian rights but drives a sports car and then abandons Roxanne's cause when she sees the finished portrait of Jemmy.

Artist and Model

One of the most fascinating aspects of the novel is the relationship between Jemmy and the artist, Otis Chapman, and how that relationship contributes to Jemmy's coming of age. Hassler effectively *suggests* more than he actually states or represents. This relationship also contains some of Hassler's own views on the purpose and end of art. Chapman, for instance, believes that the artist gives order to a world without order. This also expresses Hassler's own practice.

As Otis starts to stare at Jemmy's face, he asks her if she knows about the Maiden of Eagle Rock. The climax of the scene comes when Ann says, "'I can read your mind, Otis. You've found the face you've been looking for, haven't you?'" (52). Otis admits he has and hires Jemmy to pose for his picture of the Maiden.

A bit later, driving Jemmy home, Chapman takes the road below Eagle Rock and stops with, "'It's time to sketch'" (69). He gives Jemmy a sketch book and a pencil, and, outside the car, Chapman positions Jemmy in the place he had done *his* sketches of Eagle Rock. He shows her how to form a frame with her palms stretched outward, thumbs touching and how to hold the sketchbook as she draws the scene. Suddenly "a golden eagle had sprung from a ledge and was soaring overhead" (71). Jemmy is speechless with emotion, "as though the eagle had been sent as a sign," and "for a moment she felt very close to her mother." This is the first instance linking Jemmy, her mother, and Otis Chapman.

Later, "Painting the Maiden was the work of six days" (80). With this introduction the narrator leads the reader, in five short paragraphs, through the stages of the painting. Here Hassler's own artistic background is on display, and the reader is convinced when, at the end, Ann calls it "your best painting ever," and it gives Jemmy "the shivers to look at it." Jemmy's inner response is telling: "Never in a photo, not even in a mirror, had Jemmy seen herself so clearly." This is also one of the first indications of Jemmy's growing self-awareness. And again, "Otis's skill with shadow and color had given form to her soul" (81).[5] Jemmy's last response to Otis is: "And my hair. You've got a reddish color mixed in with the black," to which Otis says simply, "I paint what I see." This is a subtle hint of Jemmy's father's [Irish?] heritage.

At a party at the Stotts' Otis sets up an easel for Jemmy and offers to give Ann and Jemmy painting lessons. Then, in the next chapter, Ann Chapman and Jemmy share something more of their backgrounds. The reader learns of Otis Chapman's two previous marriages, his drinking problem, and the beard he grew when he stopped drinking. Ann shows Jemmy a picture of Otis without his beard ("'He looked younger without the beard,' said Jemmy").

A chapter later the reader finds Jemmy at her easel, struggling to put birch trees into her eighth painting. "Some days she lost herself in her work the way she used to become lost picking berries – but with a difference: when you were lost in a painting you weren't so eager to find your way out" (96). When Chapman arrives to take her and Candy to the New Year's party, he sees Jemmy's painting and notices the troublesome birch trees. He grabs a palette knife and "with three swipes at the canvas …

produced three birch trunks standing up from the water's edge." He tells Jemmy, "'Painting is tricks'" (97).

At the New Year's party, Jemmy and her sister become the focus of attention, but the episode's climax occurs when Chapman tells the assembled guests why he chose Jemmy for his model. He speaks about the sadness in her face but also the lack of guile and the presence of a depth and seriousness (99, 100). When midnight comes and Jemmy "was kissed four times— once by the bald man from Chicago, once by the young man in the red sweater, and twice by Otis," the narrator suggests a further significance in the artist-model relationship.

When Chapman drives the three Stott children home, he tells Jemmy of finishing her face on the mural, and how she seems to be speaking to all the people who walk through the Courtyard. When Jemmy asks, "'What do I tell them?'" Otis says, "'Your message is melancholy.'" When Jemmy tries to leave the car at home, "He reached for her hand, which she drew away from him, feeling vaguely resentful—she wasn't sure why."

Later Jemmy and Chapman argue over the meaning of the Maiden's suicide. Chapman calls it "'a romance, Jemmy. It's a pretty story.'" Jemmy responds that, as the Maiden, she'd rather be telling people, "'*Don't* give up'" (129). Chapman agrees that Jemmy "will never really fit the image of the Maiden. Instead of leaping off Eagle Rock after the battle, you would have gone home and cooked a meal for your family.'" He then praises her grace, "'Your ability to carry heavy burdens as though they weren't heavy.'" Recalling the eagle of their sketching day, he says, "'Your grace is like the grace of that eagle, Jemmy, the way you turn and climb and glide through life.'" Besides a touch of melodrama, Chapman's rhapsody might also be construed as "playing with people's lives," as Ann had said.

Later, as she paints an oak tree, Jemmy thinks of Chapman's words; "The artist finds the pattern. Most people see a random world, but the artist sees the patterns" (132). Then she recalls what her mother had said "about nature being one's guide." Reflecting on the strength and balance of the oak, she recalls what Chapman had said about the grace of the eagle, and then a telling comparison anticipates Jemmy's discovery in the final chapter. It was "as though Otis were an Indian. As though her mother were an artist." This reinforces the connection between Chapman and Jemmy's mother that has been a leitmotif to this point.

Jemmy passes up the chance to attend the opening but then takes Marty and Candy to Minneapolis. Once in the Courtyard, Jemmy feels as lonely and isolated as Ann Chapman had felt on the farm. "Not even in the forest during the blizzard had she been so alone" (144). Jemmy "sat down on a bench and gave herself up to the mural, entering it as deeply as Otis must have done while painting it." The description of the mural, and its autumnal effect, involve some excellent word painting, as well as another eagle. Then "her eyes were caught by the retreating brave." From across the courtyard she can't tell why the face looks familiar, "but the eyes of the brave were reminiscent of someone she had known, someone now just beyond her memory."

As Jemmy's focus returns to the Maiden, she ponders being "the Maiden to millions" while being just Jemmy to herself. She realizes that she has felt like two people before; at school, and even with different people. "Some days, even now, she felt more Indian than white." Her thoughts finally turn to the different sides of Otis Chapman. It is when she recalls that she had never seen the Otis behind the beard that she leaps from her bench to look more closely at the departing brave. "The brave's face, without the beard and looking younger by several years, was the face she had seen in Ann's photo album—Otis's face. She was overcome by conflicting currents of loss and joy. Loss of Otis. Loss of Ann. And yet joy at having Otis looking back at her, remembering" (146). Jemmy wants to "relieve the ache building up in her throat" by telling one of the people in the courtyard how the mural, besides telling the story of the Maiden of the Rock, "commemorated the six-month friendship between the artist and model," but as she reflects, this is not the sort of thing one tells strangers. "It was the sort of thing a girl might tell her mother and no one else." With this last understated touch, Hassler simultaneously suggests Otis's attraction to Jemmy, and once again explicitly connects Otis and Jemmy's mother.

On the bus trip out of Minneapolis, the sense of loss "came to outweigh her gladness," and [the narrator notes] "it was the same stinging emotion she had felt when she was eleven and standing at her mother's grave with a powerful urge to cry." When she was eleven, she kept from crying by looking at her father. Now she overcame it "by turning her gaze out the bus window and holding her hands up in the shape of a frame and imagining pictures that might be composed …" Even in her loss Jemmy imitates the artist and the lessons he had taught her.

Coming of Age

The culmination of Jemmy's "coming of age" story includes a number of powerful passages and evocative tropes that recall the artist-model relationship. They also suggest her growth is due to the growth of her artistic sensibility. They also suggest the continued influence of her mother. These passages also suggest the author's self-conscious artistry. Near the end of the novel's second-last chapter Jemmy prepares to go to Minneapolis to see Chapman's completed mural. Passing the high school on her way home, Jemmy reflects on how little she remembers of the day she quit; "then the blizzard came down like a curtain in a play, marking the division between acts. It marked the division between her high school days, fuzzy now in her memory, and what had happened since, all of it clear and sharp as the morning after a blizzard" (141). This sense of "distance" anticipates the greater objectivity with which she looks at her life, and the dramatic trope is one that Hassler will use repeatedly in his fiction.

After she sees the mural, Jemmy goes over all that she has learned, about friendship and about stepping back to "look at her life through a frame" (147). "She had come to understand what her mother had meant about the friendship of nature." Even without the Chapmans she will still "find other steadfast companions. She would pay more attention to the balance in trees. She would try to imitate the grace of eagles." Here the link to her mother, nature, and art is clear.

These passages prepare for the last page of the novel. Retracing her route through the blizzard, "she arrived at Eagle Rock just as the tip of the sun flamed above the horizon." Suddenly she is startled by "a golden eagle bursting out from the face of the cliff." She watches as it wheels and rides the updrafts, until it is "out of sight on the winds of sunrise." When the eagle is gone, Jemmy closes her eyes "as she committed to memory the pattern of the eagle's flight." She feels "as though by climbing to this sacred height she had transcended her other life … and had become one with the elements of nature, one with the sky and the wind and the turning globe." Though somewhat melodramatic, this scene, with its apparition and revelation, suggest at least a provisional end point to Jemmy's growth in maturity and self-consciousness.

Simon's Night

Begun in 1977 and published in 1979,[6] *Simon's Night* shares a number of features with *Staggerford*. As in *Staggerford*, a number of the characters and events are taken from real life experiences. Hassler told his friend, Joseph Plut, that Simon's character is based in part on himself. Like Hassler, Simon is an only child. Simon's earliest memory of his mother pulling him on a sled, and his voting for Franklin Pierce in the 1976 election, are from Hassler's own life (*C*, 30 f). Hassler also says that, like Simon

Shea, he used to recite poetry as he walked around <u>his</u> cabin in northern Minnesota. The failed military examination, the young man staying in St. Paul, and the buried leg are all real life events (*C*, 30 f). The novel is dedicated to James Casper, a colleague at Bemidji State University, who, Hassler said, is a model for Jay Johnson. The psalms that Simon prays at night get into the novel, Hassler says, because he was spending a fair amount of time at Blue Cloud Abbey in South Dakota while he wrote the novel (*C*, 42).

Like *Staggerford*, *Simon's Night* is about a teacher, and, like *Staggerford*, it takes place in the fall of the year. It is a time of drought and, by implication, sterility or barrenness. The setting for both novels is northern Minnesota, with some of the same towns and a number of the same physical features of the country, including the Badbattle River. As with *Staggerford*, the action of *Simon's Night* is concentrated in a single week. As Hassler told Joseph Plut, the experience of writing about seniors in *Staggerford* inspired him to "write about foolish old people." In a way *Simon's Night* is all about older people, but the emphasis on the common experience of aging: deciding to move into a retirement home and adapt, makes the theme more universal. With its focus on age and aging, *Simon's Night* is also, like *Staggerford*, haunted by deaths; the death of Donald Stearns, Jay Johnson, and intensifying on Thursday with two visits to funeral parlors. Like *Staggerford*, *Simon's Night* ends with a bizarre, and surprising, death and funeral, and a renewal of life and fertility.

Simon's Night is Hassler's second Catholic novel in that Simon Shea, age seventy-six when the novel opens, has been a faithful—and some might say overly devout—Catholic all his life. Like Agatha McGee, he grew up in a pre-Vatican II church, but, unlike Agatha, a decade into the Vatican II era, he does not have difficulties with the changes in the Church. One potential response to the changes comes when Simon shares with another character his doubts about whether God speaks exclusively through the Church. *Simon's Night* probably seems more Catholic than *Staggerford* because the novel includes a number of scenes in which Simon ends the day praying.

Just as in *Staggerford*, Hassler again employs a selectively omniscient narrator focused chiefly in Simon Shea, but with a number of significant deviations that occur, for the most part, at crucial junctures in the plot. This is especially the case when we learn how Simon met his wife, how he met and fell in love with a former student, Linda Mayo, and again when his wife, Barbara Stearns Shea re-enters the story. We also get glimpses, through the narrator, into the minds of the Indian, Smalleye, Dr. Jean Kirk, and her boyfriend, Douglas Mikklessen.

Like *Staggerford*, Simon's *Night* is about another teacher *in extremis*. Simon is a seventy-six year old college professor, eleven years retired from Rookery State College, who has recently checked himself into the Norman Home, in Ithaca Mills, a town on the edge of the northwestern Minnesota plains. The Norman Home is a family residence converted into a retirement home for seven local retirees, run by an enterprising but autocratic widow, Hattie Norman. Having misplaced a Social Security check, gotten lost in the woods near his retirement cabin, "lost" his car in St. Paul, and nearly burned down his cabin, Simon has decided that it is time to let others take care of him. The reader meets Simon, listening to the residents' conversations over coffee on a November afternoon, the day before the 1976 presidential election. Simon is bored but determined to stay at the Norman Home. The reader learns of his education and first teaching position at St. Andrew's, "a Benedictine college in the woods of central Minnesota" (97). Besides learning of Simon's early life, its disappointments and its triumphs, the reader also learns of his marriage at forty to a young widow, and of her walking out after two years, for another man—all through convincingly, and strategically situated flashbacks. This is the portrait of a perhaps *too* conscientious Catholic husband, who resolved to be, and (with one eight-day exception) actually remained celibate for thirty-three years after his wife had left him.

As with *Staggerford*, the week starts out uneventfully. Simon goes for a check-up and meets the new Ithaca Mills doctor, Jean Kirk. On Tuesday he helps one of the Norman Home residents downtown, then goes to vote in the 1976 presidential election. Late in the day he helps the same resident, the Indian Smalleye, onto the roof of the Norman Home. On Wednesday he has a proctoscopy from the young lady doctor and learns that the car he had lost in St. Paul has been found. On Thursday Simon catches a bus to St. Paul so he can retrieve his car, but he ends up having to stay overnight when the car needs repairs. He returns to Ithaca Mills on Friday to discover his wife has returned. The novel reaches its climax on Saturday when Simon fulfills a promise and then returns to his cabin in the woods.

More than *Staggerford*, which proceeds chronologically through the week, the narrative of *Simon's Night*, after the first day, proceeds episodically, with more numerous interpolated flashbacks providing exposition and a number of seemingly "discontinuous" events or episodes. Tension builds between the movement of the week's events, on the one hand, and the centrifugal force of the flashbacks, *and* the episodic "events," on the other. It might be argued that a number of the narrative "interruptions," especially the flashbacks, represent the way a senior's memory of his past operates, and this would be a plausible explanation of some of them. These episodes offer Hassler an opportunity to satirize a range of customs and values of the late 1970s.

Seen in another way, the novel has four narrative "layers." The first layer is composed of the events of the week. These include Simon's experiences in Ithaca Mills between Monday and Wednesday evening, his trip to St. Paul to retrieve his car, and his return to Ithaca Mills on Friday afternoon, culminating in a religious "errand" on Saturday morning. Interrupting this layer is a second layer, consisting of two narrative shifts. These take the reader to El Paso, Texas, where Barbara Stearns Shea prepares to leave her lucrative real estate position in order to return to Minnesota and Simon. The third narrative layer is the series of flashbacks that interrupt the events, primarily to develop Simon's history and character, as well as his relationships; first with Barbara and then with Linda Mayo. Besides deepening character and providing exposition, these flashbacks serve to slow the action, building suspense before the novel's conclusion.

The first major flashback comes after Simon has been to the Ithaca Mills Medical Center for his routine exam on Monday. Hurt by an overheard comment he believes directed at him, he searches for "another old wound that had healed" (30), and he tries to remember having failed his military examination in 1918, preventing him from serving in WWI. The flashback lasts six pages. The fourth narrative layer is a series of episodes that delay but do not interrupt the chronology. The greatest number of these occur while Simon waits to pick up his car from the repair shop in St. Paul. Repeated delays in the repair schedule motivate the additional episodes on Thursday and early Friday.

Beginning early in the novel, Hassler also introduces a larger cast of more and less fully-developed characters than in *Staggerford*. Besides Simon, there are his former wife, Barbara, Dr. Jean Kirk, and Douglas Mikklessen. Dr. Kirk is a young, liberal physician in a Republican clinic (119 f.) who combines professionalism with a streak of sentimentality. Mikklessen is a returned Vietnam veteran who has overcome alcohol and drug addiction and is now attending Rookery State. He and Dr. Kirk are living together.

The novel also offers numerous "vignettes" and "grotesques" who recall Hassler's admiration for Flannery O'Connor. These include, first and foremost, Simon's fellow residents at the Norman Home, as well as characters like T. S. Testor, the editor of Simon's regular book reviews for the St. Paul newspaper. When

Simon travels to St. Paul to retrieve his car, he meets a small host of additional "characters" who enliven the action on Thursday and Friday.

The male residents of the Norman Home are Hatch, a retired farmer who never tires of talking about the current drought that has wasted the countryside. Hatch's comments constitute a "running joke," not unlike those that caricature Wayne Workman in *Staggerford*. The other male resident, "the Indian" Smalleye, is "aloof and restless" (p. 5). He left the reservation years before, and his acculturated bartender daughter pays for his room and board at the Norman Home. Like Corinne Bingham in *Staggerford*—but more benign—the Indian is the novel's one potentially numinous character. In the very first pages Smalleye begins reminiscing about hunting season and takes up a refrain, "I'd like to shoot a goose." The "four widows" comprise the female residents of the Norman Home. These include "Spinner and Leep," identical twins in their seventies. The other two women are Mrs. Kibbikoski, who is confined to a wheelchair, and Mrs. Valentine Biggs, a sixty-nine year old "flirt." These residents fit the description of "foolish old people" that Hassler said he was emboldened to write about after having portrayed a group of seniors in *Staggerford*.

Because of Hassler's narrative skill, the reader doesn't learn Barbara Stearns' "history" until after Simon has fallen in love with and begun dating her. The story of Barbara's first marriage to Donald Stearns is told from both internal and external perspectives (101-111). In a long flashback, the reader learns that Barbara—a young bank employee—married a young quarry worker. One, internal perspective explains her attraction to Donald Stearns.

> *Donald was loud and reckless and high-spirited, and Barbara, in her demure fashion, quietly adored him for his thunderous laugh and his bullheaded opinions and the shocking pleasures he taught her on the bedless mattress. (103)*

This insight begins the development of Barbara's complex character, but a motorcycle accident leaves Donald in a coma for months. In the meantime, Barbara meets Simon and encourages his desire for companionship. When she explains her marital situation, Simon accompanies her to see Donald. A short time later Donald succumbs to his injuries, and within months Simon and Barbara are wed, on the Saturday after Easter in 1941, in the Newman chapel at Rookery State (113). Newly married, Barbara experiences delayed grief for her first husband, and then anger, and infidelity—with an artist colleague of Simon's.

An even more fascinating character is Simon's former student, Linda Mayo, who takes several courses with Simon after Barbara has left him and corresponds with him for years afterwards. She is in St. Paul, in 1950 (209), for a Mid-Century Award Dinner that Simon attends, but Simon passes up a chance to renew their relationship. Then Simon meets Linda, now an airline stewardess, in Dublin, Ireland in 1957. They have a brief affair as they travel around western Ireland, but Simon's conscience compels him to break off the relationship. He returns to the United States, alone, and resumes his celibate life, never to see Linda again.

Even as a minor character, Simon's friend and colleague, the mathematician Jay Johnson, appears in a number of key episodes. Early on he offers an objective view of Barbara, calling her "a bit of a chunk" (95), later softening it to "oval" (96). It is also Jay who first reveals to Simon that Barbara Stearns is married (100).

The physical setting of *Simon's Night*, like that of *Staggerford*, is late fall, this time, as noted, in a drought year. Though less frequent than in *Staggerford*, the descriptions are equally appropriate to the mood of barrenness and dying. Hassler situates one of the key settings of the novel, Ithaca Mills, on the prairie of northwestern Minnesota, miles from the hills and forests of Rookery, where Simon had lived and taught. "Simon was stunned each morning when he opened his curtains and took in the vast sweep of these flat fields and the atmospheric conditions prevailing over two states of the Union and one province of Canada ...(11). As in *Staggerford*, too, place and weather affect the characters' attitudes and dispositions. "In the Home, everyone's emotional changes were rung by the weather. Like the crew of a broken-masted ship, they were all at the mercy of nature, and their moods blended with the sky." Simon's contrarian view is immediately clear, and the contrast is stark. 'Give me the hills of my youth and age, thought Simon. Give me gulches and steep grades ... sandstone outcroppings and falling water and trails that lift me above the tops of trees and trails leading into ravines." When Simon looks out from the Norman Home on the plains of northwestern Minnesota, his attitude is decidedly negative. "Here, at a glance, is more than a man should see. Here, against the endless reaches of soil and cloud, I am puny."

Hinted at by the season and the details of physical setting, *Simon's Night* is, thematically, a story of revelations and renewal. At the start, Simon voluntarily accepts "exile" in the Norman Home near the figurative "desert" of a rainless November on the Minnesota prairie. In the course of the novel he rediscovers the purpose for and value of his life. Simon's revelations lead to a sense of renewal. Somewhat paradoxically, the novel becomes the story of two older people feeling young again, and starting over with their life together. As in *Staggerford*, there is also a complex interweaving of sub-themes: betrayal, disappointment, and loss. Combined with the flashbacks that interrupt the week's events, these thematic strands increase the complexity and richness of the novel's "texture."

The archetypal dimension in *Simon's Night* is both more overt and yet in some ways more hidden than was the case in *Staggerford*. Yes, Simon Shea is, at the start, like an aging hero who has given up the life of action and is preparing for death. His self-knowledge and independence shaken by events, he is ready to end his days at the Norman Home. But wounded by a chance remark and having betrayed a friend (leaving Smalleye

on the roof), Simon sets out on a series of ordeals after counseling a young "follower" (Douglas Mikklessen). Thursday
presents the central ordeal, the hero's journey through the underworld. But except for the ironic allusions to Olympus Mall,
Jupiter Service, and a waitress named Diana, it is only with
a sufficiently Olympian view that even these ordeals become
prominent as stages of the hero's journey. Fully forty pages
of Thursday are devoted to a long interruption of narrative
time as the reader listens for a second time to Simon's evening
prayers and then his recollections of Linda Mayo and the story
of their relationship. Thursday, in fact, ends with Simon abandoning Linda Mayo in Ireland and their final parting. Thursday also introduces another sub-theme as Simon acknowledges
his own tendency to see his life as a drama (197), and begins
reading the autobiography of Leonard Woolf. Friday morning presents a variation on the sub-theme in the humorous
and caustic episode with editor T.S. Testor and his own autobiography that he insists Simon read. On the way back to
the Olympus Mall, Simon's two funeral home visits, carrying
"Testor's baby" (265) with him, precipitate Simon's revelation
and the decision to leave the Norman Home. This is the start
of the hero's apotheosis and re-integration in the community.
On Saturday Simon fulfills a promise and experiences rejuvenation as he is reunited with his beloved and they find peace
in a somewhat unusual *locus amoenus*.[7]

Simon's Night is at times a quiet, domestic tale of love and
aging, and at other times an almost stunning combination of
comedy and satire. It is, in short, a successful third novel for
Hassler. It takes a common, painful experience—the decision
to move in and adapt to a retirement home—and turns it into
another parable of rejuvenation. Complicated with the improbable premise of a man remaining faithful for thirty-three years
to a wife who had left him, the story of Simon Shea's return to
his cabin with his wife will reward numerous rereadings.

The Love Hunter

The Love Hunter[8] was supposed to be Hassler's "breakthrough" novel (*C,* pp. 54-56). His new editor, Harvey Ginsberg, suggested the title *Old Friends,*[9] but Hassler "stuck to his guns" and stayed with the title that came to him after seeing the film, *The Deer Hunter.*[10] Hassler meant to write a "thriller," and he says he wrote the first half in six weeks, but then characters got in so much "hot water" that it took him two years to finish the book (*C,* 66).

It is the story of two long-time friends, Chris MacKensie and Larry Quinn. Chris, a former English teacher, is now the chair of the counseling department at Rookery State University. Larry, a former high school history teacher, had earned his Ph.D. and was teaching at Rookery State when he was struck with multiple sclerosis. With Larry now in the late stages of the disease, Chris is taking Larry on a last duck hunting trip, to Delta Marsh on Lake Manitoba, where he plans to drown Larry, ending his suffering. As Larry's condition had deteriorated, Chris has found himself falling in love with Larry's wife and chief care-giver, Rachel. At the start of the novel Chris is 45; Larry is 47; Rachel is 39.

The Love Hunter and Jon Hassler's Life

Like *Staggerford* and *Simon's Night, The Love Hunter* includes a number of autobiographical details that Hassler turned into fiction. As noted in the biography chapter, Hassler knew a colleague, Bob Nielsen, who died of multiple sclerosis (*C,* 67). Rachel is loosely modeled on Lavina Erickson, the wife of another teaching friend in Brainerd, Minnesota. Hassler said he spent a number of evenings at the Ericksons' home (*C,* 74). Hassler also identifies another friend, Dennis Nelson, who taught him how to hunt ducks. Hassler hunted with Nelson and his wife. The two couples became close.

The hunting trip to Blackie LaVoi's camp makes use of

thirty journal pages Hassler wrote about a duck-hunting trip to Canada that he took with his son, David. Blackie is modeled on the camp's owner, Rod duCharme (*C, 73*). Chris's story about a boy, Peter Ellis, dying of rheumatic fever, is based on a childhood acquaintance, Jackie Harlan, who died of rheumatic fever. Like *Simon's Night* and *Staggerford*, Hassler sets the main action of *The Love Hunter* in a definable time and place; Rookery State College, which is a combination of Bemidji State College and Brainerd Community College (*C. 56, 65*). Even the Bernard Beckwith incident has its origin in Hassler's life (*C, 78*). And, finally, Chris's Father's Day card and Bruce's Christian band have real life connections (*C. 71, 75*).

According to Plut, *The Love Hunter* is a "quantum leap" (*C, 53*) from Hassler's other novels. Part of the reason, Plut says, is the introduction of the triangular love relationship. The reader may also note that while there is no explicit sex in *Staggerford* or *Simon's Night*, *The Love Hunter* has a decidedly sexual dimension. Yet, as different as it is in these latter ways, *The Love Hunter* is also an elaboration on characters, themes and techniques found in *Staggerford* and *Simon's Night*. A number of features are similar: the Minnesota autumn setting, the academic background, debilitating illness, and the limited time span covered by the novel. The similarities also include techniques like the use of flashbacks, a selectively focused viewpoint, and—as in *Staggerford*—an epilogue. The characters of Chris MacKensie and Larry Quinn also share features of Hassler's earlier protagonists. *The Love Hunter* also continues the satiric critique of small-town American life found in *Staggerford*.

The tone can be lyrical but also almost savage. To keep the account of terminal multiple sclerosis from becoming macabre or merely depressing, Hassler subordinates the story of illness and death to a compelling and complex story of several evolving relationships. To this he adds the exploration of mercy killing. *The Love Hunter* might also be called a somewhat ironic "male bonding" novel, but published well before Robert Bly's *Iron John* made male-bonding a theme. With or without the "male bonding," it is a story of the growth and transformation of those relationships: Chris MacKensie's enduring friendship with—and love for—Larry Quinn, and the developing romantic attraction between Chris and Larry's wife, Rachel.

Decades before more popular (and political) attention became focused on debilitating medical conditions or life-changing terminal illnesses like multiple sclerosis—or drug-addiction and alcoholism—Hassler squarely faces a host of such social problems and makes of them a compelling story. In time the story becomes a "parable" of death and resurrection, and it ends with an epilogue that focuses on the love relationship born and nurtured in the midst of tragedy and grief.

The satire in the novel is less prominent, but no less trenchant. *The Love Hunter* critiques various stereotypical views of family, beginning with Chris's relationship with his wife, and the consequences of their divorce. One of the most savage critiques of family is the near archetype of the father hunting with his son. One of the hunters in Canada singled out for special treatment is a plumber from Milwaukee. The plumber has brought his twelve-year old son, Jim. The father berates the boy for calling him "Daddy." He also "abandons" Jim to Larry and Chris on the last morning of the hunt. The plumber chooses, instead, to stay in camp with "Poo Poo," a woman whose role in camp is ambiguous to say the least. The novel also caricatures Blackie Lavoi, the supposedly "legendary woodsman" who runs the camp, whose walls are plastered with newspaper articles about Blackie's exploits. In the off-season, it turns out, Blackie is an apartment owner in Anaheim, California. Another butt of satire is unassuming Bernard Beckwith, the producer at the Rookery Playhouse where Rachel Quinn has found an outlet for her creativity—and a respite from her care-giving. Near the end of the novel Beckwith causes mayhem by spreading false information on his CB radio to truckers driving through Rookery. Rachel tells the Beckwith anecdote to Chris, Larry, and thier son, Bruce on the night before Larry's death, and everyone enjoys a laugh—even Larry. Finally, there is the implicit satire on what some might call the novel's central plot: Chris's plan to murder his friend in a Canadian marsh. After holding determinedly to his plan through most of the novel, Chris realizes—when Larry regains a measure of spirit and strength during their escape from a storm on the lake—that he could not have killed Larry after all. The very foolhardiness of the idea transforms the whole murder plot into a near parody of melodramatic fiction.

Unlike *Staggerford* or *Simon's Night*, *The Love Hunter* does not have an obvious religious dimension. Except for the Quinns' son, Bruce, who is part of a Christian musical group, none of the characters explicitly manifests any religious commitments. Curiously enough, however, Hassler called *The Love Hunter* his "most Catholic" novel. That is probably because the hunting trip to Canada reaches its climax with Larry's unexpected revitalization in the storm. Hassler referred to it as a kind of resurrection (*C*, 80).

Narrative Techniques and Chapter Endings
The boldness with which Hassler handles changes in time is well in advance of *Staggerford* and *Simon's Night*. The bulk of the novel takes place in just three days, each day indicated by a separate "Part" of the novel. The two friends start off to Lake Manitoba on Thursday, October 4, 1979 and return early Sunday morning, October 7th. That is 296 of the book's 320 pages. A twenty-four page epilogue covers Larry's final decline and death between late July and early September, 1980. How does Hassler "stretch out" those three days, and still keep our interest? In large part because of the complex narrative structure. In the course of the three days we learn, almost exclusively through flashbacks presented from Chris MacKensie's point of

view, about the men's friendship (its origin, its development, its interruptions) and Chris's love for Rachel.

Hassler's growing skill as a storyteller also shows itself in the way he once again weaves together four different narrative strands to form a suspenseful and engaging whole. The first and central strand is the hunting trip to Canada. It occupies twenty chapters distributed through all three parts of the novel. The second, thinner strand is the plan to drown Larry in Delta Marsh. This appears in the first few chapters, as part of the hunt narrative, but it is also the focus of a short chapter in part three that recounts Chris's dream of murdering Larry. This strand ends abruptly with the final chapter of Part Three.

The third narrative strand is the story of the Quinn-MacKensie friendship that extends back over eighteen years to when Chris and Larry began as high school teachers in Owl Brook, Minnesota, in 1961. This narrative begins in the form of flashbacks that punctuate numerous chapters, especially in the first part of the novel. But the friendship becomes more prominent as Hassler follows Larry's illness to its inevitable end in Larry's death. The final narrative strand is the story of Chris's growing love for Rachel Quinn. Hinted at in a number of places early in the novel, this strand first becomes explicit when, early in the hunt, Larry asks Chris, "are you in love with her?" (142). This strand then occupies the long flashback in part two. It is also the chief focus of the novel's epilogue.

Through flashbacks and interruptions of the hunting narrative, Hassler develops interest in the characters' earlier lives, and a measure of suspense that exceeds that in either *Simon's Night* or *Staggerford*. The storm on Lake Manitoba (Part 3, chapter 6) is a bit of *real* suspense, leading to the climactic end of Part 3. In each of the several strands Hassler also introduces seemingly digressive events or episodes, as he had in, for instance, the Olympus Mall episodes of *Simon's Night*. These serve to enrich and amplify the point of the particular narrative strand as they create further suspense and interest.

In Part 2, the bold, seven-chapter flashback that develops Chris and Rachel's relationship in spring, 1979 includes Chris's first avowal of love, and culminates in a scene of love-making. It resembles, though it has a far different purpose and is much more subtly handled than, the long journal entry that narrates Miles Pruitt's love for Carla Carpenter, in *Staggerford*. Among the boldest writerly experiments is the epilogue. But whereas in *Staggerford* the epilogue comes after the death of the protagonist and merely records other characters' responses to that death, in *The Love Hunter* the epilogue recounts the actual death of the chief character, and the resolution of other key plot features in the story. More than the epilogue of *Staggerford*, the epilogue of *The Love Hunter* enacts a breaking free from one character's death and—further employing what is a central (theatrical) metaphor—begins a new act of a new drama.

Characters and other Stylistic Traits

The well-developed characters of *The Love Hunter* are as complex and engaging as those in *Staggerford*. There is no Agatha McGee, but the three main characters—and their complex interactions—keep the reader turning pages. Chris MacKensie begins as a high school English teacher who, when *his* marriage fails, returns to school for a graduate degree in counseling. After the divorce, Chris is lonely; so when he is offered a job as chair of the counseling department, he moves to Rookery State College, where Larry, who went back for his Ph.D. in history, is now teaching. When the Quinns open their home to him, Chris visits regularly, and this puts him into regular, close proximity to Larry's wife, which becomes a plausible reason for his falling in love with her.

From the start Larry Quinn is the more flamboyant, and aggressive, of the two friends. He marries one of his students; he is more ambitious than Chris, not only getting his Ph.D., but intending to write a history of the Minnesota lumber industry. He is a brilliant teacher, for which Chris envies him. When he is first diagnosed with multiple sclerosis, Larry tries to ignore it but ends up having to give up teaching. His two bouts of depression, in which he sits in the dark and listens to Mahler, are an important part of the novel, and a further key to his character. A psychotic break and his temporary hospitalization are a critical part of the story. Except for his insights into Chris's attraction to Rachel, however, the reader knows little about Larry's inner life, since the narrator seldom enters Larry's viewpoint.

Rachel Quinn is a more complex character than any of the younger female characters in *Staggerford* or *Simon's Night*. As a young wife she wants to join her husband when he and Chris go duck hunting, temporarily disrupting the men's friendship. When she and Chris's wife become pregnant, she temporarily disappears into a domestic role. In response to her husband's illness, however, Rachel matures rapidly. Besides care-giver, she becomes the emotional and psychological strength of the family. As Larry becomes more immobile physically, Rachel becomes a social worker and takes up jogging. As he becomes homebound, she goes out in the community, becoming, in her spare time from care-giving, an actress, and then a director at the local playhouse.

The subordinate characters are as varied and interesting as those in *Staggerford* or *Simon's Night*. Larry and Rachel's son, Bruce, combines Rachel's grace and Larry's independence. As noted, he is the only character who has a religious sensibility. Some of Chris's and Larry's students have minor—both tragic and comic—roles. At the hunting camp in Canada, Hassler's satiric imagination has free rein. Besides the owner, Blackie LaVoi (who is as exaggeratedly larger than life as the state trooper in *Staggerford*), the reader meets his three female dependents, each of whom is mysterious in an odd sort of way. Blackie's camp also gathers a variety of boastful hunters, including Sanderson Bleekman, and the plumber from Milwaukee whose antics are by turns disgusting, pathetic, and dangerous. The plumber's twelve year old son, Jim, offers the narrator an opportunity to view the two friends, and the hunt, from a child's perspective. The manager of the Rookery Playhouse, Bernard Beckwith, plays a minor role until the epilogue, when, as noted, an embarrassing incident becomes a brief, quasi-humorous distraction just before Larry's death.

Among the things that distinguish *The Love Hunter* from *Staggerford* and *Simon's Night* is the relative paucity of exaggeratedly grotesque, O'Connor-like characters. Blackie LaVoi and the other hunters in camp are the exceptions, but together these characters help turn the duck-hunting section into a tonally balanced critique of *machismo* at the same time they provide a parallel source of suspense for the story. Seen in one way, the hunting camp is like Simon's visit to Olympus Mall,[11] or Agatha McGee's attending the Cathy Hawk wedding or her visit to the senior center in *Staggerford*.

Beyond characters, the novel is appealing, and significant in Hassler's *oeuvre,* because of the further sophistication of his stylistic skills. These include continued close attention to nature and a greater emphasis on poetry, art,[12] and theater. Hassler said the theatrical "motif" is deliberate, and he complimented Joe Plut for proposing that "the whole novel is based on theater (*C*, 76). Hassler's penchant for repetition also shows itself early. To punctuate the end of chapter 3, for instance, Larry counsels the divorced Chris to use illness to get women, repeatedly telling Chris that women are "suckers for disease" (23). Other (usually humorous) repetitions such as those at Blackie LaVoi's Hassler uses rather more subtly than in the first two novels. As in *Jemmy*, Hassler also seeks to conclude chapters with striking transitional features, or minor, climactic comments or observations. In one instance a chapter ends with the phrase, "on love," and the next one begins with the same phrase. The enigmatic use of the word "Gifts," at the start of two chapters, links Part Three to the "Epilogue."

Space, Place, Tensions, and Archetypes

As noted, *The Love Hunter* can be considered a theme with variations from his two earlier, full-length novels, *Staggerford* and *Simon's Night*: Minnesota, friendship, teachers, endings, journals, and funerals. From a slightly more distant thematic perspective, *The Love Hunter* involves a series of contrastive tensions between the mundane and everyday on the one hand, and the macabre and surreal on the other. From the most distant perspective, *The Love Hunter* employs a number of familiar archetypes: isolation, violence, blood, and ritual wounding, which give universal resonance to the tale. There is also a lyrical, almost transcendent dimension, in which certain things throw light on things in a way that augments this universal quality.

Like *Staggerford* and *Simon's Night*, *The Love Hunter* makes much of the Minnesota location. Sometimes in the foreground, sometimes only part of the background, space and place are almost always significant. The emphasis begins with the drive north to the Canadian border. Then it appears—subtly—in the first flashbacks, as the "fluid" space/time of Minnesota, when teachers became "efficient movers" who could and did change jobs and move anywhere they wanted to (34). Then, once the two couples have settled down, the Quinns' and the MacKensies' homes in Rookery become the focus. After his divorce, Chris's sparse apartment contrasts with the comfortable but sometimes oppressively close-seeming Quinn home, especially Larry's den. Rookery becomes a significant place, particularly the "ravine," because it is through the ravine that Rachel and later Chris will run, and where the two will often meet. Nearby is the cemetery and, of course, the Badbattle River. The Badbattle River is a familiar "motif" from *Staggerford* and *Simon's Night*. Here, as in *Staggerford*, the river, like life, flows past a cemetery, and it is over and along the river that the characters move at various times. It is both realistic *and* potentially archetypal that Chris and Rachel descend into and meet within the valley of the Badbattle at important junctures in the story. Descent as motif is modulated into the comic register when Rachel leads Chris down through the floors of Prinn's Department Store in the long flashback of Part II. In a long flashback, Rookery becomes the Concord Street Coffee Shop and Prinn's Department Store, where Chris and Rachel meet again. Still later, the town shrinks to the theater; first at midnight in April, 1979, when Chris tells Rachel of his love, and then later, at the climactic opening performance of *Twelfth Night*. The relative "stasis" of the theater then contrasts with the hectic trip to the Rookery State Hospital, and from thence to Minneapolis and the Fawn River Health Center where Larry is hospitalized. Specific places in Minneapolis contrast with surreal events at the hospital; the Institute of Art where Chris takes Rachel contrasts with the claustrophobic space of Chris's and Rachel's hotel rooms.

For a major part of Part 2 the focus is on southern Canada and Blackie's hunting camp—like a "slat-sided cattle train, headed north, derailed" (242)—and the Delta Marsh itself, an almost claustrophobic place where Chris gets temporarily lost. In later contrast, the island near the south end of Lake Manitoba becomes the center of interest, with its "throne" of rock where Chris sits alone to think of Rachel, and contemplate his plan to drown Larry. Of course, Lake Manitoba is also the crucial location where Chris and Larry struggle in the storm. Finally, in the epilogue, the town of Rookery reappears as the ravine, the river, and the cemetery, where Larry is buried, and Chris and Rachel meet again.

Besides the contrasts in place, the novel contrasts a number of other, less tangible tensions, swinging from the mundane to the macabre or even surreal; from the clinical to the lyrical and the almost religious. Like the Badbattle River, the everyday flows on, but the surreal, the violent, the bloody, and the inevitability of Larry's death repeatedly appear and interrupt that flow. This everyday world includes Chris's job as chair of the counseling department, where he talks of teachers, budget cuts, and school visits (185). Larry's psychotic break is frighteningly real, as is the storm on Lake Manitoba. The author/narrator also emphasizes the mundane with a sharp eye for the everyday lives of Chris MacKensie, the Quinns, and their son, Bruce. Hassler also roots the novel firmly in the details of late 1970s America: the popularity of backgammon, the prevalence of CB radios, and a recession leading to layoffs and cutbacks in education (312). The pope's visit to the United States—and to Grant Park in Chicago—is a historical trip that, almost literally, pops up in the middle of the Canadian marsh (150).

Larry's illness is the chief source of the macabre or surreal and the clinical. The surreal includes some of the details of Larry's illness, including the many oddities of mood, behavior, and language, culminating in his mental breakdown and hospitalization. From shortly after the two friends arrive in Canada, Blackie LaVoi's camp, and the marsh, become a kind of macabre, if not surreal world. Part of this effect results from archetypal motifs that are not immediately apparent.

A further contrast is the way that most of the somber events take place in darkness. Unlike the sunny mornings in the duck blind vividly portrayed early in the novel (44, 45), most of Chris's "flashback" interactions with Larry, after Larry's diagnosis, take place in the darkness of Larry's den. Chris and Rachel have a significant meeting in the darkness of the Rookery Playhouse, and it is darkness through which Chris, Larry, and Rachel drive as they take Larry to the mental hospital. Some of the most significant scenes at the hunting camp take place at night. The trip back from Canada takes place between 7 p.m. Saturday and early morning, Sunday. After a final evening with Larry, Chris, Rachel, and Bruce, Larry dies at dawn the next morning.

The multiple flashbacks that radically dislocate the sense of time and tone also make the seasons of the year more meaningful. Without summer, spring and fall alternate, and winter is always threatening. The hunt takes place in fall, Larry Quinn dies in early fall. Many of the flashbacks deal with fall: the 1961 start of Chris and Larry's friendship; the 1973 disintegration of Chris's marriage; Larry's Doldrums Major and Doldrums Minor. The spring of 1979 brings the opening of *Twelfth Night* that ends with Larry's breakdown and hospitalization.

Like winter, the threat of violence, drunkenness, insanity, and sexuality are always just out of sight. The violence of the plumber's shotgun blast (243-44) and the twin wounding of Blackie and Chris prepare for the climax of the hunt narrative. In a striking instance of Hassler's "gestural symbolism," Larry appearing to hang, crucified by his hooked arms, in a straight-back chair in the hunting camp's dining room, on the night before the final hunt (233, 240), is the necessary prelude to his resurrection on Lake Manitoba. The violent storm on Lake Manitoba is a *tour de force* of nature's power.

Finally, at sufficient distance, one can see the whole novel as a journey out, into the violence and implicit sexuality of the hunting camp, where a storm transforms the threat of death into temporary restoration. The epilogue includes a different kind of restoration scene, though it too is similar to the two friends' return from the hunt, and similar, as well, to the restoration/renewal that ends both *Staggerford* and *Simon's Night*. Into this texture of the everyday, the clinical, and the surreal, Hassler weaves passages of lyrical beauty, human intimacy, and almost sacramental vision. The lyricism of the duck blind in autumn (44, 45) represents an almost transcendentally idyllic moment in the midst of otherwise mundane or tragic events. The reader shares the human intimacy of Chris and Rachel's lovemaking, even as it is the extremity of Larry's illness that seems to have forced them to this sharing. The lyricism is sometimes a blend of the serious and the comic: the midnight conversation in the Playhouse; the meeting in the Coffee Shop; the comic journey down through Prinn's Department Store. As a number of critics pointed out in 1981, *The Love Hunter* is a highpoint of Hassler's career to that point. Even as the years pass, future readers will find new surprises and marvel again at the way in which the author folds multiple motives and nuanced insights into this story of illness, love, friendship, and death.

5

MATURITY

The four novels of what I am calling Hassler's maturity —*A Green Journey*, *Grand Opening*, *North of Hope*, and *Dear James*—are not only his most popular and well-known. They *are* the work of a consummate storyteller, and well worth serious consideration. Within the broad thematic parameters established in the first four novels, these four also explore a range of new themes and situations: foreign travel, economic striving, religious vocation, family dynamics, and small-town life. They also continue Hassler's familiar preoccupations with betrayal and friendship, love and loyalty, isolation and depression.

A Green Journey was published before *Grand Opening* and *North of Hope*, but because *A Green Journey* and *Dear James* are related as premise and sequel, and because in my view *Dear James* represents a natural segue to the two campus novels, *Rookery Blues* and *The Dean's List*, I shall treat *A Green Journey* and *Dear James* together, *after* consideration of *Grand Opening* and *North of Hope*.

Grand Opening [1]

In 1978 Hassler began a journal of his childhood memories. In 1981, now at St. John's University, he began "The Book of Brendan," a manuscript that turned out to be "unpublishable" (*C*, 116-17), but from out of a combination of those two "sources" and the short story titled "Dodger's Return" came *Grand Opening*, which was published in 1986. *Grand Opening* is the only Hassler novel set wholly in the past—the fall of 1944 through the summer of 1945. It is also the most autobiographical, being loosely based on the eight years that Hassler and his family lived in Plainview, Minnesota, a rural town southwest of the Twin Cities (*C*, 121-122). It was there that Hassler's father owned a grocery store, ran for the school board, and Hassler himself went to school, playing on the Plainview High School football team. A capacious—even somewhat "baggy"—affair, with multiple moving parts and many sub-themes, Hassler makes this complexity contribute to the richness of the whole.

Grand Opening addresses, with both seriousness and satire, a number of the social issues that mark some of the earlier novels—alcoholism, parental neglect, mental instability—as well as seemingly unexplained, willful malice. As in his other earlier novels, a mix of the everyday with more momentous events, which "throw light on" each other, is one key to the novel's poignancy and appeal. Though Catholicism is an explicit context of the novel, the "Catholic decor" should not distract the reader from the novel's abidingly Incarnational and sacramental, not to mention archetypal, dimension. Proceeding, as in his previous novels, by means of episodes, mini-episodes, and brief digressive scenes, the action is cleverly and densely plotted in ways that punctuate and pace the movement of the story. The seasons, from autumn 1944 to summer 1945, provide further structure. The point of view moves through the different members of the Foster family, and then occasionally to other characters, but finally finds a stable resting place in the perspective of young Brendan Foster.

Plot

Titled *Grand Opening*, the novel *is* about the Foster family store and its numerous "Grand Opening" sales, but Hassler acknowledged in an interview (*Image*, 45) that the story really has four protagonists, Hank and Catherine Foster, Grandfather McMahon, and the Fosters' only son, Brendan. In the same interview, Hassler noted that he had begun Brendan's story in the first person but "that wasn't getting into enough of the town that I needed to know, so I changed that" (*Image*, 51). To say that the central plot of *Grand Opening* is the Foster family's efforts to adapt to small town life and try to make a success of their store is accurate, but immediately one sees how much of the novel this description leaves out. While the Foster family's struggles drive the action and give the story cohesiveness, a large part of the novel's appeal is focused in the other characters' lives and their interactions with the Fosters. In almost every chapter, the episodes and mini-episodes, with their various characters, throw light on other parts of the story being developed.

Among the sub-plots, the most important are Brendan's relationships with Dodger Hicks and Wallace Flint. Others include Wallace Flint's relationship with Catherine Foster, and Grandfather McMahon's adventures with different citizens of Plum. Together, these sub-plots provide a contrast with each other and provide a vivid and complex context for the story of the Fosters and their grocery store. Each sub-plot also includes its own thematic variations. If the theme of the family's adaptation to small town life (and the success of their grocery store) is one of perseverance, ultimate disillusionment, and then a final, bitter-sweet triumph, the theme of the Brendan sub-plot is a boy's growing from selfishness and betrayal to greater moral maturity. Grandfather's relationships with various townspeople yield a complex of thematic strands that start with errant, serendipitous curiosity and then play variations on loneliness, caring, and openness to adventure. Among the themes associated with Catherine and Wallace Flint's relationship are mistaken judgment, deception, betrayal, and temptation. Wallace Flint, through his relationship with other characters besides Catherine, also exhibits the novel's concern with the forms that evil takes in a small town. This includes jealousy of (and rivalry with) the other "only children," Brendan and Dodger Hicks.

Main Characters

While Brendan's mother and Grandfather have significant roles, his father, Hank, is (like Hassler's own father) reticent and hence, for most of the novel, a subordinate character. Catherine Foster is one of Hassler's most interesting characters. Like Rachel Quinn in *The Love Hunter*, Catherine is independent, self-reliant, and emotionally complex. Because of her husband's character, it is often Catherine who takes the initiative with her father and with Brendan, as well as speaking up to various townspeople. A city girl apprehensive about living in a small town, she finds herself stifled by the superficiality and bigotry of Plum. In time she becomes a focus of the town's attention and even an object of gossip. The reader first meets her on the road trip from Minneapolis, reading Ernest Hemingway's *For Whom the Bell Tolls*. In an apparent turnaround from other Hassler characters both male and female, the reader soon learns that Catherine "loved flat earth. She abhorred restricted vision" (12). In this she combines the preference for unrestricted vision that Simon Shea, Jemmy, and Agatha McGee found in heights. Later in the novel, the narrator does observe that Catherine too "enjoyed the long vistas offered by high ground" (193). Catherine's loneliness and her desire and hope for friendship from the town are dashed when only four people come to the Fosters' "housewarming" (ch. 17). Not counting Agatha McGee, Grandfather Michael

McMahon ("nearly eighty") is one of Hassler's first, fully-drawn, senior characters. A retired railroad man who has occasional memory lapses and an impulsive desire to roam, Grandfather is an occasion for Catherine's worry, and for some of the more humorous and poignant scenes early in the novel. As noted, it is the Foster's only child, twelve-year old Brendan, around whom most of the story's action centers. Pious and searching for both a friend and a model, Brendan does not take center stage until chapter three, with his meeting Dodger Hicks.

Rufus Ottman, Dodger Hicks, and Wallace Flint
The other three "only children" in *Grand Opening* are Rufus Ottman, Dodger Hicks, and Wallace Flint, all of whom play important parts in the novel. Rufus Ottman is the developmentally challenged son of the widow Ottman, from whom the Fosters rent their house. Until the last pages of the novel, his only role is to stand at the Ottmans' window, or behind the glass door of the Fosters' store, staring and smiling blankly. His appearance is striking and meant to remain fixed in the memory: "the eyebrows wiry and wild over hollow-looking eye sockets" (20). Rufus Ottoman's appearance, behavior, and mental disability negatively affect Brendan and become a provocation for Grandfather McMahon's second excursion. Dodger Hicks is one of Brendan's classmates in the seventh grade and the son of a single mother whose husband is serving time in a Stillwater, Minnesota prison. Dodger exhibits a paradoxical blend of qualities, starting with passivity and vulnerability. He also combines an insatiable need for love and friendship, partially explaining his obsessive generosity, with a talent and love for petty theft. In time, Dodger becomes not only an outcast, but a victim of betrayal and violence. In chapter four, Dodger is quickly connected with larceny through Hank's humorous reference to Dickens' "artful dodger," but the boy is soon privy to some of Brendan's most private thoughts about moving to

129

Plum. By the end of the chapter, however, Wallace Flint is telling Brendan he needs to "drop" Dodger Hicks, and in chapter five, after one of the most moving scenes in the novel, Brendan does precisely that.

Wallace Flint is an amazing creation. The only son of Margaret Flint, a widow, Wallace is twenty-five and works in the Foster grocery store. He was hired by the previous owner but wheedles his way into staying on with the Fosters. They keep him on, in part, because Wallace knows more about the town of Plum than anyone else they know. Abused by his mother as a child, Wallace is, like Dodger, an intelligent and complex character. Because of his epilepsy and his mother's doting, he remained in Plum after high school, even though he had opportunities for college. The reader's first view of Wallace Flint is contradictory: a "melodious voice" but a "feverish gleam" in his watery eyes (23). He exhibits "stagey movements" and an "overdramatic manner." A short time later, in the throes of jealousy at learning that Dodger Hicks has been to dinner at the Fosters', he sounds curiously modern, seeing Catherine and Hank as "bleeding hearts, suckers for anyone needy." Aloof from the village when in public, his epileptic seizures might make him seem like one of the demoniacs in the Gospels. Though proud and intellectual, he is also vulnerable, and, as a result, subject to malicious and vindictive jealousy. Why does Wallace do what he does? One explanation might be his thwarted aspirations, though "In Wallace's experience, aspiration came to nothing" (63-64). Another explanation might be the childhood abuse he suffered at his grieving mother's hands, and teeth.

Other Misfits and Outsiders
These three young men are among a number of other misfits and outsiders who also populate the novel. These include Mrs. Flint, Phyllis Clay, and Larry-the-Twitch. Larry is the young-

est child of the (generally wild) Romberg family. Called names (162) and ignored or abandoned by his siblings, he appears as an almost grotesque figure at three pivotal points in the novel. Dodger, Wallace, and Larry are, at least in part, products of their families' dysfunction. Both Dodger and Wallace suffer abuse along with isolation. But the reader may also find a strong strain of "it's their nature" in what both Wallace and Dodger are motivated to do.

Another outsider, Paul Dimmitburg, the son of Plum's Lutheran minister, has a minor though crucial role. Having had a nervous breakdown in the seminary, he returns to Plum—it is supposed to be only temporarily—to find himself. There he becomes both the "favorite" who supplants Wallace in Catherine's eyes, *and* the person who later gives the stirring sermon at Dodger's funeral (289-290). His own struggles with belief and vocation (minister or carpenter) constitute a sub-plot and attendant sub-theme.

Themes

Besides the plot and sub-plot themes, it is family, and the forces massed against the family (or at work within it) that constitute a central theme. Friendship in various forms is also significant, along with the *need* for love and kindness. The desire and need for friendship lead to mistaken judgments and misguided actions. Beneath the need for family, love, and friendship is an undertone of loneliness and isolation. Grandfather's recollections of his dead wife Sade send him on his first adventure. Brendan, lonely at a new school, becomes vulnerable to Dodger Hicks. Plut and Hassler also discuss an "intergenerational" theme (*C,* 122) that relates to loneliness, with Grandfather and Brendan as the prime examples, but Grandfather's relationships with Dodger and Phyllis Clay also show different aspects that the intergenerational theme can take.

Wallace Flint introduces a particularly somber sub-theme

in a climactic moment at the end of chapter six. After a discussion of Catholicism, heaven, and hell, Wallace the atheist first says, "there's so much religious hate in this town that nobody deserves to be saved." He concludes, "I'll tell you who's in hell, Catherine. We all are. Plum is hell" (53). This statement—along with Catherine's saying Plum is a town God might overlook—makes it tempting to see Wallace Flint as, at times, an embodiment of evil and one who, like the devil, is "in hell" wherever he goes. The narrator's observing, through Stan Kimball, that "to ignore Wallace was to turn your back on a poisonous snake" (116), adds further to that impression. But, at the same time, Wallace's own weakness (epileptic seizures) and vulnerability (crying on Hank's shoulder on his return from the induction center) pull him back into the "realistic," everyday world. When Paul Dimmitburg comes on the scene, Wallace's hatred at being supplanted only increases his desire for destruction and revenge. Much later, after Dodger's death, Catherine "saw Plum tucked into its fold of hills three miles away, two steeples, a grain elevator, and a water tower protruding above the elms." She says, "'I can't believe we live in that town. It's like having a nightmare and never waking up'" (280).

Beneath the surface of the everyday world in Plum, then, lie tensions and conflicts that are almost archetypal in their force: jealousy, envy, impulses to evil (theft and vengeance, alcoholism, infidelity), as well as venality (making money at the store), exacerbated by more petty impulses, like Cora Brask's gossip and backbiting. The Catholic vs. Lutheran tension is another form of rivalry—the Catholic men's club not wanting the Lutherans to get the old school desks for *their* school.

Imagery, Violence, and the Macabre
In another signature Hassler move, the opening of *Grand Opening* introduces death, referring to no fewer than five dead people in the first pages of chapter three. The first is Uncle

Herman's wife Margaret, the second, someone "killed" at the State School. Then a first encounter with Grandfather includes the recollection of his dead wife Sade and (in two recollected scenes) the stories of a brakeman falling from a boxcar and having both legs severed, and another of a farmer hit by a train and his body carried hundreds of miles on the cowcatcher of a locomotive.

The macabre also enters in chapter eight when Catherine visits the town library and is introduced to the novels of Edward Hodge Fleet, whose stories of pain and dismemberment excite Mrs. Brask. Later, Brendan and Jerry Franzen discuss amputation in *Gone with the Wind* before Dodger's macabre end beneath the walk-in cooler in the basement of the store. Another seemingly everyday image that becomes ominous is the prevalence of fires: first Constable Heffernand's burning a wood model of a Japanese Zero, then Wallace staring into a fire he has lighted (in an incinerator), after Paul Dimmitburg supplants him in Catherine's affections. Finally, there is the climactic Market fire and the Constable's burning more model planes in the novel's final pages.

In this novel, birds occur far less frequently as images than in Hassler's other novels, but two repetitions are worth noting. In the first, sparrows in the lilac hedge at Dodger's grave recall the sparrows seen at the State Home School for Boys, suggesting that Dodger, and the boys at the school are like the sparrows of little worth, but also—recalling the Gospel story—never forgotten by the Father. At the end of the novel, an elderly couple, the Dombrowskis, are described as being "like frightened birds." Other significant repetitions include Wallace Flint sending Brendan into an alley, early in the novel, where he nearly falls into the grease pit of a gas station, a scene which has its "resolution" at the end of the novel when Brendan saves Rufus Ottman from falling into the same pit, making Brendan's repetition a genuinely salvific action.

Literary and Artistic Allusions

Unlike the earlier novels, *Grand Opening* has no epigraph, and fewer literary allusions than any of Hassler's novels to this point. Catherine's reading Hemingway's *For Whom the Bell Tolls* is both a literary and historical allusion (Hemingway's novel was published in 1940). When, much later, she asks Bea Crowley about books (168)—seeking to find intellectual kinship in town—Mrs. Crowley scorns Hemingway's "philosophy," saying that she and her husband read only Catholic authors, like [Georges] Bernanos and [Francois] Mauriac. Of course the works of Edward Hodge Fleet (70-72; 165 f.) are a satiric criticism of certain forms of "popular fiction"—and the clientele who read it. Joseph Plut suggests a Chekhovian[2] element in the novel's many arrivals and departures, and its "autumnal" quality (*C,* 125).

Wallace Flint considering himself "deposed" from Catherine's heart (128), and his being "overthrown" and "banished from his princedom" (219) could have Shakespearean or Biblical implications, but Plut and Hassler referring to Wallace Flint as a kind of small town Iago (*C,* 124) does not make the novel a Shakespearean tragedy. Paul Dimmitburg reads Kierkegaard, but beyond that, literary allusiveness is not a significant feature of this novel, though, as will be noted, there may be a number of archetypal parallels."

For Hassler, who once painted and sold landscape paintings, any artistic allusions become thematically significant, but in *Grand Opening* these allusions present a contrast. The Deroches' "biblical painting" is an occasion for humor (167), and a possible allusion turned up by Joseph Plut in his conversation with Hassler also poses problems. Plut suggests that Brendan's Christmas Eve reference to "the peacable kingdom" (154) might allude to nineteenth-century American Quaker artist "Edward Hicks's famous painting, *The Peaceable Kingdom*" (*C,* 129), and Hassler seems to agree with him, but if Brendan's comment is an allusion to Hicks's folk painting, the sentimentality of that painting may be a further, implicit criticism of Brendan's understandably child-like idealism.

More problematic are the literary and artistic allusions associated with Wallace Flint. Wallace Flint has decorated the walls of his room (which neither his mother nor anyone else can enter) with what are first called "frescoes" (81). In chapter twelve the reader learns that they are purple and "numbered thirty-two. They were crude faces, applied with a wide brush, but with enough detail to be distinguishable one from another" (109). This artist's view of the paintings suggests Hassler's own artistic background. The faces, as the reader sees them through Wallace's eyes, include Emily Dickinson, Vincent Van Gogh, and John Keats. "The faces consoled Wallace, belonging as they did to people whose genius had not been acknowledged in their lifetimes" (109). Later, after his ignominious return from the draft induction, he paints "the faces of Axis leaders" on the walls of his mother's room (222). Then, at the end of the novel, he has also covered the kitchen walls with "enormous faces" (305), suggesting that his obsession has grown worse.

The Archetypal

How is *Grand Opening* archetypal? Most obviously, like *Jemmy*, *Grand Opening* is at least in part a "coming of age," in this case for Brendan Foster. But whereas Jemmy's growth is the central plot, in *Grand Opening* Brendan's coming of age is one of several episodically developed plots. The others have to do with the Fosters' grocery store, the family's relation to the rest of the town, Grandfather McMahon's eccentricities, and the relation of Catherine Foster to both Wallace Flint and Paul Dimmitburg.

Brendan's coming of age involves the usual tests of the young hero, as well as betrayals, struggles with antagonists, and other details of the hero's journey. As in *Staggerford* and to a lesser extent *Simon's Night*, Brendan as hero faces one principal antagonist, but whereas, for instance, Hattie Norman in *Simon's Night* is generally realistic, Wallace Flint is a bit more like *Staggerford's* Corinne Bingham, the bonewoman: full of mysterious, even uncanny, as well as evil qualities. In *Grand Opening*, however, even more than the other two novels, Brendan's struggle with Wallace Flint is woven into a fabric of everyday happenings, historical events, and details so that the archetypal "struggle" is not always apparent. Furthermore, and finally, *Grand Opening* does not end with an obvious rejuvenation or re-integration into community. Yes, it is spring, but instead of re-integration and re-assertion of community, *Grand Opening* ends—somewhat like *Huckleberry Finn*—with expulsion and exile, at least for the Foster family. But considering Brendan's story, the reader finds that Dodger Hicks and Rufus Ottman are traditional victims. For betraying Dodger at the start of the novel, Brendan "propitiates" Dodger at the end of the story by saving Rufus from a fate that Brendan himself had nearly experienced.

North Of Hope[3]

Imagine yourself in northern Minnesota, in December. Cold, snowy; dark from 5 in the afternoon to 7 the next morning. It's like that *every* day. You're in a small town; then, nineteen miles up a snowy gravel road, around a frozen lake, in a small dilapidated church on a desolate Ojibway[4] reservation. *That* is the setting for much of Jon Hassler's *North of Hope*.

Hassler's sixth major novel has much that would qualify as a "popular" novel today. A woman, Libby Girard Pearsall, is on her third husband. Her mentally unbalanced twenty-something daughter, Verna, has suffered, and continues to suffer, sexual abuse. First it was the pedophile second husband; now it's the third husband, a corrupt, alcoholic doctor. The doctor also provides drugs to a bar owner who then sells them to Native Americans on the reservation. There are numerous deaths; from suicide, drug abuse, drowning. The unlikely "savior" in this melodramatic-sounding plot is a priest who drinks too much rum and who had come to doubt his vocation after the boys' prep school where he taught was closed. The priest, it turns out, was the best friend in high school of Libby, the thrice-married woman.

North of Hope is Hassler's longest and most complex novel. It spans almost thirty years in the characters' lives, and the characters are as memorable as any he had created to that point.[5] Like all of Hassler's novels, *North of Hope* is a mixture of the comic and the tragic, the mundane and the mystical. As he does in other novels, the narrator occasionally moves from one character's viewpoint to another's. This adds to the complexity of the vision. With much humor and wry satire, Hassler again demonstrates how "things throw light on things, and all the stones have wings." Which, as noted in an earlier chapter, is just a poetic way of saying that it is the contrast, the rhythmic counterpoint of the everyday and the extraordinary, that accounts for the novel being more than "popular fiction," and lifts the whole story to a higher plane of seriousness and universality.

A sprawling chronicle that one critic[6] says, "explores and maps the bleak, spiritual north of our times," *North of Hope* and its message can apply as much to the second and third decades of the twenty-first century as it did to the 1970s, when most of the novel is set, and the late 1980s, when it was written. Thematically, *North of Hope* handles issues (drugs, alcohol, spousal and child abuse) with an openness to the realities of human suffering that seems more in tune with Jesus of the Gospel than more pious fictions. Despite the squalor, however, the anguish, and the temptation to despair, it is a novel about friendship, loyalty, and trust in the face of betrayals, abuse, deceit, and manipulation. As its title suggests, it is a novel about hope and ultimately a quest for spiritual and emotional wholeness. It succeeds by showing how goodness can be appealing, in large part by contrasting it with evil, numbing routine, and *lack* of hope. For those reasons *North of Hope* is one of Hassler's most "consoling" novels.

Composition, Autobiographical Elements, and Contemporary Details

When asked by Joseph Plut whether *North of Hope* was "an out-growth" of the unpublished "Book of Brendan," Hassler said, "Yes, it is. The first 150 pages are the teenage love story of Frank and Libby, and a lot of it had been written as 'The Book of Brendan,' so I used that to start this book" (*C*, 138). An unpublished short story, "The Backup Boyfriend" also became part of the novel (*C*. 144), and—like many of his other novels—a number of autobiographical features enter in. To Debbie Musser in 2006 he said, "I consider *North of Hope* my most Catholic novel …It was the culmination of a favorite pastime of mine—priest-watching."

Written relatively early in his tenure at St. John's University, *North of Hope,* particularly the first part, includes a vividly realized visit to Aquinas College and Seminary, details which Hassler says are taken from his experience at St. John's (*C*, 139-140). He also says that Frank's conversation on the seminary grounds with Libby Girard Jessen in her pick-up is taken from a real-life conversation he had had with another student's girlfriend. The story of accompanying a veterinarian to treat Vernon Jessen's cow is also autobiographical, as are some of the details of Fr. Adrian Lawrence, which Hassler says are based on his father (*C*, 144).

As in his other novels, historical details add "texture" to the story. Among these are movies like *A Portrait of Jennie* (4), *Asphalt Jungle* (79); *Sands of Iwo Jima* (114), *Four Faces West, Kiss of Death* (77), *Taxi Driver*, and *Lost Weekend* (238). There are several references to actors and actresses: Clark Gable, Jennifer Jones, Joseph Cotten, Ingrid Bergman and Romano Rosellini, as well as Ray Milland, and Dustin Hoffman. Songs like "Dear Hearts," "Mule Train," and "Rag Mop" at a sock hop in part one, and Tom T. Hall and Margaret Whiting at "the Homestead" add to the flavor. There are also references to John Chancellor and James Garner (315) as well as Harry

Reasoner, Debby Boone (455), and Crystal Gale (461).

Written immediately after *Grand Opening*, Hassler's use of familiar situations from "The Book of Brendan"—building model airplanes, a reticent father, boy-boy friendships, even the name "Darla"—suggest that the first part of the novel is like "comfort food" for the author. And just as in *Staggerford*, where the "Stags" always lose football games, in *North of Hope* the Linden Falls "Rockets" are always losers. Vernon Jessen and his mother cooking on a wood range (186) recalls the Flints in *Grand Opening*. Hassler also thought of *The Love Hunter* and *North of Hope* as "a pair because they deal with the dirtier side of life—drugs and things like that" (*C*, 145).

Plot

The novel comes in five parts. Part one begins in late summer, 1949 and ends in a rainy spring in the early 1950s. Parts two to five begin in Advent, 1977 (138) and end in April, 1978 (501), during Jimmy Carter's term as president. Part One uses irony and satire to contrast a romantic, coming-of-age story with a number of mystical elements. It introduces sixteen-year old Frank Healy, who falls in love with Libby Girard, a new girl in Linden Falls, MN. Because Frank believes that, on her deathbed, his mother had desired he become a priest, Frank resists a romantic involvement, but he and Libby become close friends. The climax of part one is Frank's betrayal of Libby and Libby's giving herself, first to a callow sports reporter, then to a farm boy football player named Vernon Jessen. Part one ends several months later, with a moving final meeting between Libby and Frank. Libby visits Frank in the parking lot of the seminary. She is holding her baby daughter, Verna, and she asks Frank to come away with her. Frank refuses and she leaves. Frank prays, "Dear God… please keep her out of my life." The narrator's one line quip ends Part One. "And God did, for twenty-three years" (104).

Part Two begins twenty-three years later, on the Ojibwe reservation in northern Minnesota, with another betrayal and tales
of tragic and violent death. The first death is that of Ojibwe Roger Upward, Verna's on-again off-again boyfriend, who freezes to
death. Verna has literally left him out in the (minus six degree)
cold for the owner of a backwoods bar, who is the supplier of
drugs to her, and the reservation. Roger's desire for death foreshadows other characters' similar desire. A tone of loss, betrayal,
depression, and despair (not to mention disgust) permeates part
two. It is only relieved by the joy of renewed friendship as Fr.
Frank meets Libby again, after all these years. Over the next two
hundred pages, Frank tries to support Libby, and to help Verna
who has a psychotic break and is hospitalized. Struggling with
his own depression, he nevertheless begins to suspect the source
of evil on the reservation. The first revelation is Tom Pearsall's
incestuous relationship with Verna; the second, his illegal drug
dealing. Libby moves into an apartment on her own but becomes deeply depressed. She asks Frank to spend the night with
her, but, once again, he refuses. She determines to end her life.

Characters
There are fewer main characters than in *Grand Opening*. The focus is clearly on Frank Healy and Libby Girard. Fr. (later Monsignor) Adrian Lawrence is a major supporting character. In
Frank's youth, the mechanically inept priest smokes cigars and
warns Frank, as a prospective seminarian, about criticizing the
bishop, "his boss." In the second half of the novel, the monsignor is described as having "childlike, vulnerable, wonder-filled
eyes." Even later Monsignor Adrian Lawrence becomes a source
of gentle comedy.

Libby Girard resembles the stereotypical, small-town teenage girl of the 1950s. She wants to be married by the time she
finishes high school. In the first pages she tells her friend, Sylvia
Pofford, with only slight exaggeration: "If I don't have a baby be-

fore I'm nineteen, I'll feel like I've wasted my life." Later, talking to Frank, she says, "Marriage is what makes a woman a woman." Even Frank recognizes the "obsession," calling it a "mating urge." The way the narrator represents naiveté and innocence can be seductive, but it is a tone and style that can also express savage satire. Even in the 1970s, when she and Fr. Frank meet again, Libby exhibits traces of the "romantic" young woman. When she talks to Frank, it sometimes sounds like she is still sixteen, even though she is forty-four and has gone through more dreadful experiences than most women experience in a lifetime.

When we meet her in part two, Libby's daughter Verna, an only child, is central to the plot. The reason for Libby's marriage to Vernon Jessen, Verna eventually has two step-fathers, both of whom abuse her. In the second half of the novel she is twenty-four and suffering from the emotional and psychological consequences of that abuse. Eunice Pfeiffer is Adrian Lawrence's indispensable housekeeper in Part One; Marcella Tatzig is the housekeeper in the 1970s sections. Both wield power almost equal to the mother Frank had lost when he was eleven. Through the narrator's ironic tone and attention to details, each housekeeper becomes a focus of the novel's humor as well.

Antagonists

The only significant antagonist in part one is Vernon Jessen, the self-centered football player whom Libby marries when she becomes pregnant in senior year of high school. Feared by Frank Healy in high school, Jessen becomes, in the second half of the novel, the butt of satire for his parsimoniousness and his paranoid views.

In the second half of the novel, the chief antagonist is Tom Pearsall, Libby's third husband, an alcoholic, drug-dealing doctor whose own life story evokes a sense of frustration, if not pity, at talents wasted. Like Satan in John Milton's *Paradise Lost*, Pearsall proves to be a fascinating study in evil. The reader meets him at the start of Part Two, drunk and argumentative on a Saturday night in Advent. Twisted by a ski injury that makes him appear short and awkward, he is loud, abrasive, and scornful of religion. He thinks he understands his wife, her needs, her inadequacies. On his first meeting with Frank, Pearsall even tries to analyze the priest's "needs." He is, in short, a bully and a ruthless materialist. Frank, and the narrator, however, treat him with patience, and Frank with an extra measure of caution. A few chapters later the reader accompanies Pearsall to a motel where he has sex with his step-daughter. To humanize Pearsall the narrator discloses his fear of guns and thin ice. Late in the novel, the reader also spends a substantial amount of time in Pearsall's consciousness, as he prepares to "disappear" and avoid the consequences of his illegal and immoral actions.

Judge Bigelow is the owner of "The Homestead," a local hangout just off the reservation. The Judge's shadowy but largely mundane evil still seems "oppressive" to the spirit whenever Frank meets him. Myron (Toad) Majerus is the Judge's employee, a dwarf, whose given name, self-deprecating personality, and subservient behavior make him and the Judge together an almost archetypal constellation of evil.

Secondary Characters and Native Americans

As with Hassler's other novels, *North of Hope* includes a range of often memorable secondary characters. Libby's friend, Sylvia Pofford, is the caricature of the good looking, smart, rich, bossy teenage girl. Her boyfriend, Bob Templeton, is the Rockets' quarterback and admits "I'm only half a man …" when Sylvia's not around. Ironically, he goes off to the Korean War and loses several toes. DeVaughn Smith is one of Libby's potential high school boyfriends, but whose obsession with music puts him out of the running as boyfriend. His " invisible trumpet" at the funeral of a teacher, Mr. Meyer, is one of the uncanny events in part one. The Shultenovers, who run "The Egghouse" where

Frank works, are like surrogate parents. Selma is the brains and the power; Herb Shultenover suffers from a complex because he works with eggs—a woman's work. Libby Girard's father looks like Clark Gable, but he can't hold a job because of drinking. His abusiveness may explain some of Libby's bad choices in life.

A hallmark of the novel's authenticity—and its quiet boldness—is its treatment of the Ojibwe. *North of Hope* introduces no fewer than a dozen Native American characters who play important secondary roles. Not since *Staggerford* and *Jemmy* has Hassler so thoroughly explored the lives of Native Americans. In part two the reader meets Roger Upward, the Ojibwe whose painful death is described in almost clinical detail. Because the narrator follows Roger's final moments through Roger's own perspective, the reader can't help but feel sympathy and a measure of anguish. Other Ojibwe include Caesar and Joy Pipe, Millie LaBonte and her children: Elaine, Lanny, and twin girls (never named). Caesar Pipe and his wife, Joy, represent traditional Native American culture—accommodating to the white world. Caesar is the reservation's elected leader, and its constable. Members of St. Mary's church where Frank Healy serves, he and Joy are also the Basswood parish council. Roger Upward's brothers, Johnny and Pock, appear early in part two as the object of Tom Pearsall's racist comments. Later, their suspicion that Dr. Pearsall is selling drugs precipitates the ending of the novel. Millie LaBonte, who attended grade school with Frank, suffers from anxiety. Her oldest daughter, Elaine, is sixteen, and despite Millie's frantic parenting is growing up liberated and independent. Billy Annunciation has returned from Minneapolis, where the Pipes think he has been learning too many "white" habits. Suspicions are confirmed—and Billy infuriates Caesar—when Billy insists on fishing, quite successfully, in the "white man's way," with hook and line, through the ice. Billy, along with Elaine LaBonte, represent the younger generation, and the story of their relationship contributes to both the humor and the insight into teenage behavior that constitute a further sophistication of Hassler's storytelliing. Billy and Elaine's shared passion for ice-fishing figures in the novel's dramatic climax. For those who think that Hassler doesn't handle Native Americans realistically, he reintroduces Mrs. Graham, widow of the Linden Falls undertaker. Late in the novel, she complains that her husband "buried too many Indians." When Fr. Healy mistakes her meaning ("Yes, they die untimely deaths out there"), she corrects him with a comment about their being "deadbeats."

Imagery

As in many of his earlier novels, *North of Hope* again uses seasons and seasonal change for tonal emphasis. Part one begins in the fall and ends in a rainy spring, with idyllic fall scenes as the background to the action. Part two begins on a cold December night, and most of the next three parts take place in a cold and snowy Minnesota winter. The novel concludes in another rainy, but more life-affirming spring.

Throughout the novel, significant scenes take place in enclosed or cramped spaces, adding a sense of oppressiveness. A movie theater, the Healy basement, the egghouse, the Loomis Ballroom, and the cab of a pick-up are significant in part one. Squalid motel rooms are significant locations in both part one and part two. Open spaces suggest freedom and lightness. The campus of Aguinas Academy and Seminary, the banks of the Badbattle River, and the shore of Sovereign Lake all represent the openness of nature or man-made openness in harmony with nature. The Homestead Bar, the Basswood Reservation rectory, and the rectory of St. Ann's in Linden Falls are all spaces of more and less ominous enclosure.

The religious or the mystical forms a background to the entire novel. The novel opens on a quasi-mystical note in late summer, 1949, when Frank Healy first sees beautiful Libby Girard, a newcomer to Linden Falls. Frank sees Libby a few rows ahead of him at a matinee showing of the 1948 movie, *A Portrait of Jennie*, and he keeps her beauty "in the privacy of his heart." Outside, after the sad movie, Frank sees Libby in tears and hears a voice that tells him, "*She's the one.*"

Later, the mystical returns as Sylvia and Libby watch Frank step into the Badbattle River carrying a football. "He went in slowly, up to his waist, then stopped and stood still, facing downstream, as though in a trance. He kept moving his right hand back and forth, palm down, over the surface of the water" (10). Even when he starts throwing the football upstream and waits for it to float down to him—playing a solitary game of catch—the mysterious start of his Badbattle River "ritual" remains in the reader's mind.

One of Hassler's favorite scenes (*C*, 140-41) finds Frank daydreaming at his part-time job, as he "candles" eggs in the Shultenovers' "Egghouse," There "he fell into periods of deep reverie at the egg table, eggs triggering his fantasies the way the rosary triggered his prayers" (16-17). His daydreams smoothly transition to a flashback in which the story of his mother's death from cancer reintroduces the tragic element—along with Eunice Pfeiffer's reporting that Mrs. Healy's dying wish was that her son become a priest. The mystical-uncanny reappears when, "on an afternoon in the spring of his [Frank's] freshman year" (21), Martin Healy comes to the high school and calls Frank out of class to report; "'Your mother's in heaven, Frank, it just came to me five minutes ago in the bank'" (21).

As in Hassler's other earlier novels, death is a constant background. In part one it is Frank's mother and the teacher, Mr. Meyer, who dies of hypothermia after breaking his leg while hunting. Death intrudes once more, however, with Fr. Lawrence's stories—really another series of interpolated anecdotes—which "were mostly tales of local history, with a "remarkable number of deaths in them" (70). The climactic instance in part one comes with the story of Fr. Zell, frozen to death when he loses his way trying to cross Sovereign Lake at Christmas (72). Here the violent and untimely deaths are overshadowed by what, for Frank, at least, is the story of Fr. Zell's heroism. Part two begins with Roger Upward freezing to death, and over the next several parts the reader learns of a number of suicides, gets reminders of Fr. Zell's death, and experiences the death or near death of a number of main characters.

A minor contrast of imagery involves indulgence and asceticism. Fr. Healy's rum-drinking represents indulgence. His later fastidiousness (he wonders whether he is trying to imitate Fr. Zell) represents his ascetic side. Tom Pearsall's alcoholism and Verna's outbursts are other forms of indulgence. Msgr. Lawrence's prayers for over seven hundred departed souls represents an exaggerated, excessive piety, related to "indulgence." Repetitions of and variations on the title's emphasis on "hope" include the use of the title itself and various characters expressing "hopelessness."

Fr. Healy's Religiosity

In the later (1970s) parts of the novel, the reader learns a good deal about Fr. Frank Healy's spiritual life. The reader frequently overhears him praying for various characters. The novel also follows but does not over-emphasize the "liturgical year." The reader experiences Fr. Healy as he gives homilies, hears "confessions," and is witness to a symbolic crucifixion. On a few occasions Frank assumes the role of *alter Christus* (other Christ), listening and healing other characters as Jesus had. Chapters thirty-seven and thirty-eight find Frank praying for Libby, Verna and Tom. After he tells his weekly Basswood penitents to pray "for a secret intention," he himself prays in a manner that echoes Christ in the garden of Gethsemane. "Dear God, watch out for Libby and Verna and Tom ... If there's no way for the three of them to avoid heartbreak, please see to it that they heal up in good time." But then the tone and the mystical element intensify. "Frank was not given to psychic experiences on a grand scale, but he was visited occasionally by small premonitions. A lifetime of cultivating his spiritual life had taught him… that when a prayer led to anxiety instead of peace, something ominous was looming ahead" (376).

Archetypes

North of Hope does not portray the stages of the hero's journey the way some of Hassler's earlier novels had. Unlike Miles Pruitt in *Staggerford*, Frank Healy is at best an unconventional hero, but his premonitions, his devotedness, his fidelity, and moral strength all make him heroic. His life and ordeals on occasion also suggest the heroic pattern. The novel drives forward by means of several revelations, some of which have almost archetypal significance. From his ordeals and woes the hero successfully comes to the rescue. Some of the early episodes and descriptions—Frank in the Badbattle River, and in the Egghouse, his father announcing Theresa Healy's arrival in heaven—also contribute an "otherworldly" quality that suggests the archetypal. The depiction of evil, woe, and tribulation is almost exaggeratedly excessive, and thus perhaps comes closest to achieving the archetypal effect. The ruthless and cold-blooded abusiveness of Harris Highsmith and then Dr. Tom Pearsall are shockingly almost preternatural. Tom Pearsall's jealousy and sense of rivalry for Verna's "affections" also has archetypal resonance. The later descriptions of Pearsall, Judge Bigelow, and "Toad" Majerus and their interactions add further to the archetypal aura. The way that Tom Pearsall's death (his car plunging through the ice on Lake Sovereign) calls to mind, by contrast, the death of the legendary nineteenth-century missionary, Fr. Zell, also has an archetypal quality.

Part One Key Scenes

To look at a few key scenes in each part of the novel is to get a clearer picture of the way the novel combines comedy and tragedy, the mundane and the mystical, as it explores the themes of friendship, loyalty, and trust, amid the abuse, despair and manipulation. This brief look will also help explain what makes this novel the masterpiece it is.

Three chapters (5-7) recount how Frank betrays Libby after a football game and the consequences of that betrayal. It is a pivotal moment in their friendship. After the game, Libby asks Frank to let her come into his living room. Her father has been abusive, and Libby is afraid to go home. When Frank is too afraid of his feelings for her to let Libby in his house, he betrays their friendship. Libby's response to the betrayal has an ominous tone. After Frank leaves her alone, the narrator enters Libby's viewpoint, "She turned slowly in a circle, holding back a new surge of tears. She looked at the sky. The stars seemed closer and more numerous than she'd ever seen them. They seemed caught in the webs of the bare trees" (59). When she looks at the river, she remembers Frank's Badbattle River ritual, "wishing she had the courage to do the same—and stay under until she drowned."

Libby reacts to the betrayal by offering herself to the sports writer, Dennis Hedstrom, who had come to town to cover the football game. In a squalid tourist cabin Libby loses her virginity, and this decision motivates the rest of part one. Chapter nine then recounts Libby's betrayal of Frank, as she uses him to make Vernon Jessen jealous at the Loomis Ballroom, a local dance hall. Chapter ten finds Libby pregnant, and Frank realizing that the pain of losing Libby is like that of losing his mother.

Part one concludes during a rainy May in the early 1950s, when Libby visits Frank, now in his third year in the seminary. Amid mundane chat about Frank's thinness (he is fasting), Libby tells Frank that she is lonesome for him and that she is leaving Vernon. Frank has "a momentary vision of their riding off in the pickup together" (101), but in the end he rejects her over-tures without sensitivity, betraying their friendship yet again. The final two lines of the chapter, and part one, include Frank's prayer, "Dear God, he pleaded, please keep her out of my life," and the narrator's one-line quip: "And God did, for twenty-three years" (104). It is also significant that when Libby leaves, Frank no longer hears the voice saying "*She's the one.*"

Part Two Key Scenes
Part two creates a tone of loss, betrayal, depression, despair, and death, only partially relieved by the joy of a friendship renewed. The mystical appears in a variety of overt and subtle ways, most obviously in connection with Fr. Frank Healy's priestly voca-tion. A continued emphasis on enclosures adds to the oppressive atmosphere. Structurally, part two presents a series of scenes and fuller episodes that alternate between those with a focus on Fr. Frank Healy and those that focus on Roger Upward.

The stifling enclosures are almost myriad. The first is the small Basswood rectory, then the reservation Health Clinic, and, perhaps most moving, Roger's one-room house in the woods. Later it is the rectory at St. Ann's with its cramped breakfast nook[7] and its gloomy living room. Later still, it is the Home-stead bar and the psychiatric ward in Berrington. There is also a recollection of Libby feeling "lost in murk" in the Loomis Ballroom (175). Few scenes take place "in the open," and the one that does—outside Roger Upward's house in the woods—is made oppressive by the presence of heavily falling snow.

The shocking climax of part two comes in chapter nineteen, when Tom Pearsall shows up at an unnamed motel in Linden Falls, where he has sex with Verna. The depth of Tom's evil is suggested as he refrains from telling Verna that Roger is dead, "lest the news short circuit her libido" (190). After the shock of Tom and Verna's mutual betrayal of Libby, the chapter ends as Frank arranges for the funeral of Roger Upward. There is deep irony as Libby tells Frank about her early years with Tom; how he had struggled to become a doctor but then "didn't like being a doctor" (192-94). A further incongruity: the chapter ends with a scene of tenderness reminiscent of one of the most powerful that will be examined in *A Green Journey.* As Frank leaves the clinic for Linden Falls, he kisses Libby's hand (194). His elated prayer as he returns to Linden Falls ("Dear God, am I not the happiest man in the world and doesn't life make perfect sense") forms a strong contrast to the Pearsall-Verna scene. Part two ends with the funeral of Roger Upward, viewed from the perspective of Elaine LaBonte. The service and the snack at the church afterwards are full of the everyday, except for Millie's seeing Frank and Libby "exchange a little kiss" (199).

Part Three Key Scenes

Feelings of hopelessness and depression fill part three. An example occurs in chapter 22 as the reader accompanies the Pearsalls as they return from Chicago on a cold. Sunday in January. The scene combines Libby's recollections (an internal flashback) of the six months in Basswood, beginning with hope but ending with downheartedness and "one or two awful days and nights, in fact, when suicide seemed as reasonable as staying alive" (215). Back at the Basswood health clinic, the banality of the Judge's phone call reporting Verna's psychotic break constitutes the chapter's climax. The chapter ends as Libby considers leaving Tom, and her hopes that Frank will accompany her to visit Verna.

Subsequent chapters continue to complicate the narrative with contrasting tones. Chapter twenty-three begins with everyday comedy: Marcella's violent cooking, some gentle satire on the Monsignor's interest in a TV anchorwoman. Then the tone changes as Frank and Adrian repair to the "large and somber" living room, where the paneling was "the color of mud" (227). The chapter ends with a brief scene of potential tragedy, balanced by the comic-mystical. As a grade school teacher, Mrs. Pettit, introduces Msgr. Lawrence to the fifth and sixth grade, "she was horrified to see him leaning sideways, far to his left, with his eyes shut tight as though in pain" (238). When he "tipped over—slowly and carefully—and lay on the floor," she tries to hear the words he is saying—or singing. "Up and down went the old man's quavery voice. He was reciting a line over and over that Mrs. Pettit recognized from this morning's liturgy: 'The spirit of the Lord God is upon me, the spirit of the Lord God is upon me'" (239). Monsignor Lawrence has experienced a heart attack.

Part Four Key Scenes

Though part four maintains the contrast of comedy and tragedy, the blend of mystical and mundane, and furthers the themes of friendship, loyalty, and trust, the plot structure dramatizes the suspense-filled revelation of Tom's various betrayals, and the working out of his plan to escape prosecution. But part four also concentrates on Frank's efforts to re-ignite a fervor for his vocation, which happens largely through his pastoral work and his continued loyalty to Libby *and* Verna. Accounts of his pastoral duties are the occasion for much of the mundane humor that balances the greater intensity of the Pearsall family drama. Subtly and gradually, the reader also witnesses the deepening and transformation of the two high school sweethearts' mature friendship.

Chapter thirty-seven shows Hassler's skill with indirection. In his apprehension about the coming Tuesday meeting with Dr. Pella, Frank prays for Libby and Verna. When he thinks of Tom he only gets as far as "Dear God –" (372). Then, talking with Billy Annunciation—whom he has come to like—Frank and Billy take a detour into theology. Billy's reflections on Adrian and his notebook of intentions lead to a discussion of God and his/her attributes. When Billy asks, "'What's he like?'" Frank "called to mind his four years of graduate theology and reduced them to a word: 'Merciful'" (374). When Billy conjectures that "'maybe God's like the monsignor'"—which idea Frank likes—Billy continues, "'Sort of vague in the head, I mean. That wouldn't be so great, would it?'" To which Frank says, "'But so full of concern for everyone's soul. That would be ideal'" (374).

The latter part of chapter thirty-seven intensifies the Frank and Libby friendship as they argue on the phone about their relationship (377-380), even as Frank has to lie about the reason for the meeting with Dr. Pella.

The meeting with Dr. Pella is a crisis of part four. An ominous, mystical dimension is hinted at in Frank's prayer at the beginning of chapter thirty-nine: "Dear God, does one continue to live with one's husband after a horror like this comes to light?" (393). The fallout after Verna confesses, "'Tom's been screwing me ...'" (387) further strains the loyalty and friendship of Frank, Libby, and Verna. After the meeting, Frank invites Libby and Verna to stay at the rectory, but this precipitates a blow-up between mother and daughter (408).

Part four builds slowly to a crescendo. Frank and Libby share dinner in Berrington, with the sounds of freight trains punctuating the meal. Libby acknowledges their enduring love. "Think of it, Frank, our love goes back twenty-five years"(441). Frank feels "a vague sense of spiritual unity taking shape around him" (442) that comes with acknowledging their common love. He feels nurtured by two communities, St. Ann's and St. Mary's.

Chapter 49 is a final, complex demonstration of Frank's friendship and loyalty as he tries to console Libby following the news of Tom's death. Grief stricken, Libby is on her own and feels both loneliness and futility, but she has also grown dependent on Frank and wants a closer relationship. Frank visits her in her apartment in Berrington. As he holds her hand, she asks:

"Frank, would you go to bed with me?"
His turn to ponder – not his decision but his phrasing. He settled on "No."

"Please." She was still gazing at the yellow wall.
"I can't"(408).

After a few minutes Libby goes into the bedroom for some names and addresses. "She was in the bedroom a minute or more before she called to him and he went to the door and saw her standing naked beside the bed" (409). She puts out her hand to him and says "Lie down with me, Frank."

He steps into the room, but lowers his eyes. When she asks him to look up, he does so, but still refuses her request.

He picked up her robe off the bed and draped it around her shoulders, guiding her hands into the sleeves. She was trembling. As he drew the lapels together over her breasts he reflected not with regret so much as wonder on the superhuman perversity expected of the priest, the contrariness of covering the sublime nakedness of a woman other men – normal men – would naturally disrobe. And yet this did not feel like perversity to Frank. Not tonight. Not with Libby so distracted, so desperate, so vulnerable. It felt like common sense (409).

This scene verges on being melodramatic cliché. Yet the close observation, and the reflection, measured out in carefully constructed sentences, holds it in emotional balance. In this way the narrator confirms the sense of Frank's care, and a sense of a loyalty and fidelity that does not need, perhaps even positively precludes sex.

After he refuses her grief-motivated offering of herself to him, and Frank sets off for Linden Falls, he turns his car around when he has another premonition. He arrives in Berrington in time to save her from throwing herself beneath one of the freight trains whose names she kept repeating. After Frank has saved her, Libby asks if Frank has ever felt hopeless. Her response is a final reminder of the novel's title. "It's like hope doesn't reach this far north" (498).

Conclusion

Hassler said that conclusions often caused him problems. In *Simon's Night* he adapts the ending of James Joyce's *The Dead*. *Jemmy* ends with a vision of freedom and a return to the mundane. More and less "understated" conclusions characterize *The Love Hunter* and *Grand Opening*. *North of Hope* has one of the most serene and understated endings of any of his novels. Part of the dramatic balance in *North of Hope* comes from the way Hassler juxtaposes scenes with different tonal qualities. Like a good watercolor or acrylic, *North of Hope* blends shades of light and dark; soft and hard edges and colors both bright and drab; the comic and the tragic, the mundane and the mystical.

In the final episode of the novel, it is spring, and the reader is back at the St. Ann's rectory, where the narrator enters Mrs. Tatzig's point of view as she finishes some late-night tasks. As the reader will recall, during the critical months of Verna's psychiatric treatment, Libby was in the habit of calling Frank at the Linden Falls rectory every midnight to talk. He would lift the receiver after the first ring. Even when Frank dismisses Libby's plea for a physical relationship, he acknowledges their friendship and says he welcomes the calls. In the relatively short, understated final paragraph of the novel, the reader gets a glimpse of Frank and Libby's continuing relationship—and a final sign of hope. Once in bed, Mrs. Tatzig listens to the quiet of the house. "A car passing in the street. The clock on the mantel marking midnight. The furnace kicking in as the temperature dropped. The phone ringing. Once."

It is tempting to say that *North of Hope* is so reassuring partly because, in telling a complex, compelling story, it is still so well-made. Yes, the novel contains ugly, violent, and despicable events. It presents varieties of mental instability and depicts with great vividness the effects of out of control psychosis. Yes, on occasion the novel exhibits some of the melodrama of "grocery store fiction." Libby can be almost sentimental and occasionally superficial. Yet *North of Hope* is one of Hassler's most poignant and reassuring novels. As the great French novelist Gustav Flaubert might have argued, it is the technique—the distance that technique gives—that saves things; makes even the ugly and the despicable manageable, endurable, if not actually beautiful. Hassler continues to contrast the mundane and the mystical; the humdrum everyday with the intense and genuinely dramatic. It is his *skill* on a number of levels that makes the novel as a whole —its effect, its impact—rise above the sometimes quotidian elements, attitudes, and even the language of specific characters. It is Hassler's skill as novelist and his fallible but completely credible hero, Frank Healy, that make the consolation with which the novel ends both real, and memorable.

A Green Journey [8]

Approaching fifty years of age, Hassler writes a novel about a woman preparing for her retirement. That woman is Agatha McGee, a major character from his first novel, *Staggerford*. In *A Green Journey* Hassler makes Agatha the protagonist. She has now been teaching sixth grade at St. Isidore's Catholic school in the Northern Minnesota town of Staggerford for over forty years. In the course of the novel she will retire, take a trip to Ireland to meet the man, James O'Hannon, with whom she had been corresponding for years, and this will precipitate a momentous revelation about both herself and O'Hannon. Continuing to employ his characteristically shifting point of view, Hassler also uses new spatial and temporal arrangements to affect pace, spicing the narrative with his usual humor, satire, and compassionate insight. A cast of subordinate characters provides further variety, humor, and breadth of social commentary. *Staggerford* has a remarkable epigraph. While the epigraphs for *Simon's Night* and *The Love Hunter* are equally apt, only *AGJ* has an epigraph that really occurs *within* the novel—and in fact becomes a link between a crucial chapter and the novel's conclusion. As will be seen, this conclusion also suggests the thematic resolution of the novel.

Accompanying Agatha on her trip is a young woman, Janet Raft—a former student whom she befriended when Janet stayed with Agatha during the last weeks of her unwed pregnancy. With her son now four years old, and married to Randy Meers, Janet is a young wife and mother with both hopes and apprehensions. These two characters, joined together by bonds of friendship for the trip to Ireland, make *A Green Journey* simultaneously a story of age and youth. In time, with its shifting focus on other characters both old and young, the novel also explores a sub-theme present from the very start: the different forms that loneliness can take.

Joseph Plut notes (*C*, 103) that some readers found *AGJ* "lightweight," especially compared to *The Love Hunter*. This is perhaps because the two books really belong to different genres (as Hassler implicitly points out in his interview with Plut). Might readers consider the novel "lightweight" because the theme is less a matter of "life and death" than the story of Larry Quinn's multiple sclerosis? Perhaps in part. Is it because Agatha McGee's *milieu* involves more everyday events and apparently "trivial" concerns? Again, perhaps. The satire of *AGJ* makes it more akin to that in *Staggerford*, but the novel's "weight" and tone are really a matter of greater balance. As a counterweight to Agatha's severity—and the serious personal transformation she experiences—there has to be more humor. This includes episodes with Agatha's friend, Lillian Kite, as well as episodes both in Ireland and back in Staggerford, most prominently, the humor involving Janet's husband, Randy Meers. Even at the height of Agatha's transformation a number of humorous episodes in Ireland balance intensity with comedy. *AGJ* is more "episodic" than many of the earlier novels. The reader experiences Agatha's transformation as Hassler develops her story intermittently, in chapters separated by chapters set back in Staggerford. Hassler uses the different episodes to maintain the pace and create contrasting moods or tones, always balancing comedy and drama.

To take one of Hassler's most serious earlier novels as a contrast: if *The Love Hunter*'s comedy is more Dantean in the way it explores the depths of despair and chronicles the sometimes painful ecstasy of love, then *AGJ*'s comedy is more Chaucerian. There are as many fools, knaves, and ninnies as there are admirable characters. It also makes more sophisticated use of comic and serious suspense. Comic suspense comes, early on, in the long-awaited birth of Janet's son Stephen, and later, as the reader follows the adventures of Randy Meers—especially with the vacuum salesman Eugene Westerman and the new Staggerford pharmacist, Connie Eklund. In Ireland, the comic episodes include the interactions with the Plunketts. Agatha's journey to find James O'Hannon in the fictional village of Ballybegs uses sustained comic suspense with serious implications. Bishop Baker's visit to the rectory in Ballybegs is a long, suspense-filled joke.

Autobiographical Elements

Like most of his other novels, *AGJ* contains a number of details taken from Hassler's own life. While many of the most crucial come from two trips to Ireland that he took before writing the book, a number of them come from his life in northern Minnesota. Though the reader can find all these references discussed in *Conversations*, I include them here in summary fashion. Hassler notes that Agatha McGee is "much like my mother" and "a maiden aunt I had who used to teach school" (*C*, 88). Agatha's early love, Preston Warner, was someone Hassler knew in Plainview, MN (*C*, 90). Hassler heard about the confirmation "trick" that Agatha pulls on Bishop Baker in the diocese of Duluth (*C*, 91). He was also familiar with a number of priests from Ireland who had come to serve in the Duluth diocese (*C*, 91). The Brass Fox bar is based on "Paulette's," a place that Hassler and

Joe Plut had frequented (*C*, 93). The magazine (*The Fortress*) in which Agatha reads a letter from James O'Hannon is based on the conservative Catholic magazine, *The Wanderer* (*C*, 93). The story of Lady Wellington the cat derives from a story Hassler heard at St. John's University (*C*, 95). Agatha's encounter with the Quimby girl, whom she recalls when leaving Ballybegs (*AGJ*, 163-65) comes from a similar experience Hassler had in Plainview (*C*, 99).

Details derived from Hassler's Ireland trips include the Plunketts and their Bed & Breakfast in Knob (*C*, 94). Hassler saw the Breughel and the Last Supper paintings (chapter 16) at the National Gallery of Ireland, in Dublin (*C*, 96-97). Janet's experiences in Belfast were Hassler's own (*C*, 102). Finally, Joe Plut documents Hassler's having seen Sam Shepard's *Buried Child* (a performance of which Agatha and the Bishop attend in chapter 26) at the Peacock Theater in Dublin in May, 1981.

Like some of Hassler's earlier novels, *AGJ* also incorporates a number of previously written or published short stories. "The Holy War of Agatha McGee" and "The Midnight Vigil of Agatha McGee appeared in *McCall's*. A third story about Agatha McGee, "Agatha McGee and the St. Isidore Seven," later appeared in *Rufus at the Door*. Hassler even says that "'The Midnight Vigil of Agatha McGee' had been the origin of this book actually. I wrote that before I wrote the book'" (*C*, 88).

Characters

The story opens "On the night before Christmas," sometime in the later 1970s. In the later parts of the novel, allusions to "Pac-Man," *Star Wars*, and Linda Ronstandt's *On Blue Bayou* (279) suggest the novel ends in late spring, sometime around 1980. On that Christmas Eve, Janet and her father Frank (another of Agatha's former students) arrive on Agatha's porch. Their coming has been arranged. Janet will stay with Agatha during the last days of her pregnancy, because a winter storm is threatening, and her doctor does not want her out in the country on her father's small farm in case the storm should close the roads.

Hassler's introduction of Frank and Janet Raft is highly skillful, and its apparent casualness belies the effort needed to have created it. The reader learns in a few paragraphs a great deal about the father, the daughter, and their situation. Like Jemmy's father, Stott, Frank has been in the army and even was at least a part-time house painter. He is around forty years of age, about the age of Stott, and like Stott, his wife has died and left him a single father to a large family. He fathered his oldest daughter, Janet, at about age twenty-four. Like the Stotts, the family has no phone. Like the Stotts, too, the Rafts take welfare, but not regularly. When his farm produces hay, Frank is satisfied. When he can't make enough from the sixty acres, he will "go on the county" (46).

Though Janet at the start is roughly the same age as Jemmy, her character is a world apart from Jemmy's. Like Jemmy, Janet has no friends in town that she can think of. But, unlike Jemmy, the reader learns that Janet loves sex and thinks she loves Eddie Lofgren, the man who made her pregnant. She also knows it was her destiny to have a husband and children, even if they don't come in that order (16). The reader soon learns that Janet does have as much determination and initiative as Jemmy, though of a different kind. Agatha and Janet become somewhat unusual friends, despite the fact that Agatha harbors misgivings about Janet's unwed condition and later about her judgment and her husband's lack of ambition. Still, she agrees to be godparent to Janet's son, Stephen, who is born on New Year's Day, the first Staggerford baby born of the new year.

What all three characters have in common is an element of loneliness. Janet and Randy are young and married, but in many ways lonely as well. Randy's lack of "pep" and our interior view of his self-doubts make him out as something of a loner. His jealousy of his stepson further isolates him from his wife. Chapter six finds Agatha reflecting on forty-six years as a teacher. Her exchanges with Frank Raft and her misgivings about Janet's marriage have caused her to wonder about her life alone. A letter from James O'Hannon, whose theme is loneliness, precipitates Agatha's decision to retire and go to Ireland to meet James.

Once Agatha has decided to go to Ireland, Hassler shifts the focus and complicates the plot by bringing along her friend, Lillian Kite, and Bishop ("call me Dick") Baker, a liberal prelate who had made a number of changes to his diocese, which have infuriated Agatha. Like Randy Meers, Baker is an only child, and having been a "mother's boy," he manifests an almost constant desire for companionship and camaraderie. Bishop Baker is the focal point of one of the important subplots of the novel. On the trip to Ireland Agatha, Janet, and Bishop Baker meet the Plunketts, a sister and two brothers who run a Bed & Breakfast in Knob, Ireland. The Plunketts are middle-aged and for all their working together seem to lack a genuine family life.

Once in Dublin, both the youthful dimension and the everyday and trivial reappear as Janet is paired with Evelyn Fermoyle, the young daughter of Alexander and Nora Fermoyle. The Fermoyles are acquaintances of the Meers family. Alexander is in the newspaper business and provides a view of Ireland in the early days of "the troubles" between the Republic and Northern Ireland. Evelyn introduces Janet to her circle of (single) friends, and the episodes involving Janet, Evelyn, and Evelyn's friends provide youthful balance to the episodes involving Agatha, James, and Bishop Baker.

The Rhythm of the Plot
Chapters developing the main plot (Agatha McGee and James O'Hannon) alternate with chapters devoted to Randy Meers

MATURITY

and his efforts to succeed as a salesman, and finally a real estate agent working for his father. Like what used to be called "comic relief" in Shakespeare, the Randy Meers chapters animate and move the novel forward in interesting, often hilarious, and occasionally suspenseful ways. As is the function of many comic scenes in Shakespeare, a number of transitional chapters often present a contrast in tone to what came before.

Chapters four and six represent a first major juncture in the story of Agatha's self-discovery. They also re-emphasize the themes of loneliness and friendship. Picking up the theme of discontent and loneliness with which chapter three ends, chapter four stresses Agatha's lack of enthusiasm for school and teaching. In a digression, the reader learns of Agatha's two-week retirement the previous year, and her determination to retire in four years, at sixty-eight. A few paragraphs on, Agatha's conservative Catholicism provide a segue to her correspondence with James O'Hannon.

Writing to O'Hannon about the Raft family, Agatha introduces the term "hardscrabble girl," here applied to Janet. That leads smoothly into a quasi-flashback to the previous summer and a revealing conversation with Janet's father, Frank. They meet on a hot August day when Agatha is out looking for wild chokecherries, and she stops to talk with Frank. Frank shows Agatha "a secret clump of chokecherries" on an abandoned farm. Their conversation as Frank helps Agatha pick the berries is revelatory. Frank's greater candor with her since she began visiting Janet and her baby leads him to a question.

It's got to be hard never letting your hair down. Always being up to snuff yourself and expecting everybody else to be up to snuff. When do you let your hair down, Miss McGee?" (45)

Sounding defensive, Agatha tells Frank about making and drinking chokecherry wine and getting tipsy.[9] The conversation ends with Frank acknowledging his hard life on the farm but

161

concluding "we each of us have our own natures and it's no sense going against them," and Agatha's grudging respect as she mutters, "Oh, to be so reconciled."[10]

The chapter has accomplished a number of things. It has raised the issue of Agatha's retirement and introduced James O'Hannon and their common interests, starting with the Church. It has also shown Agatha reflecting on her own high standards, especially *vis à vis* hardscrabble families like the Rafts. Such self-scrutiny is the first phase of the transformation that Agatha will experience in the course of the novel.

Chapter six begins, "The first year of Janet's marriage was Agatha's forty-sixth and final year of teaching" (55). It is Agatha's eavesdropping on two exchanges between Randy and Janet (one on the phone and one in person) that re-introduces the theme of loneliness. Then a letter from James ending, "Are you ever lonely, Agatha, living alone?" (60) brings loneliness to the forefront. Feeling that James's question is "brazen," Agatha reflects on the terms of their relationship.

> *If she replied with the whole truth—why wouldn't she feel lonely at times?—he might be encouraged to do more probing and destroy one of the qualities she most enjoyed about this correspondence: giving or withholding at will. Wasn't that the great advantage of living one's life alone, the control? (60)*

Reserve and control are also characteristics implicit in her conversation with Frank Raft. It is Agatha's reflecting on her teaching career and her loneliness that precipitates her decision to visit Ireland and James O'Hannon (61). Ten pages later Agatha has joined a tour to Ireland. "Lillian Kite would travel with the group. Janet Meers would stay with the Fermoyles and Agatha McGee would meet the man in her life" (71).

Chapters fourteen through sixteen develop and confirm the Agatha-O'Hannon friendship and kindle Agatha's—and the reader's—expectations through euphoria, revelation, and finally betrayal. With everyday details that develop character and scene, the eight-page chapter fourteen is a teaser, before the more intense two chapters that will follow it. Their meeting is a convincing start to their in person friendship. An intimate dinner begins with more everyday details, including talk of marriage and the single life. He asks what childhood incident had led her to remain single. The dinner's climax is O'Hannon's claiming they are "kindred spirits" and that "There's always a bond between Irish hearts" (144). The chapter closes with a taxi ride, Agatha's expectation of "an intimate question" (146). But at the hotel elevator he embraces her, and she ascends "to the realm of her happiest dreams."

Chapter fifteen is composed of several mini-episodes that build to a surprising climax. On the second day of their time together, James takes Agatha to the National Gallery of Ireland, where they view a Brueghel and an unattributed "mammoth" Last Supper. The reader sees James's reaction, and the painting itself, through Agatha's eyes. "For the first time this morning he seemed relaxed. The painting was a peasant wedding with a lot of dancing and kissing going on. Heavy bellies, round cheeks, wine and food spilling. Treetop leaves turned by a breeze" (149). Agatha confronts her friend: "'Tell me what it is about Brueghel that people admire, James. I've never understood.'" He is surprised and answers, "'Life.'" Their differing views highlight their different responses to life. For Agatha, "heavy bellies, round cheeks, wine and food spilling"—not to mention dancing and kissing—are not prime values. Like the scene with Frank Raft, this exchange with James O'Hannon is revelatory of Agatha's deeper character.

Viewing the mammoth Last Supper, Agatha is reminded of Mass and thinks to ask James if they could attend Sunday Mass together the next day. But then she is distracted by noticing there are only eleven apostles around the table. James hadn't noticed, and it is Agatha who "found the hint of a face in the upper right corner" (150). They speculate that the face "all but erased by reason of the betrayal" (150) is Judas. When Agatha then asks about Sunday Mass, James moves them on to another painting. Lunch at Bewley's culminates her pleasure in the day, but also makes her, almost unaccountably, think of Preston Warner, the man who proposed to her in 1938. The recollection is like a "death's head" or *memento mori*. The narrator dwells on Warner's empty life and recent strange behavior.

In the afternoon they take a train to Dun Laoghaire then stroll along the pier. On the way back they share a bench, and James tells of his sister's and his mother's last years and their deaths. Agatha tells James about Miles Pruitt and Beverly Bingham; both tales of sorrow and loneliness. At the end James and Agatha are holding hands in silence. The chapter's climax comes when James says, "I dare say you've never seen a whirlpool of gulls" (156). He takes her to the Ha'penny Bridge and throws crumbled bread to a rapidly increasing flock of seagulls.

As he continued flinging the bread, the birds flew round and round, dozens of them, some higher some lower, and with each pass near the bridge they slowed or speeded up to snatch the morsels in mid-air. Circling, circling, they formed a white-winged whirlpool above the dark water.[11]

At the end of this spectacular show, Agatha "felt airborne herself," but James brings her down, telling her that a crisis has come up and "'We'll be in touch before you leave'" (157). When Agatha presses him, he says, "'For now let me just say how very much you mean to me'" and "'I trust we'll continue to write to each other.'" He turned and walked away." Agatha "felt as if she'd been struck," and all she can do is watch him "flow away with the crowd."

Chapter sixteen brings the Agatha-O'Hannon story to a different and surprising juncture. At seven pages, it is one of the most economical yet most intense of the book. Her morning thought, tinged with the author's characteristic irony, is to help James in his crisis and then "sit stand and kneel in church beside the man she loved. Loved? Yes, the pain in her breast had to be love. Either that or a coronary" (159). As she recalls their time together, the reader and Agatha experience the swift bus trip to Ballybegs, the moaning sound of the sea, gulls overhead, and a young couple "running barefoot in the froth." Then, in St. Brigid's church, the priest, wearing white for Corpus Christi ("He was James") brings the first shock of the chapter. Fleeing the church with a "bitter laugh," she is, somewhat anomalously, carried back in memory to childhood and a long recollection of the Quimby family's daughter, "the idiot girl." The image and her recollections culminate in Agatha asking herself: "Where did she [the idiot girl] fit in God's plan?"(165). The shock of the memory ("Agatha lay awake for a long time that night, feeling sick to her stomach the way she felt now, leaving Ballybegs"), transferred to the revelation about James O'Hannon, has ominous and ambiguous overtones.

Shifting the focus as he modulates the tone, the narrator follows Agatha back to Dublin and out again to Dun Laoghaire. "She must see the sea. To keep her balance, she must fix her eyes on the perfect horizontal of the sea." There, facing eastward and speaking to God, "the only friend within earshot," she cries, "'Who said there are no snakes in Ireland?'" In this way the chapter brings together places, past and present, joyful memories, tragic recollections, and betrayal, ending on a comic but deeply ironic note.

An oblique continuation of the Agatha-James theme, chapter eighteen represents another crucial juncture in the novel. It also includes a revelation and a further confirmation of the friendship theme, even as it reinforces the confrontation of age and youth. It is also thematically rich in other ways and includes a fascinating meta-comment on the novel. The day after her discovery that James is a priest, Agatha meets Janet in front of The General Post Office, where a demonstration against British police brutality is taking place. Together they take a bus out to Howth Castle, where they climb to the crest. "The view from high ground was spectacular—the gardens and lawns of a swank hotel, thousands and thousands of rhododendron blossoms big as cheerleaders' pompons [sic]" (186). Agatha comments, "'I can't get enough of the sea,'" prompting Janet to say she prefers the smaller lakes back home in Minnesota. "'They don't remind you how big the world is, the way this does.'" To which Agatha's whispered, "Yes, there's so much more to the world than we realize" (186) is also a reference to the revelations of chapter fifteen—the sharing of which is the conclusion toward which this chapter will drive.

Walking down to the harbor, where they sit on a bench, Agatha takes out her sketch tablet and shares her latest work with Janet. Acknowledging that "'I'm an artist by default'" (187), Agatha explains how she had taught art in school. "'My strong point was always composition.'" This evokes a recollection—in Janet's perspective—of Agatha's artistic principles.

> It was the artist's job to rearrange nature, she said; life as you met it needed a great deal of straightening and fixing. Everything in nature had once had its place, she explained, but some things since the Fall of Man had been misplaced, and the artist had to set everything right."[12]

Agatha then concentrates on a sketch of the harbor and the cliffs, meanwhile asking Janet how her visit with the Fermoyles is going. This prompts Janet to ask about Agatha's meeting with James O'Hannon. In the midst of acknowledging the good things of the visit, her eyes fall "on an elderly couple leaving the town and walking down toward the pier" (as she and James had done). When her sketch is done, Agatha shows it to Janet saying, "'It isn't very good, is it, Janet? The cliffs haven't any depth to them.'" Janet agrees, but "with an impulsive stroke she put a gliding gull high in the sky over the headland. Suddenly the sketch was better. The bird for some reason gave depth to the scene."

Suddenly the teacher again, Agatha says: "'Now answer me this, Janet: Why should that bird make such a difference?'" As Janet searches for an answer, "Agatha wondered if there was an artistic principle about providing the viewer with some distraction in order for the core of the work to come into focus. She recalls the tantalizing, elusive image of Judas in the Last supper painting," but rather than focusing on Judas's betrayal, this reflection prompts a surprising—and revealing—one: "In the past four years hadn't she come to a fuller understanding of her own life by concentrating on the life of James O'Hannon?" Like her conversation with Frank Raft while picking chokecherries, this conversation with Janet is a further stage of Agatha's self-reflexive transformation.

The culmination of Agatha's reflections—and her answering her own question, "'Things throw light on things'"—prompts Janet to follow with the next line, "'And all the stones have wings'" (189). Agatha repeats the phrase, "this time more softly and to herself. It was a line she favored not only because it seemed true, but also because the man who wrote it, the son of a nurseryman, had grown up among flowers, as Agatha had." The Roethke lines articulate in a slightly different way the artistic principle that Agatha was pondering. In a kind of meta-comment on the novel, it may also explain why and how the many subplots of *A Green Journey* work; "providing the viewer [reader] with some distraction in order for the core of the work to come into focus."

Immediately following Agatha's reflection, "The elderly couple, their heads bent in rapt conversation, came strolling toward Agatha and Janet." The couple's presence prompts Janet to ask if she and Randy would "look like that someday," thus reasserting the age-youth theme in a different way. Janet's view is in contrast to Agatha's imagining the couple's "harmonious marriage" and

"If the world had been ordered more perfectly they might have been herself and James."

Janet's questions move Agatha toward further revelation. "'It takes time to be like that,'" she says, immediately thinking, "Yet weren't she and James like that on the pier at Dun Laoghaire?" When Janet renews her questions about James, Agatha's reflection on the old couple, in turn, prompts her to reveal that James O'Hannon is a priest. Janet exclaims, "'I didn't know that, Miss McGee.'" And then, "'Oh, Miss McGee, you didn't know either, did you?'" (191). This becomes a shared revelation of a shared unknown, further cementing the two women's bond.

After this revelation and Janet's consoling Agatha by putting "her arm around Agatha's sharp, bony shoulders," Agatha says, "'I know a place downtown that has the best coffee and rolls.'" Asked if she will see James again, or if she wishes to, Agatha answers "no," but then she acknowledges,

> *"But we were kindred spirits, Janet. James said it himself. He said our hearts were alike in so many ways, and he wasn't surprised, because we were Irish. There's always a bond between Irish hearts, he said."*

The chapter ends with Janet pondering and finally saying, "'I'm part Irish, you know'," a typical youthful response that further intensifies the novel's theme of friendship. It is tempting to call chapter eighteen a *tour de force*, but so many of the crucial chapters of this novel might be called that. In the course of a day trip to Howth, Agatha and Janet complete a work of art together, even as their bond of friendship strengthens. What is clear is that Hassler has taken everyday events—a climb, a sketch, an elderly couple, and a conversation—and made of them the stuff of everyday mystery, showing how "things throw light on things," even as they suggest a spiritual but, even more, an immensely valuable human reality.

Chapter twenty-five presents the economical but quietly intense and dramatic resolution of the Agatha-O'Hannon story. It begins with the everyday. Eating breakfast at Rosella Coyle's bed-and-breakfast and pondering whether or not to take Bishop Baker's offer of being principal, Agatha is surprised when Rosella tells her a priest is there to see her. It turns out to be James O'Hannon, and he has come to apologize for his not having told her he was a priest. Hassler handles the beginning of the apology with consummate skill, seeing into Agatha's mind while James O'Hannon tells Agatha what her friendship has meant, weeping as he asks for her forgiveness. Hassler then breaks the scene into two mini-episodes, prolonging the apology, and its emotional intensity. When Agatha says nothing to his first plea for forgiveness, O'Hannon gets up and leaves the room, but reappears immediately to hand Agatha a note for Bishop Baker. After he leaves the second time, Agatha gets up and calls to him from the front door. "'James, about this message. I feel like a girl being sent home with a note from her teacher. Is it about me?'" (263). When James assures her it is not, she says she wants to go out shopping and asks if he will "walk with me as far as St. Stephen's Green?"

This initiates the second half of the apology. In the middle of St. Stephen's Green they sit down on a bench, and Agatha is able to speak about what James and his letters have meant to *her*. "They meant more to me than they should have, I admit it now. I should not have allowed them to mean so much." Her explanation fits with that sense of reserve and control noted in her relationship with Frank Raft, and her reaction to James's epistolary query about loneliness. James's response is more straight forward. "For my part I cannot say that, Agatha. Your letters have been worth the world to me." He then asks if they will resume writing. When Agatha does not answer—and meantime "a well-dressed man comes to sit at the far end of the bench where James and Agatha are sitting—Hassler moves into O'Hannon's perspective. "Well, he thought, why not blunder back over forgiveness again?

Nothing to lose." When he repeats his apology, Agatha's response is a moment of genuine self-revelation. "Oh dear, must I tell you this minute? Forgiving is not one of my skills." Like her admission to Frank Raft that she doesn't give people the benefit of the doubt, this admission, that she doesn't forgive easily, represents a significant further growth in her self-awareness.

Breaking into this moment of high emotional intensity, Hassler introduces a fourth character, "a derelict with a cane" (264), who comes to occupy the bench on which Agatha, O'Hannon, and the other man are sitting. The derelict tells an Irish joke that bears upon the "well dressed man's" bus schedule. "Agatha and James smiled. The man with the bus book laughed." After a few moments Agatha says she is going shopping, and James asks, "'Am I forgiven then?'" Agatha says "'Yes'" but refuses to commit to further letter-writing. As they are about to part, James "pointed and said, "'You'll be wanting to go that way to Grafton Street.'" To which Agatha, in a one sentence paragraph that ends the chapter with a trademark significant gesture "took the hand he was pointing with and kissed the back of it. 'Good-bye, James.'" The awkwardness and cross-purposes that Agatha and James exhibit, as well as their inability to speak or to respond at different times, make this one of the most tonally complex chapters in the novel. The "business" of their sitting, not looking at each other, standing, taking leave, and Agatha finally and impulsively kissing the back of James's hand also make it one of the most dramatic and emotionally charged as well.

A Typical Hassler Denouement

Hassler orchestrates many of the sub-themes to a crescendo in the novel's final chapter, where, as in a fugue, the different melodies—Agatha-O'Hannon, Baker-Agatha, and Randy Meers's real estate deal—converge in three mini-episodes. By the third paragraph of the chapter Hassler is tying up loose ends. Back in Knob, and standing "on top of the three concrete steps leading down to the pier" (275), Agatha sees clearly how she will handle being St. Isidore's principal, deliberately applying "things throw light on things" and thus resolving the first part of the epigraph. She watches Janet along the stony breakwater where "there were dazzling white stones among the gray."[13] Returning from a flower shop, Agatha "watched in amazement as Janet, with a shout and a flap of her arms, turned all the white stones into gulls and sent them flying out over the water" (277). Like the talk of artistic principles, this symbolic resolution of the epigraph's second line ("and all the stones have wings") suggests not only how deeper (lighter) meaning can happen suddenly, surprisingly, but how the two are necessary to highlight the radiant insights of the novel.

The second mini-episode, starting in Shannon airport, resolves the minor Agatha-Lillian sub-theme. Lillian has "swallowed Ireland whole" (277) and has a stack of picture postcards to show for it, while Agatha thinks of Dun Laoghaire and the Ha'Penny Bridge with James, the Wicklow Hills with Bishop Baker, and her and Janet on a double-decker bus out to Howth. When Lillian asks Agatha what *she* got for her seven hundred dollar trip, Agatha responds, "I saw the essence of the Emerald Isle." Another page reprises the Baker-O'Hannon sub-theme.

The final mini-episode of the novel belongs exclusively to Randy Meers and "the final phase of his plan" to close the Vaughn real estate deal. Like the chapter's opening, the start of this mini-episode begins with everyday details. His mother, Louise Meers, gives Randy a blank check and tells him to stop at Southdale Mall to buy her Elizabeth Arden cosmetics. Randy is delayed in picking up Stephen at the farm by "a Denver sandwich with pickles and soup." But finally they are on their way, and Randy is determined to please Janet by bringing her son to the airport. At the Noznicks' second drive-in theater, the *Meteor*, he writes a check to cover the difference between the seller's firm price and the buyer's final offer. But it is the blank check his mother had given him. The reader closes the book having to imagine the outcome of all three mini-episodes.

The novel thus ends on an unresolved cadence. Agatha has forgiven Fr. James O'Hannon for his deception, but the reader doesn't know whether they will ever correspond again. The reader knows no more about Agatha's decision to accept the bishop's offer than that she will fight to keep St. Isidore's open. And about Randy Meers little more is known than that he closed the Vaughn deal, and that he thinks that bringing Stephen to the airport will please his wife. His thought, "Randy felt like Eugene Westerman, only smarter" is deeply ironic. His final thought is similarly ironic. "From now on Randy would sell himself to Janet through her weakness. Not a bad kid, Stephen. His voice was sensational on the high notes."[14]

Dear James [15]

The inspiration for *Dear James*, Hassler's seventh novel, occurred in Rome on Epiphany Sunday, 1986, when the author was viewing Michelangelo's *Pièta* in St. Peter's Basilica (*C*, 174). "I suddenly imagined Agatha McGee and James O'Hannon standing beside me. I recorded the moment in my journal" (*C*, 174). Among the autobiographical elements that enter into the novel are a ten-day St. John's University tour to Rome in 1986—of which this inspiration was a part—and two trips to Ireland in the early 1990s (*C*, 194-196). The novel also includes a number of details and incidents that connect with the author, his childhood, and his conception of himself as a writer.

Dear James is a true sequel to *A Green Journey*. Besides characters, it shares a similar structure and tone with *AGJ*. Like *AGJ*, it begins at a holiday in Minnesota but, like *AGJ*, soon develops two parallel stories; that of Agatha and James O'Hannon in Rome and Assisi, and Frederick ("French") Lopat and Imogene Kite in Staggerford. The tone of the Italy thread is elegiac, religious, romantic, sometimes humorous, and occasionally satiric.

The tone of the Staggerford thread is comic, satiric, and at times slightly sinister. Further similarities to *AGJ* include renewed attention to "the Troubles" in Ireland, a focus on art, views of the sea, and a continued critique of some aspects of post-Vatican II Catholicism. Imagery familiar from other novels includes views from heights, views of the sea, and natural descriptions generally. Where *Dear James* diverges from *AGJ* is in the last third of the novel. It is in these pages, Parts 3 and 4, that Agatha returns to Staggerford, then leaves again for Ireland, where she helps James and then engages in a kind of "peace" mission to the troubled island by bringing home a traumatized Irish boy, Bobby O'Malley.

Like *AGJ*, *Dear James* covers a discrete and limited span of time; in this case from November to the next July. There are fewer movie references than in other novels, but the two most important—*Bonnie and Clyde* (1968) and *Out of Africa* (1985)—help locate the action. Together with references to "the Troubles," an athletic Pope John Paul II, Princess Di, "Donahue," and terrorism against an Israeli airline, the historical time is an often vivid but vague mid-1980s.

Thematically, the novel focuses again on loneliness and depression, love and friendship, rivalry and betrayal, and the tribulations of marriage. The love and friendship come in the form of Agatha's renewed relationship with James; the rivalry takes the form of Imogene's "betrayal" of Agatha that her envy brings about. Like *A Green Journey*, *Dear James* also begins as another astute analysis of depression, in this case Agatha McGee's. Of her decision to make what *she* sees as a pilgrimage to Rome, Agatha notes: "It's not easy putting an idea into effect when you're depressed" (7). Later, she reflects on how she has "no energy" to wait out the "New Dark Age" that she sees threatening the Church (40-41).

Once again Hassler employs the opportunistic narrator, occasionally inhabiting minor characters like Agatha's pastor, Fr. Finn, her long-time neighbor Sylvester Juba, his daughter Sister

Judith Juba, and others, in addition to the principal characters, Agatha, James, French, and Imogene. The tour-guide, Fr. Finn's brother, is an agnostic professor driven by frustration and two failed marriages (263). As the title suggests, letters, as in *AGJ*, play a prominent role. They include letters to James O'Hannon that Agatha writes and then tears up; a letter from James, conveyed from Bishop Baker to Fr. Finn, and thence from Fr. Finn to Agatha. Later, Agatha's letter to James re-initiates their correspondence. These letters provide a climax to the opening Thanksgiving dinner and anticipate the tour to Rome. Later in the novel the author uses letters to punctuate the rhythm and pace of the novel, to introduce transitions, and to foreshorten time.

Brief Plot Summary

The double-plot is simple to outline. Following a lengthy and often humorous account of Thanksgiving dinner at Agatha Mc-Gee's house, the novel moves swiftly to the new year and Agatha's ten-day trip to Rome, where James O'Hannon surprises Agatha by meeting her at her hotel (after a letter announcing his intentions never reaches her in Staggerford). Agatha, James, and Fr. Finn leave the tour temporarily in order to spend two extra days in Assisi. In Assisi James reveals his intention to work for peace in Ireland. Meanwhile, back in Staggerford, Imogene Kite and French are up to mischief while French "house-sits" for Agatha. Over the course of several chapters that alternate between Rome and Staggerford, Imogene discovers Agatha's letters to James and, out of vindictiveness and envy, reveals their contents to Sister Judith Juba, who has come to record an interview with Imogene for the *Staggerford Weekly*.

On her return from Italy, Agatha discovers that copies of the taped interview have circulated in Staggerford. Her isolation from the townspeople renders James's visit to Staggerford at Easter a tense proposition. Then, after his departure, and unable to endure continued ostracism, Agatha herself departs, without telling anyone but Janet Meers, for a month-long trip to Ireland. There she helps James with his mission of peace, driving him, over the course of three weeks, to several speaking engagements both in the Irish Republic and Ulster. She also meets a boy, Bobby O'Malley, who has been traumatized by "the Troubles," and she determines to take him back to Staggerford for the summer. Returning with Bobby to Staggerford for a mid-July library board meeting to choose a new librarian, Agatha surprises a number of the townspeople (and the reader) by voting to hire Imogene Kite. The novel ends as Staggerford, in a sign of reconciliation with Agatha, celebrates, with an outdoor library tea, Agatha's thirty-five years on the library board.

Dear James as meta-novel

Dear James is somewhat unusual in that it emphasizes a number of features that refer to the art of narrative or storytelling. I want to suggest—though little more—that *DJ* is one of the most self-reflexive novels Hassler ever wrote. With a letter writer and a storyteller as the chief characters, and a villain who *reads* letters in order to gain advantage over the letter writer, the novel is ripe for sophisticated literary critical analysis. As seen in *AGJ*, both the principal letter writer and the storyteller, like Hassler himself, also have artistic tastes.

One particularly striking instance of the self-reflexive moment comes during James and Agatha's visit to the Vatican. To pique the agnostic Professor Finn, who has scoffed at the practice of pilgrims kissing the foot of Michelangelo's statue, James kisses Peter's foot and then does a "Jimmy Durante" move in front of Finn. When Agatha says that he is "light on his feet," James replies—and then repeats—"It's all in the timing." James's admission to Agatha is a hint that James/Hassler is "wooing" his muse, Agatha McGee. Later, when James describes his "mission" to work for peace in Ireland, he says, "The right story, well told, goes straight to the heart" (238). Here, too, one can imagine the storyteller James O'Hannon "standing in" for the storyteller, Jon Hassler.

Characters

The cast of characters in *Dear James* is as rich and varied as in any Hassler novel. Among those from earlier books, Lillian Kite is probably the most familiar. For most of the novel Lillian is what she has been since *Staggerford*, Agatha McGee's neighbor and best friend. Early in the novel the reader hears Agatha's assessment of Lillian's strengths and weaknesses: "Lillian was a dear and virtuous soul, but she seldom spoke—or listened—from the heart." Despite various—mostly gentle—satiric comments like this, Lillian is still portrayed as loyal, if slightly obtuse. Only when she learns through the interview tape what Agatha presumably had said about her in a letter to James does she respond as something other than a two-dimensional character. At the end of the novel, when Agatha surprisingly votes to hire Imogene as Staggerford's librarian, Lillian responds with "What a friend you've been to me all these years, Agatha," to which Agatha says, "And likewise" (429).

Another character familiar from as far back as *Staggerford* is Lillian's daughter, Imogene. Described in chapter thirteen as "noisy, pushy" and "gruff," as well as "strident in her opinions," she is also "tense, loud, and unattractive," a "tall horse-faced woman with rough edges" (112). In this novel, Imogene is a different kind of villain than those found in most of Hassler's other novels. Less malicious and more vulnerable from the start, she is certainly not the sinister and self-centered Tom Pearsall, or the quasi-diabolic Wallace Flint. As she seduces French, she shows her vulnerability in her desire for a husband, children, and job security. In chapter 26, however, Imogene becomes "larger than life" as she calls Agatha "a whited sepulcher" and determines to expose the older woman's supposed hypocrisy.

Though Sister Judith Juba appeared in *A Green Journey*,

she only comes into her own in *Dear James*. Beginning with a satiric portrait of her at the Thanksgiving dinner, Sister Judith and her post-Vatican II ideas become a further source of satire and humor. In the midst of her efforts to discredit Agatha, it is Imogene who provides an acerbic assessment of Sister Judith's character, calling her a "magpie," that is, "a sucker for anything bright and shiny" (272). A bit later Imogene adds complexity to Sister Judith's character as she thinks to herself, "She was a mental lightweight, but not treacherous. Quite honest, actually. Quite dependable, in the way such innocent souls often were."

Though Frederick ("French") Lopat is a new character in *Dear James*, he is not a totally new creation, having first appeared in Hassler's early short story, "Willowby's Indian." Hassler incorporates almost the whole short story as part of chapter 12. In the course of the novel, "French" grows well beyond the confines of the short story, becoming a key part of the Staggerford sub-plot, involving him and Imogene, and as an important part of the novel's archetypal dimension. French, who suffers from "post-traumatic shock," following service in Vietnam, has myriad weaknesses. These include lack of ambition and care about his appearance. He lies at the unemployment office in order to get his bi-weekly check. Later in the novel, his conscience tells him to resist Imogene in her efforts to discredit Agatha, but he doesn't follow through on these moral impulses. He is weak but not malicious.

The reader might be tempted to call Sister Judith's father, "the old lumberman" (45) Sylvester Juba, the ill-fated star of the novel's opening. He is certainly one of Hassler's greatest hypberbolically comic creations. As Fr. Finn sees him Sylvester is "short and stout," wears a "lint-collecting wool suit," a necktie "spotted with food," and lapels "decorated with the tiny metallic emblems of the Rotary Club and the Knights of Columbus." After noting his jowls and the bags under his eyes, Fr. Finn reports a number of rumors about Sylvester, including one that "had him sweet on Agatha McGee" (21).

With the latter in place (and a sample of Sylvester's crudely "poking his fingers into" a fruit salad), the perspective shifts to Sylvester and his desire to marry Agatha. A quick rehearsal of Sylvester's proposal to Agatha the previous June leads to Agatha's imagining how James O'Hannon would see Sr. Judith's father. "*And her father is a case as well, standing there in a kind of alcoholic stupor.*"

When French greets Sylvester, "The color of the old man's bulbous nose and sunken cheeks gave French the impression—based on a magazine article he'd read recently—of heavy drinking or high blood pressure or both," prompting French (who lacks tact) to ask, "What's your blood pressure?" (31). When, a bit later, Sylvester asks his daughter what his blood pressure is, she ends the chapter with the equally indelicate "stroke city." All this prepares for Sylvester's attempt to charm Agatha at the dinner table. At the end of chapter five, as Agatha comes to fill his water glass, Sylvester says, "You look like an angel today." Agatha stiffens but accepts the compliment. But then he follows it with "I'll bet you're a little devil in bed" (44).

Agatha breaks down as Sylvester, pursuing her, decides to "cut out the sweet talk," shifting to his other obsession (the end of life), as he suggests, "'The sooner you order your coffin, the better you'll feel.'" This causes Agatha to break down even further. When it appears that Sylvester will join the tour to Rome, Judith assures an incredulous Fr. Finn. "'Oh, he's going all right. He'd follow Agatha to Hell. He's got it in his bonnet that she'd make him a nice little wife in his old age. Didn't you know, he's proposed to her?'" When Fr. Finn thinks Sylvester was kidding, Judith ends another chapter, this time with, "'Kidding, hell, he's in heat'" (55). Luckily, this plot complication never materializes. At the end of chapter thirteen, as the tour is about to leave Chicago for Rome, Sylvester bows out with a final protestation of his love, saying he is too "sick" to go. We get Agatha's sympathetic perspective on what is left of "the handsome, blue-eyed ladies' man of a generation ago" (120), and this serves to temper somewhat the exaggerative picture of Sylvester Juba.

Other minor characters include an older and a younger priest who interact with James O'Hannon in Rome, a sprinkling of students on the tour, and Professor Albert Finn, a burnt-out professor of physics from Rookery State College, who leads the tour. One student, whom the reader only knows as "Paula the pixie," contributes to the grotesque atmosphere. Like one of the lesser figures in a Fra Lippo Lippi painting (as depicted by Robert Browning's dramatic monologue), Paula, with her fragility, her emotional outbursts, and her naively uninformed feminism (253) adds to the real, and hence uncanny aura. As Agatha sees her face in the window of the bus departing from Assisi, she notes Paula "gritting her teeth in pain or happiness, you could never tell which" (275). The author ties up this loose end in the final chapter. Another uncanny touch is the case of Albert Finn, which James refers to, wryly, as "One of those cases of sudden conversion, only the reverse of St. Paul's. Christian one minute, agnostic the next" (254). Though, in typical Hasslerian hyperbolic fashion, James goes on, "A voice from nowhere saying the Creed's a fraud." Near the end of the novel the reader meets Liam O'Malley and his son Billy, and we learn about Billy's grandmother, and James O'Hannon's cousin, Con Stitch and his wife Suzanne. Altogether, the secondary characters add color to the narrative, and depth to some of the novel's social-critical insights.

The Grotesque and the Mystical

At first glance, and despite the episodes in Rome and Assisi, *Dear James* seems a far less Catholic novel, and has fewer instances of the grotesque or the macabre than many of the earlier novels. Of course St. Clare's preserved body (261, 264-65) is one of the most startling "macabre" events. A number of scenes, however, establish a powerful religious dimension as they remain in the memory and affect one's reading of the entire novel. But, as in *North of Hope*, the religious here, too, often appears embedded in the everyday, making "things throw light on things," as they did in several previous novels. A presage of later uncanniness comes early in the novel when Agatha finally opens the letter that Fr. Finn has brought from the bishop. The letter from James O'Hannon causes such perturbation that, in a melodramatic moment, she wakes up in the middle of the night to burn it in her trashcan.

One of the first and most striking religious scenes occurs in Rome, when James tells an old seminary classmate, Monsignor Andrew Corcoran, about Lourdes and its aura of holiness. Fr. Corcoran scoffs, "A thick layer of fraud lies over the place" (172). James counters with, "It's a holy place, Andy." In a recollection of his spring visits to Lourdes in the south of France, James describes "a sacred aura you could almost see, almost smell, almost reach out and run your hand over, like silk." Then, remembering how "by the end of the second day, the spell…began to evaporate," he muses how "reality broke in." But then, returning a year or two later "in order to verify that the uplifting otherworldliness created by religious pilgrims gathered at a holy site had not been some kind of hallucination," he asks, rhetorically: "'Reality broke in? Indeed, the feeling of holiness was so overpowering, so tangible, that it might have been reality that was broken into.'" This curious reversal suggests that "otherworldliness" may be the normal, real way to look at the world, and that the mundane and prosaic—what we usually term "reality"—is what is broken into. Many of the religious, and uncanny events in the novel have this effect.

What might be called Agatha's "premonition" of James's presence in Rome is another clever detail—and a potentially melodramatic moment—suggesting a mystical dimension. In chapter 22, on the day when James spends the afternoon at St. Peter's pillar waiting or her, Agatha returns to the Hotel Bellarmino and begins a letter to James in which she notes: "This noon I was sitting on a low wall of the Villa Borghese when you imposed yourself so forcefully on my thinking that I murmured your name aloud" (204). James also contrasts the "malcontents" (*vis à vis* Professor Finn) to "the lovable side of the Church" which attracts "all walks of life." Agatha's response to the religious dimension in Rome is instructive, and complex. When she looks out over Rome, she sees that "the thousand colors of Roman buildings blended into one color. The shade was that of a ripe apricot" (223). This observation is a kind of symbolic "coda" to James's description of the Church.

The most obvious, and most prominent "religious" scene in the novel is James's presence at an audience with Pope John Paul II. It is also quite melodramatic. The scene is described from Agatha's perspective.

> *Then an amazing thing happened. The Pope, drawing abreast of them, stopped, lifted his eyes and gazed directly at James for a full five seconds. He then lifted his right hand and beckoned to him ... James turned to Agatha with an incredulous, uncertain look.*
>
> *"Go," she told him.*
>
> *John Paul stepped forward, took James's face in his hands, turned it to the left and spoke briefly into his ear ... Then he moved on (309).*

Following the description, Agatha ponders "the possibility of something mystical or extrasensory having taken place." The author/narrator brackets this "mystical" interpretation with a characteristic bit of Hassler irony and use of bird imagery.[16] A replicated gesture, John Paul II's cupping James's face, and then Agatha asking James to do the same add a further symbolic, if not necessarily mystical, exclamation mark to the scene, the chapter, and Part 2.

One of the most powerful, though also most ambiguous,

scenes in the novel occurs in the third-last chapter, when Agatha, waiting for James to complete one of his talks about "the Troubles," walks by the sea with Bobby O'Malley. There is even a kind of subtle "spirituality" in the way Agatha "exorcises" Bobby's "demons" on their walk.[17] A bit later, after his talk, James enters a church and prays for Bobby, Bobby's grandmother, Belfast, and Agatha (413) in a way that provides a subtle and touching culmination to Agatha's seemingly miraculous transformation of the boy. There is also a subtle ominousness lent by the atmosphere of fear and danger that Hassler has created.

The Archetypal Dimension

Dear James is less an archetypal novel than *Staggerford*, but familiar features and patterns of the hero's journey, even when they are dislocated or transferred, should be included in any appreciative evaluation of the novel. To review a few of those features: in this novel, unlike most traditional epics or fairy tales, it is not the hero whose identity or origin is unknown. It is Frederick (French) Lopat, a comic victim, who does not know his identity. But like Superintendent Stevenson in *Staggerford*, he is debilitated—here by post-traumatic shock—lacking any vitality or ambition. There is also a very traditional epic suggestion of contamination, impurity, or guilt. James O'Hannon's cancer might also be seen in archetypal terms. And when, during his and Agatha's visit to Assisi, he apologizes for his lack of strength, he does so in arguably archetypal terms. "'My strength ebbs and flows like the tide, Agatha'" (258). The metaphor is strengthened when he asks, "'Will we have a cup of tea while we wait for the tide to come in?'" Agatha and James find a similar comfort from the simplicity of the sea.

Another classic feature is the hero's—in this case the heroine's—estrangement from the community. Since the closing of St. Isidore's, Agatha has been reclusive. It is because of, or as response to, Agatha's sense of estrangement and lack of purpose that she decides to make a journey (which becomes a pilgrimage). The first journey results in a number of revelatory experiences or visions: in Rome, in Assisi, and (on a second journey) in northern Ireland. When it turns out that Agatha and French are related by blood (a revelation shared late in the novel, at Easter), the two come to be seen as almost paired characters.

Further "dislocations" or "modulations" of archetypal features occur in that James O'Hannon—not the heroine—has suffered a wound (his surgery for intestinal cancer). The pope's "miraculous" insight only confirms the transformation that has taken place in James. Transformation itself has archetypal overtones. James's "conversion" to peacemaker puts him in the line of other heroes who are transformed by their ordeals. It is Imogene whose treachery causes a second estrangement for Agatha, and hence a second journey. This journey ends, not unlike *A Green Journey*, with a walk by the sea, where her regained poise, self-possession, and resourcefulness facilitate the beginning of a veritable exorcism of Bobby O'Malley's demons.

Conclusion

Despite greater than usual diffuseness of details from everyday life, *Dear James* manifests a clear and coherent direction and purpose: a sustained re-consideration of Agatha McGee at age seventy. From out of depression and lost direction, Agatha embarks on a pilgrimage that, surprisingly, re-unites her with her friend and "soul mate," Fr. James O'Hannon. After enduring an attack on her reputation, self-esteem, and privacy, she sets off on another journey that gives her a new purpose and opportunities to help both James and a little boy twisted by the same Irish "troubles" that James has made it his mission to oppose. On her return to Staggerford she surprises Lillian, the town, and herself by discovering the inner resources to forgive Imogene Kite for the attack that transformed her relationship to the town. The conclusion some may find understated; others, disappointing, but looked at closely, it constitutes a genuine reconciliation and Agatha's successful re-integration with her community. Though Catholic in many external details, the fundamentally Christian dimension of the novel is most present in its themes of peace, forgiveness, and community. Some may choose to see in this retreat from more overt Catholicism the trajectory that readers can trace through *Rookery Blues* and *The Dean's List*, but one can also see, instead, the deepening of a more thoroughly—and more capacious—Incarnational vision that is the hallmark of Hassler's whole career.

6

BACK TO CAMPUS [1]

In his later years, Hassler figuratively returned to school with two "campus" novels, *Rookery Blues* and *The Dean's List*. The first follows five friends—college teachers all—as they struggle through a cold winter and a teachers' strike in northern Minnesota. The title refers obliquely to music and "the Icejam Quintet," a musical ensemble that the five friends form, and which comes to occupy more than their leisure hours. After adventures aplenty, a disbanding of the quintet because of the strike, and some other dark happenings, the five are re-united at the end in a near apotheosis of the quintet.

The Dean's List takes place twenty-five years after *Rookery Blues* and includes some of the same characters, as well as a number of familiar villains and grotesque denizens of the northern Minnesota college world. A troubled teen, Laura Connor, and her boyfriend become a source of problems for Leland Edwards, the only first-person narrator in all of Hassler's adult novels. A visit from the renowned poet, Richard Falcon, becomes a trial and an inspiration for Leland, and after more adventures—including a Christmas Open House in Leland's mother's home and several sinister encounters—Leland receives the poet's blessing on his impending (second) marriage to a former colleague.

Rookery Blues

Written in its entirety after he had taken the position at St. John's University that he would hold until his retirement, *Rookery Blues* (1995) is Hassler's first novel about academia since *The Love Hunter*. It also makes more use of autobiographical elements than any other of his novels, yet, for all that, it is, paradoxically, a more impersonal and artistic structure as well. A Minneapolis *Star-Tribune* reviewer called it "academic satire, and it's a hoot." Readers will appreciate the treatment of academic administrators, teachers, and students. They will also enjoy the humorous take on small-town know-it-alls, and citizens who wonder what college teachers do, as well as the insightful treatment of relationships, youthful, mature, and intergenerational. But *Rookery Blues* is more than a "campus novel," and more worthwhile for that. Though its five central characters are all academics at small, northern Minnesota Rookery State College, many come to their jobs from backgrounds that don't bode well for their job satisfaction, or their becoming friends, let alone fellow-musicians in a jazz combo called "The Icejam Quintet."

But it is precisely the story of their growing friendship, and the disruption to that musical friendship that a campus strike occasions, that makes *Rookery Blues* an unobtrusively Incarnational narrative. That may seem an outlandish claim, but starting with Hassler's own statement that "all of them have these spiritual longings—all those five people exhibit them in their own ways" (*C*, 222), this chapter will show that *Rookery Blues* represents a search for community that at times resembles an almost "mystical body." I am convinced that the protagonist's dream of an uncommon (and often unusual) musical friendship is the heart of the novel: the dream, its single, fleeting achievement, its dissolution, and its final, brief re-incarnation, if not apotheosis, charting the course of the novel's main action.

With five main characters and multiple plot lines, the novel can be a challenging read. The story spans a period between

January and July, 1969. This setting and the faculty strike that forms the principal action make use of many of Hassler's experiences while teaching at Bemidji State University (1965-1968) and Brainerd Community College (1968-1980). The model for the Icejam Quintet was a support group of teachers at Bemidji who got together to drink beer. The strike it recounts is patterned on a strike for higher wages at Brainerd in March, 1979 (*C*, 216). The fishing trip with which the novel opens is modeled on a fishing trip that took place while Hassler was teaching high school in Fosston, MN in 1958 (*C*, 214). The basement apartment of one character, Neil Novotny, is based on a colleague's basement apartment in Bemidji.

There are fewer topical allusions, relatively fewer movie titles, and—oddly enough for a novel many of whose characters are English faculty—fewer literary allusions than other of his novels. The Vietnam War does form a dark background that affects at least two of the characters directly. But, as the title suggests, music plays a central part, especially "Big Band" and jazz titles from the 1940s and 1950s.

Each of four main characters, Leland Edwards, Neil Novotny, Victor Dash, and Connor, shares certain life experiences with the author, but because these experiences are spread over those four different individuals, the temptation to read autobiographically is dissipated or displaced. Because the narrative point of view is at times in each of the main characters, the overall effect is more impersonal. Connor's marriage difficulties, Victor Dash's being minimally qualified for college teaching, and the conflict between Neil's obsession with his writing and his teaching obligations all have analogies to Hassler's life. Like Hassler, Leland Edwards is an only child. Add to this his shy introversion and his years of painstaking piano practices, and some would say the novel presents a fragmented portrait of the author. Only Peggy Benoit does not appear to have an obvious autobiographical analogue.

A comic novel that moves from disorder to seeming chaos and then back to a semblance of order while indulging in satire, exaggeration, and a measure of the bizarre—if not grotesque— *Rookery Blues* fits comfortably into Hassler's developing *oeuvre* to that point. In contrast to the humor are a host of darker issues. Depression, loneliness and (in)fidelity, with insanity on the side; unexplained illness, a gritty, semi-humorous treatment of alcoholism, a number of suicide attempts, and—as always— various forms of betrayal all further complicate the thematic texture. Vindictiveness (Peggy's husband, Gene Benoit, and Dean Zastrow) and Gary Oberholtzer's pointless rebellion and hormonally-driven desire to despoil innocence round out the all too familiar social issues. Gary's obscene phone calls also hint at even deeper disorder. There are also scenes of unalloyed misery: Connor after Marcy's first suicide attempt; Peggy when she hears of Connor's alleged "death." Still, the abiding impression is of a comedy that the author enjoyed writing, and that readers will continue to enjoy.

Plot Summary

Rookery Blues seems in some ways a leaner book than previous Hassler novels. It intersperses short passages of exposition within the action without impeding it. Within each of the five named "Parts" (instead of chapters), a few italicized pages highlight certain key aspects of each main character's childhood. There is also more intensity, and more complicated implications, in the treatment of everyday, domestic scenes than in the previous novels.

So how does this, at first unlikely, friendship begin? Not well. Because it *is* complex, an overview of the plot is useful. Part 1 (titled "These Foolish Things") begins in January, 1969 with three of the future quintet (Leland, Connor, and Victor) visiting the fourth member, Neil Novotny's basement apartment to pick him up for an ice-fishing trip to Liberty Lake. Leland Edwards, a tenured member of the English faculty, wants to find an occasion for "bonding" with new faculty members. He also has hopes of forming a musical combo to play "Big Band" compositions—a fervent dream since he was a shy, eighteen year-old piano student. Victor Dash is a former pipeline worker turned business English instructor, and Connor is an alcoholic artist in residence. In Neil's basement the three meet not only Neil but the future fifth member, Dr. Peggy Benoit, assistant professor of music. After an interlude of drinking, music, and a hint of romance between Connor and Peggy, the three go off to Liberty Lake without Neil or Peggy, where Connor, who has continued to drink, passes out. Returning to Rookery in a snowstorm, the three fishermen leave Connor on his doorstep. That night his wife and daughter check him into the hospital with a case of pneumonia. The first part ends with an inaugural jam session by the "Icejam Quintet," minus Connor, who is still in the hospital. In one of several digressions that interrupt the fishing trip narrative, Justine Gengler, the wife of the college president, while routinely opening her husband's mail, discovers a nude photo of Peggy Benoit. This photo will become a minor narrative thread that weaves through the story.

Part 2 ("I'll Get By") begins as the quintet gathers for a first rehearsal with Connor present and resolved to remain sober. The reader learns, through the various characters' perspectives, the value that the quintet holds for each. At the same time, Connor advises Neil to share his novel manuscript with students and to send it to an outside reader. The newly organized union, the Faculty Alliance, becomes the faculty bargaining unit by a close vote of 59-53, and a focus on Neil's students and teaching provides occasions for humor and satire. Part 2 also traces how Leland, Neil, and Connor each falls in love with Peggy to varying degrees. For Connor, it is one of his reasons for remaining sober. The reader also becomes acquainted with Connor's wife, Marcy, their daughter Laura, and Gary Oberholtzer, the delinquent twenty-one year old son of the department chair. Part 2 ends, after an intense musical interlude, with Connor and Peggy having sex in her office, while Laura hitchhikes to an unsavory roadhouse with Gary.

Part 3 ("Mood Indigo") recounts Marcy Connor's hospitalization following a suicide attempt and the strike vote by the Faculty Alliance. Tension builds as the quintet is divided over the strike. Victor and Peggy strongly support it; Leland opposes it. Connor and Neil try to ignore it. Switching to Neil's troubles in the classroom, a moment of high tension—and high humor—occurs when Neil explodes and tells off the chairman and the dean, assuring his termination from Rookery State. This event coincides with the arrival of Connor's former drinking partner, the author-editor Emerson Tate, who comes to town to talk with Neil about his novel. Connor relapses in a colossal drinking binge that evolves into the climax of Part 3 as Neil's (also drunken) negotiations with Emerson take place at Culpepper's Supper Club. There Neil betrays his artistic vision by accepting the pseudonym "Cornelia Niven" and agreeing to make a number of changes in his manuscript's characters and plot, turning it into a cheap romance. Part 3 ends with Victor Dash, pleased with the strike, but hoping for a job in Milwaukee, after what he sees as his own inevitable dismissal from Rookery State.

The beginning of Part 4 ("Don't Blame Me") records the early successes of the strike, Marcy Connor's stabilization and discharge from the hospital, and the further development of Connor and Peggy's romance. The high points come as the quintet rehearses at the Edwards' home and then plays for her Saturday afternoon radio show. But by the end of part four, the strike is collapsing, a "summit" with college administrators becomes a fiasco, and the quintet breaks up as a result of their disagreement over the strike. Then Marcy Connor starts to volunteer at the hospital as she contemplates divorce, Gary Oberholtzer and Laura Connor send Peggy's nude photo to the English department chair, and—in a sentimental interlude—Leland plays for

Peggy the song he had composed for her. The section ends as Leland, learning that C. Mortimer Oberholtzer has been showing the photo to select visitors, goes to the chairman's house and manages to burn the photo while the chair is out of the room. Part 4 concludes with the end of the strike and the effective end of the quintet.

Part 5 ("My Blue Heaven") will impress the reader by the skill and efficiency with which the novel concludes the strike. It also manages Marcy's separation from Connor by having her move in with Eldora Sparks (amid humor and further betrayal). It also presents Peggy Benoit's spring concert and the reduction of the quintet to a duo. It then moves Connor to Minneapolis, sends the Dashes off to Milwaukee, and prepares for Leland and Peggy to perform at Georgina Gold and Ron Hunsinger's July wedding. Part 5 also provides a twist to the novel's conclusion as Laura enlists Gary Oberholtzer, home from basic training, in a malicious and vindictive, but also bizarre, plot to spread the rumor of Connor's death. This "news" dampens as it darkens and upsets preparations for the wedding, and plans that a reunited quintet play for the reception. The hoax is uncovered as Connor appears, and the Icejam Quintet plays "into the small hours of morning" (481).

Characters
Rookery Blues includes three only children, two of whom, Leland Edwards and Neil Novotny, are central characters. An attentive son after the death of his history professor father, Leland is, as previously noted, "the most Hassler-like" character in the novel (*C*, 208, 212). A piano student from the age of six, he longs for the community and camaraderie of fellow musicians. The first of five italicized "digressions" (55-58) recounts the tale of Leland's final high school piano recital and his desire to form a jazz combo. Like other interpolated diaries and seemingly discrete episodes, these italicized episodes in *Rookery Blues* are both

familiar from Hassler's other novels but serve their own unique function here.

Though he is one of the main characters, Neil is sometimes portrayed as a fool (434). A bit like Randy Meers in *A Green Journey*, his self-absorption and obsession with his novel are a meta-element: Hassler's own self-deprecatory impulse directed to a comic character. Neil's obsession with his first novel is humorous and a subject for satire, but his devotion to his art and his artistic vision is genuine, if sometimes misplaced and inordinately pursued. His obsession is what makes his betrayal of that vision both tragic, and ironic.

It is loneliness, the desire for genuine companionship—and compensation for his failings—that makes Connor a painter of mothers and daughters. One could say that his artistic insight is driven by the misery and anguish of his personal life. The italicized look at Connor's childhood (316-18) explains his lonely childhood in a single-parent family, his befriending by an itinerant bandleader, and his early introduction to music and drinking. It also explains his gift for comic strips and portraiture. Like the artist Otis Chapman's single-minded focus on portraying the Indian princess in *Jemmy*, Connor's exclusive focus on "mother-daughter" portraits could be explained as part of his own anguished relation to Marcy and Laura. Connor's roller coaster of emotions *vis à vis* Marcy and Laura is true to the experience of deep anguish—and alcoholism.

Peggy Benoit is a thirty-something Ph.D. who grew up in a large family and experiences bouts of extreme loneliness at this, her first job, in far-away Rookery. A cousin by marriage to Neil, she initially finds some comfort in spending time with him. Her early cultivation of music—voice, sax, and choral directing—derives in part from the loneliness and longing for family, community, and the personal appreciation that her marriage to Gene Benoit had lacked. The second italicized section in the novel (156-160), devoted to her musical—and sexual—awakening by a music teacher named Tillemans, is like a short story in itself. The interlude describes this awakening to her awareness of her talent in terms both lyrical and erotic.

Victor Dash, in his energetic approach to life, also longs for camaraderie, but for him it is the community and conflict he had experienced as a union member working on an oil pipeline. He organizes the Faculty Alliance and the strike in Rookery, in part, to achieve that goal. His drum playing is a further expression of the energy that drives his union work. The short italicized interlude (416-418) explaining Victor's childhood interest in boxing and drums helps to illustrate his temperament and his aggressive approach to life.

Leland's mother Lolly is one of Hassler's most fully-drawn comic characters, but though she is mother of a main character, the reader doesn't really see into her at any great depth. But the narrator gives her plenty to do. As the host of "Lolly Speaking" on KRKU, she is mouthpiece for the community's attitudes and opinions. She is part of the "summit" between the Alliance and the administration, and says she would have supported the union had it stayed in existence long enough. Like Lillian Kite in two of the earlier novels, however, she comes in for a fair degree of comic/satiric criticism.

Hassler lavishes as much attention on the creation of his "everyday villain," Laura Connor, as he had on Wallace Flint in *Grand Opening*. Like Flint, Laura is a bundle of contradictions: vulnerability, malice, and scheming. And, like Flint, she doesn't go away. Laura is capable of sensitivity, and her contradictory relation to her father makes for a significant portion of the novel's underlying tension and complexity. At first she scorns her mother for not loving him. Later she becomes jealous of Peggy, and this jealousy becomes the occasion for a form of betrayal as she passes the photo of Peggy to Gary Oberholtzer (351). As her father notes, she has "a talent for attracting sinister companions" (165). Still later she reaches out to her father, subtly challenging him to set limits, to show her more attention (363), which is attended by the irony of Connor's not wanting to interfere in her friendships. In a final betrayal, she follows her mother when Marcy moves in with a hospital cleaning woman and militant divorcee, Eldora Sparks.

There is Swiftian "grime" and savage satire in Hassler's portrayal of Gary Oberholtzer, the chairman's only child. The portrayal of this "rebel without a cause" is sometimes overwritten, as if there is personal animus here. Though he doesn't say it to Joseph Plut, it is clear that Hassler relished depiction of the disgusting Gary, putting into his character all of the despicable behaviors, and language, of a spoiled juvenile delinquent. When, to his mother Honey's despair, Gary is drafted into the army, it is like poetic justice.

For the other minor characters that Hassler invents, the Robert Browning analogy first used for *Staggerford* applies. The author seems to delight in creating a host of striking characters, many present only in vignette, and not since *Simon's Night* has Hassler so skewered the editorial profession. Here it is the "discreet alcoholic," Emerson Tate, whose unkempt appearance and ruthless behavior make him rank with Hassler's other more and less petty villains. The academic administrators, Zastrow and Oberholtzer, come in for their share of satire. For readers familiar with Hassler's first novel, *Staggerford*, Dean Zastrow is the Wayne Workman of this novel (356). Then there are the many minor characters in the several sub-plots or episodes. Veteran teacher Kimberly Kraft is a woman of independent means; so she walks the picket line, along with her friend, the masculine female athletic director, Alex Bolus. Though she is Peggy and Kimberly's friend, Fellow English teacher, Georgina Gold, does not strike because she is engaged to the single-minded Rookery businessman, Ron Hunsinger. Then, after the strike, the "shapely" administrative assistant (167-168) Delane Villars (whom Dean Zastrow likes), ends up replacing the union-sympathizing executive secretary, Lorraine Kibbee, who returns to her pig farm near the Rookery airport. A number of students have minor, but significant roles; like Chuck Lucking and Dickie Donaldson and their friend, Sandy Hupstad. Helen Culpepper and her eleven year-old daughter, Alison, as well as her ex-husband, Sammy Culpepper, the bartender and owner of Culpepper's Supper Club, also form the nucleus of a number of significant subplots. Eldora Sparks, the outspoken divorcée with whom Marcy Connor goes to live, has a number of episodes in which to dramatize herself. And, finally, there is even brief mention of Peggy's therapist, whose chief characteristic is her incongruous name, Lois Latitude (192).

Themes and Transformations

The five main characters' various needs account for a proliferation of thematic threads. As the narrator contrasts their deep desires with a series of sometimes comic "shticks" and running gags, he is in danger of turning this novel into something more complex than a mere "serio-comic" romp.

Leland's loneliness, introversion, and the desire for a musical combo motivate his actions up to the time of the strike vote, when his speech before a faculty gathering results in a transformation. His unexpressed love for Peggy adds poignancy to his solitary suffering. Peggy, seeking an escape from loneliness, and her twin desires to do well at Rookery *and* to leave for an east coast school, make her longing for intimacy both intense and yet potentially aloof. When she falls in love with Connor, those twin desires undergo a transformation that opens up her life in unusual ways. Connor is oppressed by his wife's mental illness and his soon-to-be teenage daughter's needs. His decision to give up landscapes in order to paint mothers and daughters appears to be a compensatory reaction to his family problems. When he falls in love with Peggy, the complexity of his life increases, but his determination to stop drinking represents a transformation for him as well. For Neil, who is also pointlessly in love with Peggy, it is his obsession with his novel and his artistic "vision" that provides a comic-satiric picture of the single-minded artist, but his capitulation to Emerson Tate represents a transformation that has serio-comic consequences.

In trying to organize the Faculty Alliance, Victor Dash seeks to recreate the sense of community he formerly felt as a pipeline worker and union member. His crude and aggressive intensity often creates crises (as well as opportunities for humor), but his credible everyday love for his wife, Annie, and their children makes for a striking contrast to the other—more and less intensely—love-struck main characters. Victor's initial success with the strike and his pride of achievement work a transformation that ultimately carries him out of Rookery and on to a career in labor organizing.

The desires of the supporting characters also drive much of the subsidiary action. Lolly Edwards, as "the consciousness of Rookery," is both a comic/satiric character, but also a power-wielding force in the community. Her desires to find a husband for Leland and to remain at the cusp of what is happening in Rookery add detail and texture to the interstices of the main action. Of the other supporting characters, Dean Zastrow's determination to oppose the strike and his putative desire to weed out the deadwood from among the college faculty provide additional tension, and opportunities for humor, while C. Mortimer Oberholtzer's implicit desire to appear as the benevolent, fatherly chair motivates other scenes in the novel.

The Bizarre, the Grotesque, Blood, and Other Imagery

Instances of the bizarre are markedly less prevalent than in other novels, but President Gengler's rash is part of it. Connor's recollection of his mother's death (348) is another instance. Helen Culpepper's outbursts, and Neil Novotny's blowing up at the dean and department chair in part 3 are exaggerative scenes that might be termed grotesque, in a Flannery O'Connor manner, given the tone of the rest of the novel. The arrival of Dean Zastrow's wife at the faculty-administration" summit" (376) is also grotesque. If one is looking for the signature "blood-letting" that is found in most Hassler novels, it could be when Gary Oberholtzer falls and hits his head on a rock under the bridge over the Badbattle River (352) and walks on without wiping the blood away.

Rookery Blues includes a variety of natural imagery (some of it associated with the quintet's music), but unlike most of the earlier novels, it has very few references to birds.[2] One of the first references to the "needy" sparrows that Justine Gengler "appreciates" for their neediness (30) suggests that such analogies might have greater significance. The narrator notes, through Peggy's viewpoint, that chairman Oberholtzer "liked to preen before all young and youngish women" (53). Otherwise, there are no more bird references until robin sightings occur just before Peggy's spring concert (428). The final instance of bird imagery occurs when a hawk appears in a significant scene near the novel's conclusion.

Humor, Satire, and Television Techniques

Once again, the novel is full of repetitions, frequently in the form of one of Hassler's favorite techniques, the running gag. These include Victor's expressions like the gross "shit in your hat" and the cliché, "write your own ticket" (293; 296). Victor also repeatedly makes bicycles for his children a rallying cry for the Alliance. The "steel plate" in Victor's head comes in early and is then mentioned again late in the novel (430). On a cruder level, there is Gary Oberholtzer's obsession with "humping," which first occurs when he seeks to interest Laura Connor in sex. In a conversation about Peggy and Laura's father, Gary's comment is, "'You mean he's humping her'?" Such repetitiveness, as has been seen, is a feature of Hassler's style.

197

A good deal of the satire is directed at 1970s academia. Starting with out-of-date airplanes and swimsuits on posters in the language laboratory at Rookery State (151), the satire includes faculty like Reginald Fix, the chemist, and his experiment with fingernail clippings as compost (343 et. al.). Like the descriptions of Gary Oberholtzer, this, too, has an almost Swiftian dimension. But the narrator also takes a satiric look at townspeople like the utilitarian businessman, Ron Huinsinger. During the strike he argues with Historian Quinn about academics (224). There are also references to Lolly Edwards' avocado-colored stove (353) and other fashions of the late 1960s.

As he had in a number of previous novels, Hassler makes increasing use of what might be termed television[3] techniques to vary the pace and maintain interest through a contrast of everyday events with misery, humor, and music. With five main characters and at least half again as many subplots, the narration, like many a television series, frequently switches from story to story, adding details and capitalizing on opportunities for humor, romance, pathos, or the contrast between them.

Contrast and Paradox

As was also the case in earlier novels, Hassler's use of contrast and paradox in *RB* also operates on both the "macro" and the "micro" level, with scenes of the everyday and the humorous punctuating, as they separate, scenes of greater intensity, or intimacy. These contrasts are particularly noticeable as the counterpoint to scenes of intense musical camaraderie and communion, thus further highlighting the sense of music's "transcendent" quality.

An example of contrast and paradox on the "macro" level would be the structure of the novel's start. Opening with the ice-fishing trip to Liberty Lake, the narrator breaks up that story by introducing 1) the visit to Neil Novotny's basement, 2) Peggy Benoit advising a student, 3) Justine Gengler opening her husband's mail to find the nude photograph of Peggy Benoit, and

4) Gary Oberholtzer calling in to Lolly Edwards' radio show with an obscene question. Only then does the narrative return to the fishing trip.

As just two examples of contrast on the micro level: accounting professor, Aaron Cordero, is, paradoxically, a financial planner but also an officer in the faculty union (140-41). Laura Connor's innocence and vulnerability contrast with her duplicity and scheming. After initially fearing Gary Oberholtzer, she later looks at him and thinks, "Here was an ignorant man-child she could lead around like a dog" (245). Also, from being dour and depressive, Laura can suddenly appear almost light-hearted. Later in the novel, when she comes upon Peggy and Connor during a rehearsal, she says, "'Hi, you two.' The girl breezed into the room with unusual grace, unusual cheer" (249). Such contrasts, on the micro-level of character, also contribute to the verisimilitude of everyday life that marks the novel.

Narrative Structure and Archetypes
Northrop Frye has argued convincingly that the structure of Shakespeare's comedies is often archetypal in that each play recapitulates universal aspects of human social life. As the reader has seen in previous chapters, Hassler's novels, too, exhibit archetypal features. In *RB* the first hint of an archetypal dimension comes with a debilitated administrator, President Herbert Gengler, who resembles Superintendent Stevenson in *Staggerford*. As noted earlier, there are also betrayals and, by the end, two "expulsions" (Neil's and Victor's) before a final "re-integration." Seen at sufficient distance and in overview, *Rookery Blues* also displays the archetypal comic "disorder to order" pattern. The fishing trip opening is a first, decidedly comic example of disorder. The remainder of the novel struggles to bring order out of disorder, often in the form of music being played, with the final wedding and reception representing the "classic" comic ending. Connor's supposed death reminds one of how Shakespeare, too,

often used "mock" deaths and re-appearances to add punch to the final scenes of *his* comedies.

In terms of conventional dramatic structure (conflict, complication, crisis, climax, denouement), the KRKU Saturday radio performance in Part 4, punctuated by commercials and ultimately truncated by the program's time constraints, can be read as an ironic anti-climactic climax of the novel, while the wedding reception "love fest" of the quintet is a dream-like, almost mythic experience that has little connection with reality. The quintet's final performance is a kind of "post-resurrection" "apparition," mirroring Connor's own "miraculous" reappearance after his reported death.

Religion and Music

Rookery Blues is unusual in that it is the first of Hassler's novels that does not have as much as an implicitly Catholic background. Leland Edwards is an Episcopalian, but little more is made of that fact. In a moment I shall argue that, in this novel, the enactment of musical intimacy takes the place of religious experience. Besides the 30s and 40s big band music that the quintet plays, the novel provides occasional reference to contemporary (1960s) musicians such as Patsy Cline (294) and Joni Mitchell (331). Otherwise, the chief examples of music are the quintet's rehearsals and performances, most of which strive toward an almost transcendent dimension of camaraderie, community, and almost spiritual union. At times the descriptions are sensual, bordering on the sexual, and in the case of Peggy and Connor, music becomes an incitement to sex. As with many earlier Hassler novels, certain episodes and passages provide not only the flavor of the novel, but insight into its themes and its perennial appeal.

Music Episodes in *Rookery Blues*

One critic, Roger Sheffer, says that the best parts of the novel are those involving art and music (*C*, 211). The scenes in which

"The Icejam Quintet" becomes a musical ensemble and experiences the intimacy, musical and otherwise, that such a community provides are among the most powerful in the novel. When looked at together, they distill the essence of the novel's Incarnational vision. There are compelling musical "set pieces" in each part, but here I treat only a few in detail.

The first rehearsal, at the end of Part 1, is an unusually deft and suggestive example; one which also prepares in a number of ways for subsequent musical scenes. With Connor still in the hospital, the four remaining members gather in a rehearsal room in McCall Hall, which Peggy has prepared in advance. With Leland at the piano, Neil on clarinet, and Victor on drums —and Peggy preparing to play the saxophone or sing—the four musicians warm up. After snatches of "Ain't Misbehavin'" and other tunes,

> *the noise died away and a kind of embarrassed silence filled the room. Peggy was surprised to see the three men looking expectantly at her – acknowledging her as their leader, she realized. Their expression amused her, like those of three little boys asking permission to go ahead with some vaguely illicit fun, and she laughed her short, stuttering laugh, lifted at last out of the sadness she'd felt at Connor's bedside (102).*

Embarrassed silence, Peggy's leadership, and reference to "illicit fun" all suggest an unusual event. The potentially sexual innuendo of "illicit" prepares for the end of part 2.

When Peggy urges Leland to lead the group into a simpler rendition of "These Foolish Things" than he had played in Neil's basement, the lyricism mounts as the narrator—in Peggy's perspective—invites Neil to join in.

> *Then she nodded at Neil, evidently before he was ready, for he joined in out of control, his clarinet unsure of itself, its voice like a pubescent boy's, changing register without warning, blaring where it should have been soft, momentarily disap-*

*pearing when he meant it to sing. He dropped out in shame
and waited for Peggy to lead the way back in (102-03).*

Neil's unsuccessful response to Peggy's invitation has more than
a quasi-sexual innuendo to it. Then, when Peggy comes in with
her sax, the narration waxes poetic as she "felt enormously relieved, almost euphoric to think it was working, they were staying together, they were a team. They were out for a walk in the
country on a fine summer day. Look at the green fields, look
at the cows grazing in clover at the top of the hill, look at the
birds swooping above them, look at the puffy white clouds." The
natural descriptions, metaphors for almost inexpressible emotion, are also suggestive of deeper communion. Paradoxically,
the effect on Peggy reinforces the theme of loneliness, and by
the end the reader sees that *her* desire for the quintet is the same
as Leland's.

> *She couldn't give up the warm, sisterly affection she was feel-
> ing for the quintet, each chorus binding her closer to her four
> companions: the shy and serious pianist, his head bent low
> over the keys again, brow to brow with the Steinway; the
> emaciated novelist, her cousin-in-law, tooting earnestly along
> with an expectant, approval-seeking look on his face; Victor
> the wild man, tamed and absorbed by his drums ...*

In an almost archetypal fashion, Peggy has become something
of a mother-figure, even capable of "taming" Victor. At the end
of the song, it is as if her imagination is capable of conjuring a
vision, a ghost:

> *and Connor – even in his absence, she could hear the deep
> underpinning he would provide with his bass. Connor, she
> knew, would be their foundation.*

This final suggestion of an almost preternatural element in her
sensibility also prepares for much that follows.

Second Jam Session

The second jam session, with Connor present, opens Part 2. In contrast to Part 1's two-page exposition, this time the narration of the quintet's playing together takes five pages. Because, the narrator notes, "they wanted him to feel welcome," it is just Peggy singing "Stormy Weather" with Connor on the bass, Victor "shushing along softly with his brushes" (107), and Neil and Leland minimally present. When the quintet finishes the song, however, Peggy "led them through it again."

> *"Stormy Weather," this second time through, grew slower and bluer, strictly a duet now, Peggy's voice and Connor's bass growling along together. She sang frowning, as though worried or in pain. No strolling through fresh green meadows this time. No chirping birds, no puffy summer clouds. This was a trudging, sorrowful progress through the night, with far-off thunder heading this way, Connor slogging along at her side, slumped over his bass as though about to embrace it or collapse upon it …*

The deliberate contrast to the first jam session's natural imagery, augmented by the song's title, heightens the drama. The dark metaphors referring primarily to Connor and Peggy also subtly anticipate their future relationship. The group's reaction suggests the bond that is forming.

> *When it ended, no one spoke. Nobody's eyes sought out other eyes. Usually upon finishing a piece they had a dozen things to say about it, except Victor, who had two dozen, but their rendition of this one had been too tragic and wonderful to talk about.*

The narrator then records four of the quintet's individual responses, but it is Connor's that is most telling. "He'd only heard Peggy, and he was still hearing her. Putting his ear to his strings, tightening them and quietly strumming them, he went back over 'Stormy Weather' in his head, noting where next time he would better anticipate her subtle changes of tempo" (109-110). And a moment later: "So fresh was her singing that even an old standard like 'Stormy Weather' became something you'd never heard before."

Over others' suggestions, then, Peggy suggests they play "Goody, Goody," of which they make a "ragged," "furious" mess, but Peggy's response is not unexpected. "To Peggy, who came from a large family, her friendship with Victor, Neil, and Leland had come to feel like the loose but everlasting union between brothers and sisters, and tonight there was the added dimension of her adoration for Connor." When "Goody, Goody" finally "came apart and collapsed like an old wooden shed," the narrator describes the quintet's responses in terms that are suggestive. "Leland moaned with delight and Victor laughed silently, wiping his eyes on his sleeve. Peggy cast her highly charged smile on Connor, who responded in kind." It is only when the narrator, however, notes that Laura Connor "looked on with a face of stone, sensing the current running between Peggy and her father," that the reader once again picks up the thread of the novel's action. The moments of musical communion are over, and all the real world tensions return.

Third Musical Interlude

The rest of Part 2 builds a crescendo toward the climax in Peggy and Connor's musical and erotic relationship. It begins, however, somewhat obliquely, as the reader learns of Leland's love for Peggy and the inspiration to compose a piece for her (143-44). Then the second of the five italicized sections tells of Peggy's musical (and more or less broadly sexual) awakening by Tillemans, the lonely outsider, the "mysterious and handsome new music teacher"(156-60).

Tillemans takes an interest in her playing and particularly her voice. At one piano lesson, after laying his hand on her arm and "brushing his fingertips lightly across her breast as he did so," Tillemans tells Peggy, "'you owe the world ... the gift of your voice.'" He even begins composing a piece of music for her. It is a bagatelle that he plays for her, so slowly that it sounds like a lullaby. But Peggy notices that "his advances were carefully timed to be interrupted." "For the rest of that week she thought of little else but her body and how its various parts would feel if touched by the hand of the composer."

After the italicized flashback, reference to Connor's solitary practice on the bass as "a holy time" (162) prepares for the second intense musical interlude. After they meet and talk in the student center, Connor asks Peggy if she has records he can practice with (167). After he affirms her musical talent—"you've got the perfect voice for the pieces we do, and we're all trying to be good enough for you"—Peggy implicitly acquiesces as she says, "I've got time to be Ella [Fitzgerald] myself."

In a practice room, with the piano between them, she sings "I'll Get By" three times, each time more emotionally fraught than the one before. In the first "her voice quavered with emotion. He [Connor] assumed this was stage emotion, manufactured and rehearsed ..." But, switching to Peggy's perspective, the reader learns, "It wasn't stage emotion ... Singing without the rest of the quintet, she was feeling so close to Connor, so helplessly entangled in his strings, and at the same time so lonely and sad, that she was moved nearly to tears" (169-170).

After trying unsuccessfully to pick up the tempo the second time through, at the third she "made a dirge of it, sang low and slow and a little on the sour side." But when she stops, just before the finish, and Connor tries an improvised "cadenza" as he waits for her to conclude, she turns to him with tears in her eyes. She then explains her sadness (recollection of her husband's leaving her), and, coming around the piano, she stands in front of Connor, who has sat down on the piano bench to hear her story. Interrupted by the secretary with a message from a student, Peggy remains standing in front of Connor. "Connor made a move to rise from the bench, but she stood so close in front of him that their knees were practically touching" (172). He thanks her for the song, and she says "Sure."

> Before embracing her around the hips, he sat there for a moment, prudently making sure her closeness was an invitation and not necessitated by the smallness of the room. It had been months since his wife had allowed him to touch her, and so the feel of this woman's flesh through her wool skirt caused a roaring in his ears that intensified when she dropped her coat, lowered herself to her knees, pressed herself between his legs, and kissed him.

As a sharp tonal contrast to this first, intensely intimate scene in Peggy and Connor's relationship, the narrative then presents an episode involving Connor, his mentally ill wife, and his daughter, Laura.

Fourth Musical Interlude
Like the radio concert that will be interrupted in Part 4, the last musical interlude of part 2 is interrupted several times before its understated finale, but the prelude to that interlude actually begins several pages and several episodes earlier, when Peggy takes her Wednesday dinner back to the band room where she plays all the records she and Connor had found there. Leland arrives early for rehearsal in order to ask about the quintet's readiness to play on his mother's radio show. After several interruptions, Connor and Laura arrive, and Laura again "settled into a corner with her homework" (197). Leland starts to pick out "a one-finger rendition of 'Bye Bye Blackbird" that Connor picks up on, and Peggy sings, "filling in the lines she couldn't remember with scat singing." The narrator interprets the effect in a way that recalls the earlier musical episodes. "The wildness in her voice was startling. It spurred

the two men to play louder and faster." (199). The "wildness" of Peggy's voice, the aggressive "pounding" of the piano, and Connor's "reckless rhythm"—with his "slapping his strings roughly"—all add a suggestive element.

Playing the song a second time, Peggy picks up her sax and "'Bye Bye Blackbird' grew very elemental, very deliberate." Then, when Leland and Connor again pick up the tempo, Peggy puts down her sax "and began to move her hips with the beat. She didn't sing, but stood there with her eyes closed, facing away from both men, transported by their playing." At this point the depiction of the rehearsal again turns almost poetic.

> *Leland's eyes were fixed on his keyboard. His pounding in the lower register was starting up again, while his right hand kept approaching the melody and backing away from it. Connor set up a rumble in his strings (200).*

The aggressive "pounding" and the "rumble" of the strings have ominous suggestions. A striking contrast to "a walk in the country" in part 1, this passage conveys how the music feels. Connor's response anticipates the end of the chapter.

> *Connor couldn't take his eyes off Peggy's movements, her rhythmic knee bend, her ankle turning in, turning out, her black hair falling forward, hiding her face whenever she dipped her head.*

When the music stops, "Peggy opened her eyes and faced Connor with a self-conscious smile, aware that he'd been concentrating on her." Then, in two rapid changes of perspective, the focus on Peggy and Connor switches to Laura's absence from the practice room. With Leland gone, and after a long flashback that resolves Laura's whereabouts—building suspense—the understated climax comes as Laura returns to campus to find her father, and the last sentence of part two implies that Peggy and Connor have made love in her office.

Music in Parts 3, 4, and 5

Part 3 has the fewest episodes devoted to music. The first is a brief, again metaphoric, taste of the music when the trio rehearses on the Sunday afternoon of the strike vote. "Lacking Neil's off-key piping, 'Mood Indigo' became as shadowy and touching as rain in the night. 'Little White Lies,' without Victor's frenzied drumming, went bubbling along like a clear little brook" (231). The nature analogies connect this rehearsal with the earlier ones. After a number of interruptions, the trio gets back to rehearsing, but "Connor was continually off the beat and Peggy was flat" (245). After feeling "like a virtuoso," Leland fails with "Little White Lies" and "Mood Indigo," makes an excuse, and leaves, but from outside the band room he hears Peggy and Connor doing "I'll get By." "He stood and listened. No sax. Just the words against the soft thud of the string bass ... It was actually quite wonderful. It couldn't be luck that produced such an exquisite harmony of voice and strings; anything this polished had obviously been rehearsed." When Leland leaves, he feels lonely and left out, reinforcing the theme of loneliness as well as the Peggy-Connor relationship.

In part 4 the focus is on the rehearsal for and the – ultimately truncated – Saturday radio performance on KRKU. Invited to the Edwards' house and the sleeping porch where they will perform, the quintet warms up with "Don't Blame Me." But when the quintet finally gets to perform, "ten minutes of their half hour were gone by the time the quintet began 'These Foolish Things,' and half the show was over before they finished it" (369). To deflate further the effect of the afternoon, the reader learns that the phone calls that had threatened to interrupt the performance were unanimously negative.

The next practice spells the end of the quintet. When three of the five don't show up at Leland's house on the Sunday afternoon after the Alliance's summit with college administration, Peggy asks Leland to play the song he had composed for her.

"He sat down at the piano and did so, but stopped after a few measures." The narrator shares Leland's thoughts, "He felt as though the bottom were dropping out of his heart. He felt like weeping" (389). When he won't tell Peggy why he can't play the song again, they work up "a passionate rendition of 'After You're Gone,'" and Leland makes a request. "If we're doomed [referring to the quintet], I don't think I could stand to stop playing these songs all at once" (395). Calling him "my friend," Peggy assures him that the two of them will go on playing.

The earlier sections of Part 5 are not without music. The chief instance is the spring concert. But there are no nature analogies; no descriptions of the "section from Handel's *Israel in Egypt*" that the chorus, under Peggy's direction, performed "flawlessly." During the intermission Leland also thinks about the future of the "Icejam Duo," which means he and Peggy playing two dates at the Van Buren Hotel and the reception for Georgina Gold and Ron Hunsinger's wedding.

Peggy on the Heights

Before considering the climactic instance of musical communion, it is worth considering another familiar scene that Hassler introduces just before that climax, as a way of preparing for it. As occurs in many of Hassler's novels, a main character ascends high ground to survey the surrounding area and reflect on the circumstances s/he faces. In *Rookery Blues* this scene occurs near the beginning of part five, while Peggy is under the mistaken impression that Connor is dead. The main action of the novel has moved forward. The semester is over; Neil has gone to Minneapolis to pursue his writing career, and the Dashes have moved to Milwaukee. Peggy herself has made a short trip to visit her sister in Boston.

Returned to Rookery for Georgina Gold's wedding, Peggy takes time following the rehearsal to walk out into the country.

She climbed a path through a grassy field to a height afford-

ing a broad view of the river bottom. At the crest she found a boulder to sit on, under an oak tree for shade. Resting there, looking back over the way she'd come, she regretted the course she'd taken with Connor.

Note the presence of a river and the submerged metaphor of journey and water in her use of "the course" in reference to her relationship with Connor. Then, like Jemmy Stott in Hassler's young adult novel, Peggy sees a bird whose apparent freedom from cares contrasts with her own. The scene, and Peggy's reflections, border on the melodramatic.

A hawk rode the air currents high above her. Grasshoppers jumped about at her feet. She sat there for a long time, imagining the life she might have had with her genius artist. When she finally roused herself and came down from the height, it was much later than she thought, and she arrived back at the hotel with scarcely enough time to dress for the wedding (474).

This return to the real world of Rookery and the Gold-Hunsinger wedding is not unlike similar returns to reality earlier in this novel, as well as in other Hassler novels, after quiet moments of reflection.

Conclusion
Other episodes in part five had also prepared for the conclusion of the novel by anticipating Neil's and Victor's return to Rookery for the wedding. Then the focus is on Peggy singing at the wedding, Leland and Peggy providing dance music at the reception, and the quintet, minus one, playing a number of pieces (474-478). When Connor appears and Peggy leaves with him (to pick up a string bass), Leland, Neil, and Victor try to do "Bye Bye Blackbird," "which wasn't very good."

On Peggy's return to the reception with Connor and the bass violin, and with the quintet once again all together, Peggy thinks, "they played astonishingly well." The subsequent descriptions emphasize the effect of the music, not on the performers, but on a variety of listeners. No more nature imagery, just Peggy Benoit seeing the quintet as "a single entity producing a sound so unified and reliable that their audience kept up an almost constant patter of applause. She saw even those who'd drunk too much sit up and take notice, sensing themselves in the hands of professionals." Several paragraphs in the perspective of each combo-member in succession reveal the final significance of the reunion. Victor's drumming is "relaxed and unforced," Leland has regained the "stage presence"—and the ability to smile at his audience—that he had had at eighteen, Neil "played like someone going deep into himself," and Connor "was feeling euphoric."

Then the narrator, stepping in, shifts the scale[4] again (as he had with Peggy on the heights) and views the combo's music as it drifts out beyond the confines of Culpepper's Supper Club.

> *And so the Icejam Quintet played until everyone had gone home, and they kept playing long after that, into the small hours of the morning ...*
> *Their music drifted out over the water and across the railroad yards and flowed downtown by way of Division Street, faint strains of it were heard by a policeman sitting on the steps of the city hall . . . heard by a late night disc jockey locking up KRKU and then unlocking it again to check his turntable and the tape player because he thought the beautiful strains of "My Blue Heaven" might be coming from inside, heard by a man living in the apartment Peggy used to occupy over the J C Penney store, a solitary insomniac who wished he had a woman to turn to and say, "Ain't that music pretty?" (481).*

Like Miles Pruitt imagining the Badbattle on its course to the Red River and Canada, or Simon Shea imagining the snow falling out over the plains, here the narrator imagines the Icejam Quintet's music drifting far out beyond Culpepper's Supper Club, having a mysterious, almost supernatural effect on those who heard it in the surrounding area. Like an apotheosis, or like the song of John Keats's nightingale fading to a dream, the music at the end of *Rookery Blues* is the equivalent of the many other "mysterious," or religious, scenes in Hassler's previous novels.

The Dean's List[5]

The Dean's List, published in 1997, is a kind of sequel to *Rookery Blues*, but it takes place twenty-five years after the events of the earlier novel. It is another satire on academic life, but with an element of mystery tied to the re-appearance of a literary celebrity. As a companion to *Rookery Blues*, *The Dean's List* is, like the earlier novel, also in many ways a return to the satiric style and academic focus of *Staggerford*, and perhaps *Grand Opening*, though *DL* exhibits greater thematic diversity than *Staggerford*. Many of the characters are familiar from *Rookery Blues*. The protagonist, Dr. Leland Edwards, age 58, is now dean of Rookery State College, where he continues to teach English as well as perform the duties of dean.[6] The story is told in the first person, from Leland's perspective. Readers will enjoy the satiric look at college administration, the faculty hand-holding, and the political in-fighting. Also humorous is the way Leland Edwards handles (or "tunes out") meetings that he has to attend as he makes his various "lists." Leland's continued love of teaching, and his desire to return full-time to the classroom, adds a realistic dimension. Though reviewer Diana Postlethwaite found the novel "disappointingly flat,"[7] Hassler himself thought it "one of my best books" (C, 246). I hope that this closer reading will convincingly demonstrate some of the novel's richness.

Autobiographical Elements

Like *Rookery* Blues, *The Dean's List* uses a number of details from the author's life. Though never an administrator, Hassler exploits his high school and college experiences, as well as a variety of events from his time at St. John's University and elsewhere, to add realism and enliven the humor of the novel. The charge of sexual harassment that occurs in the first pages comes from a colleague's experience at St. John's (*C*, 234).[8] President Zastrow's having a personal toilet installed in his office is a detail related to a president at St. John's. Leland and Mary Sue Bloom playing piano together (373) is taken from Hassler and his wife Gretchen "working up duets" (*C*, 256).

The Sylvan Senior Hi-Rise—a key location in the novel—is modeled on the retirement home where Hassler's mother spent her final years. The story of Rev. Worthington Pyle backing his car through a neighbor's all-season parlor (107-108) is based on an event in Brainerd, Minnesota, and Leland's mother's radio show is taken from a similar show that aired in Brainerd. The idea of celebrating a wake before one's own death derives from a Mrs. Humphrey in St. Cloud, MN (*C*, 254). Hassler credits one of his favorite minor characters, Johnny Hancock, to a friend, Lee Hanley, at St. John's (*C*, 258). One significant character who does not have a real-life analogue is Angelo Corelli, the dean's assistant and "enthusiastic young teacher" (C, 43). Perhaps the most important autobiographical element: Hassler admitted to Joseph Plut that the "unhappy break-up of his first marriage" (*C*, 234) is part of Leland's background that he takes from his own life.

Allusions

Once again, literary and pop culture allusions also provide ballast, orientation, and true-life texture. Herman Melville's "Bartleby the Scrivener" is the first. Then, a more contemporary allusion is Toni Morrison's 1993 receiving the Nobel prize in literature. Among many other allusions are those to Norman Maclean's *A River Runs Through It*, poets Ezra Pound, T. S. Eliot, Wallace Stevens, John Ashbery, and Carl Sandburg; and movies like *Naked Gun Two*, *Robocop*, and *Mrs. Doubtfire*. There are also references to Mike Tyson and Saddam Hussein, as well as the TV show, *Roseanne* and Madonna. Lolly Edwards' favorite music is Vivaldi, Purcell, and the Carpenters.

Plot

Hassler told Joseph Plut that history wasn't important in the novel, but historical markers and chronology remain an important and subtle orientation. The action takes place between December 18, 1993 and Thursday, June 22, 1994. WWII is a shadowy presence during a visit to Omaha. In time, flashbacks to Leland's earlier life, including the death of his father, Leland's marriage to divorcée Sally McNaughton, and the death of their son, Joey, also cast long shadows over the story. As Hassler noted to Plut (*C*, 254), he does not, in his later novels, leave characters by themselves as much as he had in earlier books, saying, "I guess I'm more concerned with plot now and keeping the action going." Like *Rookery Blues*, *The Dean's List* exhibits complex plotting, with many flashbacks and episodes and, if possible, an even larger cast of characters than in *Rookery Blues*.

The Dean's List is artfully plotted. Just opening *The Dean's List* and reading the first two and a half pages should convince the reader that s/he is again in the hands of a skilled storyteller. The opening scene presents a committee discussing a possible fund-raising celebrity. The dean, who is narrator, informs the reader that President O. F. Zastrow will be retiring. When the dean leaves the meeting to teach his Freshman English class, he has to answer a phone call from his mother, Lolly, reminding him of her regular Friday afternoon appearance at the Sylvan Senior Hi-Rise, to which Leland is to drive her. At the end of the phone call, the dean's "unkempt" secretary reminds him of his lunch—and what the campus sees as his "budding romance"— with colleague, Mary Sue Bloom.

The second episode of the novel develops out of Leland's composition class: a "staged reading" of a scene from Herman

Melville's "Bartleby the Scrivener." In it, Leland takes the role of Martin Ferguson, while a somewhat "odd looking" and challenged student, Carol Thelen, plays his long-lost youthful admirer, Charlene Trent. The climax of the scene is supposed to be Ferguson's embrace of Trent. When—because he "hams up" his part—Leland forgets the embrace and, after class, tries to console Carol Thelen with a brief embrace, the incident is seen by L. P. Connor, a thirty-something woman who has been the dean's "nemesis" for years, and who seems always to be lurking about, waiting to catch the dean in some compromising behavior.

Even with this brief summary, the reader can see all the principal components of the novel's plot laid out. The celebrity fund-raiser will lead to the choice of Richard Falcon; Lolly's lung disease introduces the focus on Leland's care for his mother as well as his relationship with his ex-wife, Sally McNaughton, who runs the Sylvan Senior Hi-Rise. The lunch with Mary Sue Bloom will initiate the story of *that* relationship. L. P. Connor's "witnessing" Leland's embrace of Carol Thelen leads to her filing a sexual harassment charge against Leland, a process that spins itself out through most of the novel.

But the central plot concerns the surprise arrival and subsequent preparations for a reading by the famous, reclusive poet, Richard Falcon.[9] As early as the first few pages the episodes are a complex preparation for Falcon's appearance.[10] Though Falcon's traditional verse is no longer *au courant* (hence the English Department chair, Sandor Hemm's snubbing him), the general public's love of Falcon's poems makes his appearance at Rookery State College a one-of-a-kind event, and the climax of the novel.

The dramatic climax of *The Dean's List* is unquestionably Falcon's reading, on February 4, 1994. It occupies six pages near the end of the chapter titled "The Feast of St. Blaise." Sneaking the poet into the hockey stadium from the visiting team's locker room, Leland becomes the more and less attentive auditor/observer of the entire performance. Leland's comments and insights punctuate—and serve to lengthen, for dramatic effect—the reading itself. Falcon reads for something over an hour (2:15 to after 3:20, by Leland's watch), which surprises Leland, who at the end thinks it's only twenty to three.

The poet begins by having the audience recite a familiar poem, "Squatters' Rights," which makes Leland observe, "He's a showman" (286). Then there are familiar and unfamiliar, older and some recent works. He ends with some poems for children, for which he again invites the audience to join in. The audience's response is understated. "He closes his book. Nobody claps. More stirring than applause is the utter silence of these adoring readers. Not a cough, not a murmur, not the scrape of a foot. It's a silence so complete that you can actually hear the rustle of his loose pages as he gathers them up."

There is something distinctly "meta" about this event. Hassler has invented a character, a middle-aged writer (poet) with Parkinson's disease. He is a cross between T. S. Eliot and Robert Frost. He has assumed the persona of a folksy, country philosopher-artist. His poems are about everyday events, in a genre and style that are no longer fashionable.[11] But Hassler has also carefully "created" the sense of a following so large that it fills the 4,000-seat hockey stadium of RSC. Into this setting steps the almost frail poet. Inasmuch as Leland resembles Hassler, and Leland finds in Falcon a brother/father, it is not hard to infer that Falcon is an image, a metaphor for Hassler the novelist, the popular writer, who can charm an audience with his readings. At one point, when Falcon takes the stage to a "wild ovation," Leland observes, "Were I Richard Falcon himself I couldn't feel more gratified" (285). While somewhat melodramatic, this highpoint of Leland's career, and the novel, is also Hassler's imaginative projection of himself.

As has been the case with a number of previous novels, however, through this central plot Hassler weaves multiple strands relating to Leland's past and the history of Rookery

State College in the years Leland has been there. Other threads concern Leland's short, unsuccessful marriage, the loss of his two-year old son, his mother's celebrity as a radio talk-show host in Rookery, and her worsening lung disease. The comic climax of this latter thread, following her near-fatal respiratory crisis after a Christmas visit to relatives, is Lolly Edwards' decision to celebrate her wake while she is still alive. In conventional comic fashion, the novel wraps up with a re-uniting and healing as Leland Edwards assumes the presidency of Rookery State College and determines to make a new life with colleague, Mary Sue Bloom. Like *Rookery Blues*, this novel is not overtly religious, but poetry becomes a powerful medium of communication and a symbol of reconciliation both public and private. Richard Falcon's reading, and the inauguration of Leland Edwards as president also offer an intimation of a potentially transcendent, transformative dimension in individual and communal life (*C*, 232-33)

As in his other novels, episodes and flashbacks vary the pace: the story of Leland's depression, of an autumn evening in 1970 at his cabin with Sally McNaughton; of his helping Pug Patnode build a wilderness Casbah; of the Christmas trip to Lolly's relatives in Nebraska, are all part of varying, while maintaining the pace. Like *Staggerford*, the experiences of burn-out, depression, and lack of direction form a point of departure. The novel opens in the midst of a select committee's efforts to bring a fund-raising celebrity to campus. The accusation of sexual harassment further complicates the opening and provides an initial cause of tension that will follow Leland through much of the story. The novel also involves illness, drugs, and the threat of death in the Christmas break trip to Grimsby and Omaha.

Social Gatherings
As Plut and Hassler note in their conversation (*C*, 252-53), the novel highlights a number of smaller and larger gatherings.

Besides the meeting of the select committee, the novel moves through a Friday gathering at the Sylvan Senior Hi-Rise and later the Edwards Christmas Open House. One could discuss at length the structure and complex effects of the Open House, the only event in the novel besides the inauguration that occupies an entire chapter. It is tempting to see the Open House as a kind of holiday *saturnalia*,[12] similar to the Halloween party in *Staggerford*. Composed of guests and humor, flashbacks, and running gags, as well as the Dean's inebriation, it culminates with Leland's Christmas ebullience, and ends abruptly with Rev. Worthington Pyle's auto accident. A predictable post-drinking plunge into moroseness and a flashback to the death of his son Joey makes Leland seek sexual solace with Sally at the Sylvan Hi-Rise. There his memories after Sally falls asleep introduce the concluding four-page flashback that describes how former dean, Pug Patnode, deceived the campus as he fooled faculty and seduced faculty wives.

The author makes the story of Sally's infidelity with Patnode the tragic-comic climax of the tales of disordered relationships. The culprit is Theodore ("Pug") Patnode, a former dean and rival of Leland Edwards. But to prepare for this episode, he places it after the story of Joey's death, and the episode of Worthington Pyle's car going into the Coopers' four-season porch, with the four-page Pug Patnode episode ending the chapter. The portrait of Pug Patnode—loud, opinionated, and scatological—is classic Hassler humor. All of these characters to some degree pick on or exploit the shy and quiet Leland in a way that suggests an archetypal comedy. Leland even admits, "I guess I've always been too innocent for my own good" (113), which is later echoed by the mysterious Kimberly Kraft (210). The final social gathering of the novel occurs with the early summer inauguration of Leland as the sixth president of Rookery State College and an inauguration celebration back at the Sylvan.

Season, Setting, and Movement

As in *Staggerford* and other novels, the seasons are significant. *The Dean's List* begins as winter sets in, and it ends on an unusually warm June day. Spatially, Hassler moves the reader from the administrative offices, classrooms, and student union of Rookery State to the Sylvan Senior Hi-Rise and back; then on to the Edwards home, where Leland lives with his mother. From there the novel takes the reader to Grimsby and Omaha, Nebraska, and back to Rookery, where the poet Richard Falcon suddenly appears. Thereafter, the plot focuses on Falcon, his need for privacy, lodgings, and ultimately a hiding place from supposed pursuers. Along the way the reader, through the narrator, also enters a reclusive couple's riverside dwelling, an ice-fishing shack, and a reclusive retiree's musty Victorian house.

Like some of his previous novels, *The Dean's List* also uses car travel to vary the novel's action. The trips to and from Grimsby and Omaha; the "flight" with Aunt Mary and Richard Falcon from Rookery to Fargo, then to Nebraska, are all part of the peripatetic element in Hassler's fiction, and an aid to variety. The trip to Bismarck to pick up Mary Sue Bloom that occurs near the end of the novel has an almost idyllic quality.

Themes

As in many of his earlier novels, loneliness and loss, the struggle for personal integrity, a devotion to one's art, and care for one's elders are all themes. While betrayal is less central than in earlier novels, deceit—especially Richard Falcon's—is prominent. Leland's betrayal of Lolly on various occasions becomes a somewhat somber kind of "running gag." The revelation, and resolution, of Falcon's many lies is downplayed, and the L. P. Connor and Peggy Benoit threads are somewhat summarily tied off.

Once again death assumes a significant place in the novel. Leland's father's death was a defining event for Leland, and recollection of his father's life and death color the visit to Omaha.

Son Joey's accidental death, for which Leland feels culpable, also looms over the Edwards Christmas Open House. Lolly's near-fatal respiratory attack after leaving Omaha is another intimation. The reader also learns of the deaths of Connor and Eldora Sparks. Then, near the end of the novel, the deaths of Nettie Firehammer and Rev. Worthington Pyle are final, somewhat surprising reminders of death's constant presence. A signature reference to "maiming" occurs when, during the Omaha and Grimsby episode, Leland recalls his Uncle Herbert O'Kelly, a butcher who had lost a finger in a slicer.

One prominent example of the outright macabre comes in the form of a minor character, Dorcas Muldoon (who is battling terminal stomach cancer). Dorcas appears again and again, her emaciated appearance as a clerk in the student union becoming a kind of "death's head" every time Leland sees her. Before Richard Falcon's reading, not only Peggy Benoit, but many of Leland's in-laws react to Dorcas's appearance. Then, at his inauguration celebration in the student union, her "finger-wiggle of congratulations," accompanied by her emaciated smile creates a further macabre image, "like a message from beyond the grave."

One of the earliest instances of the grotesque is the introduction of a couple Leland calls Mr. and Mrs. Roman. Mr. Roman and his wife, "Dee," live in a house Roman built on railroad land on the far side of the Badbattle River, where they live on fish and game they catch or kill (some of it illegally), and raise a seven-acre vegetable garden. They are reclusive, reticent, and lovers of Lolly Edwards' radio show. Mr. Roman recounts how he met his wife, "Dee," a hobo who got off a train from Montana. Leland fishes with the Romans, and later in the novel he enlists their help in hiding Richard Falcon from Peggy Benoit and the tax authorities that Leland believes are following Falcon.

Also bizarre is some of Richard Falcon's behavior. At a dinner with Leland and his mother he dominates conversation, and at the end he more or less deliberately confuses Angelo Corelli with a "flunky" named Phillips, who did odd jobs for him. Falcon calling Corelli "Phillips" then becomes a running gag through much of the rest of the novel. One of the most intensely realized grotesque features relates to the multiple descriptions of Kimberly Kraft, a character from *Rookery Blues* whom President Zastrow had forced to retire from teaching. Now she is a reclusive, somewhat embittered woman who lives alone with a stuffed parrot. Leland visits Kimberly repeatedly during the latter part of the novel, and each time the sense of the grotesque is re-evoked.

Imagery and Language

As in almost all Hassler novels, there are descriptions of the seasons; the Badbattle in winter, the coming of spring in the Dakotas; the unusually warm June day of Leland's inauguration. The few bird images have varied weight. A "buzzard-like" Dorcas Muldoon is a throw-away, but the description of a blue-jay in December, with "its beak buried in its puffed-out breast feathers" (64), shows Hassler's signature deftness. The description of Kimberly Kraft, who "cocks her head left and right like a wren" (216), falls somewhere between the two. There are also references to chickadees and geese (250), and Richard Falcon is described as having "the sleeping habits of a bird" (339). Hassler also uses nuanced language that affects the tone and texture of the novel. In a brief look back at the history of RSC, for instance, he observes that now, "there are nearly three hundred members of what I like to call our college family and President Zastrow refers to as his labor force" (5-6). The irony here cuts both ways. Leland's referring to "family" borders on sentimental idealism, while Zastrow's "labor force" is clearly meant as a satiric comment on the president's view of those working in higher education. Some surprising uses of language also relate to other features in the novel. Early on Mary Sue Bloom complains, "I feel like my soul has turned to chalk. Like everything I ever believed and felt is dusty and erasable" (60). While possessing an edge of humor, this description both depicts the extent of Mary Sue's mental and emotional state, while it contributes to the archetypal dimension of the novel.

Humor

The Dean's List employs a wide range of humor. There are the usual "running gags" and humorous names, like "Petey's Price-Fighter Foods," the "Spect-O-Cheer scoreboard," and even names like Nettie Firehammer and Faith Crowninshield—the latter a "tall, broad-shouldered ex-nun" who is the human rights officer. There are Coach Hokanson's malapropisms (he speaks of an "illegible" goalie) and, explaining his third string players winning and losing, he says, "'They been erotic like that all year.'" Later, he says, "'Did you know that a single hockey game turned our president into an invertebrate fan?'" There are also possible symbolic names, like Kimberly Kraft's address on "Bellwether Drive."

Hassler's humorous treatment of senior citizens begins with the first visit to the Sylvan Hi-Rise. There Leland observes the oddities of old age, culminating in a visit to arthritic Twyla Thorp's room, where Twyla's slow uptake and tendency to repeat, added to Leland and Lolly's gently malicious efforts to confuse Twyla and Nettie Firehammer, result in some of the novel's best humorous episodes. There is also the outlandish, bordering on the bizarre and grotesque. One of the first is Leland's encounter with the Romans. When Leland finds the entrails of a deer in the dump—an illegal kill—the punch line comes when Roman and his wife invite Leland for a venison dinner. When he politely says, "some other time," Roman says, "The venison won't be as fresh" (79).

Another instance of bizarre humor is the creation of Theodore ("Pug") Patnode, the previous dean. Composed of often seemingly contradictory details, the Pug Patnode "episode" (is it a genuine flashback?) is almost a *tour de force*. And the punch line is that Leland Edwards helps Pug build a "casbah" in the woods, miles from anywhere, where Pug can take his many conquests, seductions of RSC faculty and faculty wives, including Leland's wife of scarcely more than three years, Sally McNaughton.

There are as many sight-gags and instances of slapstick humor as in the early novels like *Staggerford* and *Simon's Night*. An early instance of slapstick—some might call it TV sit-com—humor comes at the end of the Edwards Christmas Open House. It comes as the climax or punch line of an elaborate narrative that weaves in Leland's inebriated state, his parting insult to Rev. Worthington Pyle, and a "pastoral" description of the neighbor couple's four-season parlor. When Leland offers to drive the Sylvan Senior Hi-Rise residents back home, Worthington Pyle says Leland is too drunk to drive, and the residents pile into Pyle's small sports car. But when Rev. Pyle puts the car in reverse to leave the Edwards driveway, the car continues across the street, up onto the lawn, and part way through the wall of the Coopers' parlor. The crash brings together and confounds all the previous narrative.

Another humorous scene occurs during the "Spring Term" chapter, when the Richard Falcon plot is building toward a climax. Mary Sue Bloom has had a breakdown, and the L.P. Connor harassment hearing takes another plodding step forward. Then, in a scene of humorous contrast, the dean confronts the athletic director and the hockey coach with two infractions: an ineligible goalie and an unapproved advertisement for Heim's Beer on the hockey stadium marquee. This latter scene allows Hassler to indulge his satiric gift, directing it at uneducated former athletes "going to pot" (219). The coach's malapropisms are a further highlight. With respect to playing the ineligible goalie, Jeff Todd, the dean methodically destroys the coach's and the athletic director's arguments, ending with a brusque announcement of his decision: to report the infraction and "pull the plug on the message board" (224).

One of Hassler's favorite minor characters, Johnny Hancock, is the focus of an elaborate running gag. Hancock is a resident of the Sylvan Senior Hi-Rise. A former farmer, one in a long line that extends back to "Nelson" in Hassler's first published short story, Johnny goes around in bib overalls asking people if they'd like to buy a bat house. He builds both seventy-five and one-hundred bat models (18). This story is varied over the course of the novel. When he can't sell bat houses, he starts calling them blue martin houses. As a kind of punch line, at the end of the novel, he tells Leland that he has now sold two and a half houses. This should cause the reader to pause. Two and a half? Then Johnny explains. He couldn't sell his constructions as either bat or martin houses; so he cut them in half and sold them to Hi-Rise residents as dollhouses for their grandchildren.

Johnny is also the focus of another, somewhat grotesque running gag that ends with a surprising punch line. Because he chews tobacco, Johnny is always looking for a place to spit the juice. He carries an empty orange juice concentrate can in the front pocket of his bib overalls and spits into it. At the Edwards Christmas Open House, the first thing he asks Leland is whether he has made more orange juice; he wants an empty can. Near the end of the novel, Johnny is jailed for shoplifting. Leland goes to the police station to bail him out. When he sees the evidence of Johnny's shoplifting (an orange juice can kept frozen in the station's fridge), he explains to the police that this is where Johnny spits tobacco juice. The police release Johnny, handing over the "evidence" to Leland. When Leland drops Johnny at the Hi-Rise, he gives Johnny the can. Johnny refuses it and walks away. It is only then that Leland sees: the seal on the can is not broken; this is a can of frozen orange juice concentrate.

A final source of humor comes in the spring, when the RSC writers' week gives Hassler an opportunity to satirize writers and writers' conferences. Besides one Jimmy Olsen—of whom Angelo says, "what a pain in the ass" (372)—the particular focus is Neil Novotny, a character from *Rookery Blues*, who returns to speak as Mary Magdalen Peterson and Delphinia White, the pseudonyms under which he wrote a number of pulp romances.

The Archetypes

Though in their conversation on *The Dean's List*, the first thing Hassler and Joseph Plut talk about is the place of art, poetry and healing, the implication is that, like a number of his other novels, *The Dean's List* is a conventional comedy, with relative disorder—if not exactly chaos—ending in restored order, harmony, and "healing." And comedy, as Northrop Frye pointed out, often employs archetypal elements. To review, briefly: archetypes are those recurrent characters, situations, and patterns of imagery found throughout literature and history. Originally they related to fertility rites, the cycle of seasons, and the stages of life. T. S. Eliot purportedly used the ancient story of the fisher-king—his weakness and his later transformation—as the pattern/structure for his long poem, *The Waste Land*. Many of Hassler's novels gain added power and effect by employing such archetypes.

At first glance, *The Dean's List*, as a campus novel, seems without such an archetypal dimension. Yes, the seasons are important; as the novel proceeds from December to June, the reader experiences the end of fall, then winter, and the slow coming of spring. But what of other archetypal patterns? Yes, Richard Falcon *is* the sick prince. Afflicted with Parkinson's disease and self-medicating unwisely, Falcon also purports to be hounded by a species of the Furies. In the course of the novel he seeks ever-greater isolation to complete his life's work, even resorting to disguise and flight. In the end, the Furies are placated, or at least diverted, the illness abates, and the prince's "savior" heals him.

But the "hero" or "savior," Leland Edwards, is also sick. At the start of the story, he is, like many Hassler characters at the start of his novels, depressed and feeling isolated, directionless.

Like the archetypal hero, he carries wounds of regret, guilt, and grief, and he worries about the current state of his mother, Rookery State College, his relationship with his ex-wife, and his psychologically fragile colleague, Mary Sue Bloom. Throughout the novel, Leland, as protagonist, struggles against death and the coming of death—his father's and his son's death, his mother's impending death, Dorcas Muldoon's impending death from cancer; the deaths of Nettie Firehammer and Worthington Pyle.

But Leland is also a classic "fall guy," "patsy," or victim, the ironic "butt" of comedy. This, too, is archetypal. His innocence and naiveté (not to mention his shyness) are all on display. One could argue that part of the novel's thematic core is the story of the fifty-eight year old dean becoming more consciously aware of his own strengths and limitations—what C. G. Jung would call a story of "individuation." Leland finally finds purpose and orientation and casts off his depression with the arrival of Richard Falcon, who becomes at first a kind of brother and then a father-figure. Both of these "figures," father and brother, and their subsequent relationship are so conventional as to be almost archetypal as well.

What form does "regeneration" take in this novel? First, Richard Falcon is finally freed from the "furies" (318) that were chasing him: Peggy Benoit and his autistic grandson, Jonathan. There is even the suggestion that Falcon will "settle down" in Kimberly Kraft's house: a species of "homecoming" that would have archetypal resonance. The final example of regeneration or renewal comes with the inauguration of the new president. Richard Falcon offers a "poet's blessing" to Leland and Mary Sue, saying, "Nobody deserves good fortune more than you, Leland" (394). Leland's response sounds very much like the rejuvenation that the archetypal pattern demands. "The words [of the poet] work on me like brandy. I'm much, much taller than ever before, and I'm imbued at last with the very sort of benevolent presidential power I'd expected to—but didn't—pick up at my installation ceremony." As if by a kind of magic Leland Edwards "grows taller," genuine proof of the archetypal structure of not only the inauguration ceremony, but, looking back, certain other aspects of the novel as well. With the reminder of a poet-father's blessing, which is a classic archetypal gesture (and Falcon's promise to write a poem for their wedding[13]), the novel ends. Despite some reviewers' negative comments, the reader should find that *The Dean's List* continues to provide both entertainment and further insight concerning Hassler's skills as a storyteller and a creator of comic, not to mention archetypal, journeys of self-discovery and consolation.

7

The Final Years[1]

The three books treated in this chapter, "The Final Years," represent a kind of "farewell" on many counts. In *The Staggerford Flood* and *The New Woman* the author bids goodbye to Agatha McGee, his longest-lived and most beloved character. Both *The Staggerford Flood* and *The New Woman* bring back characters from earlier novels. In the first, a number of them are stranded with Agatha McGee in her large house in Staggerford, high above the flooding waters of the Badbattle River. *The New Woman* finds Agatha McGee moving into a retirement home where, like Simon Shea, she manages to upset routines, introduce novelty, and even solve a mystery, while the narrator gently satirizes old age, retirement homes, and contemporary culture. Here, too, characters from earlier novels provide familiarity as well as often shocking surprise.

The Staggerford Murders, two novellas, bound as a single work, is a different matter. The title novel is an adaptation of an adaptation. Originally written as a short story,[2] Hassler expanded it and turned it into what is ostensibly a murder-mystery play, which was first produced in 1999 at the Lyric Theater in Minneapolis. Then he re-cast the play in the form of a prose narrative, told from five different perspectives, transforming the stage script into a comic romp; a send-up of crime thrillers, set in the familiar Minnesota town of Staggerford. The second novella, *The Life and Death of Nancy Clancy's Nephew*, expands and transforms another short story,[3] making it a genuine farewell. *The Life and Death of Nancy Clancy's Nephew* presents a last portrait of old age in the person of W. T. Nestor, a retired turkey farmer who, in the course of his life, has lost his son, his wife, and his livelihood. His only consolation is the friendship of a former latchkey kid, and the anticipation with which he undertakes a trip to visit the aged matriarch of his family, Aunt Nancy Clancy. The result is an amazing performance, combining an empathetic narrator whose sensitivity to his protagonist, the insensitive W.D. Nestor, creates a dual perspective that is subtly ironic without being cynical.

The Staggerford Flood

At 199 pages, *The Staggerford Flood* is Jon Hassler's shortest novel since *Jemmy*. His not explicitly connecting this novel to a larger *historical* context (as had been his consistent habit right through *The Dean's List*) may be explained by health, and haste to complete another novel. Although *The Staggerford Flood* lacks explicit orientation to events in the wider, historical world, the narrator supplies this lack through often digressive glimpses into a number of different lives. These include the women Agatha has helped (Beverly and Janet), the Willoughby community that surrounds and supports Agatha's friends, the Holisters, and finally the citizens of Staggerford, old and new, with whom Agatha and her friends interact.

The use of familiar characters, familiar techniques, and a greater reliance on the details of everyday events and experiences might all be evidence that the author is working quickly. While his busyness at the time of its writing might belie the "health" argument, together, the author's health and busyness might explain why *The Staggerford Flood* turned out to be the kind of book it is. Though not manifesting the breadth and quality of earlier novels, *The Staggerford Flood* shows the skill and canniness of an author who may be just past the top of his game, but, except perhaps for some overly detailed parts, the novel maintains interest from start to finish.

Published by Viking in 2002, *The Staggerford Flood* remains special on a number of counts. The reader will find much that is familiar and therefore reassuring. To begin with, the novel brings back Agatha McGee, one of Hassler's favorite characters, and the protagonist in two earlier novels. Agatha is now seventy-nine years old and conscious of her many diminishments. The greater emphasis on Agatha's past and her Irish background recall as they augment what the reader learned about her in *Staggerford*, *A Green Journey*, and *Dear James*. The reader meets a number of other characters from earlier novels as well, many of them Agatha's former students. The reader also gets a glimpse into her friend, Lillian Kite, in a way not realized before.

Hassler is still a master storyteller, in clear control of all his usual techniques. As in *Staggerford*, the story of a flood in the fictional town of Staggerford unfolds over a single week (Thursday to Thursday, during Holy Week, sometime around 1996). This week is bracketed by two days from a year after the flood. Each chapter (named for each day of the week) has its particular dynamics; its crescendos, crises, and climaxes. To aid the effects, in each chapter the narration switches location and point of view, character, or time. Again, anecdotes, recollections, prayers, conversations at cross-purposes, a humorous phone call full of misinterpretations, more or less elaborate, and detailed, meals, running gags, and other familiar instances of repetition form the staples of the style. As expected, the narrator includes two views from places of height, one reference to blood, and at least two instances of the mysterious or the uncanny. And, throughout it all, the perceptive reader will notice Hassler's familiar technique of contrasting humor or satire with serious insights; a contrast of the mundane or everyday with something like an Olympian, authorial insight. Agatha's Catholicism makes religious belief and matters of conscience thematic.

Though the first impression is that this novel, like *Rookery Blues* and *The Dean's List,* is all action, there is really quite a lot of interior reflection. Yes, the twin focus of the novel is the flood and Agatha's aging. It is also about Agatha's coming out of an early spring depression through the agency of friends and those whom she has helped, and those she seeks to help. Once again, it is also about other forms of illness, addiction, and death, and the way that friendship, and helping others, becomes a way to respond to such "evils" and make life worthwhile. The narrator constructs the novel from a number of larger and smaller visits and gatherings: Janet's lunch with Agatha, a trip downtown; a visit from the Edwardses, a trip out to the small town of Willoughby. During the flood there are arguments, frugal meals, and the flood-stranded visitors "making do." Agatha spends a lot of time pondering her past as she worries about food for her guests and adjusts the sleeping arrangements in her house. The reader gets the "feel" of the rain, the impending flood, and then the experience of being "stuck" in a house with all these women —with no power and no working toilet facilities. When Agatha goes to bed during the flood, she reflects on her past life, and on the people who depend on her. Carefully placed descriptions introduce lyricism as they develop the tone of isolation, danger and fear: fear of starvation, fear of eternal punishment. The novel ends with a celebratory meal that—it is suggested—will become a kind of tradition.

The novel introduces relatively few new characters. One striking feature of *The Staggerford Flood* is the reappearance of characters from other Hassler novels. There are so many, in fact, that it is hard not to imagine Hassler deliberately seeking to revisit and reconnect with some of his favorite characters. Because it is a story about the town of Staggerford and Agatha McGee, some of these reappearances are not surprising. But the number of characters who "show up" at Agatha's house, or who are otherwise mentioned in the course of the novel, make such appearances less plausible than the novel's familiar location might suggest. One of the first familiar characters to arrive is Fr. Frank Healy (from *North of Hope*). As the new pastor in Staggerford, he visits Agatha who is one of the "shut-ins" to whom he ministers. When Agatha tells him about attending the Dublin funeral of James O'Hannon (from *A Green Journey* and *Dear James*), it is travel agent Verna Jessen (another character from *NoH*) who made her reservation for Ireland.

Lillian Kite is still Agatha's best friend, and Janet Raft Meers (from *AGJ*) is again Agatha's confidant and helper. Janet's teenage daughter, Sara, is a new character. Janet's husband Randy (*AGJ*)—of whom Agatha has never approved—has a walk-on part. Agatha's nephew, Frederick Lopat (also from *AGJ* and *Dear James*) now lives with Agatha and helps not only Agatha but the plot as well. Lillian's daughter, Imogene (*Staggerford*, *AGJ*, and *DJ*), returns as a predictably peevish annoyance to Agatha and almost everyone else.

An early point of tension and puzzlement is Agatha's supposed illness, reported in *The Staggerford Weekly*. In Agatha's one trip into Staggerford—to shop and to get to the bottom of the report—she confronts Lee Fremling (a hapless football player in *Staggerford*) who has inherited not only the newspaper, but his father's inclination to drink. Lee is now the "publisher" of the *Staggerford Weekly* and three other local newspapers. The editor, Leslie Hokanson, is a new character. Agatha's illness also brings out Lolly Edwards and her son, Leland (from *Rockery Blues* and *The Dean's List*). On an early visit to Agatha's house, Lolly makes the first of two suggestions that Agatha plan her own Memorial Service, before she passes away. Later Leland's wife, Mary Sue Bloom (an important character in *DL*), also makes a brief appearance.

Agatha's new neighbor is the strikingly well-dressed funeral director, Linda Schwartzman, who turns out to be the former Linda Mayo from *Simon's Night*. *She* makes reference to a distant cousin, Libby Girard Pearsall (from *North of Hope*). The former Beverly Bingham, from *Staggerford*, returns to town as the twice-divorced Beverly Cooper, whose constant worry is her grown son, the schizophrenic Owen. Other minor characters include William Muhlolland from *Staggerford* and Stephen Meers from *A Green Journey*. Near the end of the novel, in a somewhat contrived way, Beverly assuages her loneliness by copying down what she (and her husband of one year, William) knows about their former high school classmates, all characters in *Staggerford*. This becomes a list that includes Nadine Oppegaard, Roxie Booth, Peter Gibbon, Jeff Norquist, Superintendent Lionel Stevenson, and former principal, Wayne Workman, whose wife, Anna Thea Workman, we learn, divorced him. Beverly also writes a short *What I Wish* essay that recalls one of the final assignments given by Miles Pruitt, the chief character in *Staggerford*.

Three other new characters who occupy prominent places are the Holister siblings: Dort, Calista, and Howard. Like Eunice Pfeiffer and her two brothers in *North of Hope*, the three Holisters live together. They reside in the small town of Willoughby. It is Agatha's efforts to save the Holisters' livelihood (they run the town post office) that, along with the flood, constitute the major plot lines of the novel.

Plot

The action of the novel derives from the spring rains and the consequent rising of the Badbattle River. The river's overflowing makes it necessary for residents of Staggerford, and much of the surrounding countryside, to leave and seek higher ground. Only Agatha chooses to stay in her house, which occupies the highest ground on River Street. Then, for various reasons, seven friends and acquaintances join her to wait out the flood in her house.

An early visit to Willoughby introduces the Holisters, whose hold on the post office job is contingent on Dort's remaining the postmistress. When Dort dies suddenly, Agatha proposes that her sister, Calista, assume Dort's identity and continue as postmistress. This initial deception breeds various serious, and sometimes comic, consequences. The return to Staggerford of Beverly Bingham Cooper comes as a surprise to Agatha, and her subsequent, temporary disappearance constitutes a minor mystery early in the novel.

The heart of the story, from Sunday night until Tuesday morning, finds the seven women "holed up" in Agatha's house, trying to get along. Visitors by boat include Howie Holister and Frederick Lopat, who for one night swell the house's occupants to ten. After the water recedes and phone service resumes, the city clerk, William Muhlholland calls. Hassler, still a master at juggling plot elements, is able to keep all the balls in the air as he adds a new one: Beverly's budding "romance" with her former high school classmate, William. The week concludes with the Holy Thursday burial of Dort Holister, which includes an appearance from Lee Fremling, Leslie Hokanson, and Lolly Edwards doing a "remote" interview from Willoughby. The final chapter picks up where the first chapter left off, a year later, and chronicles the flood survivors' response to Agatha's invitation to brunch, and the brunch itself.

Themes

Thematically, the story is about age and its diminishments, as well as a general decline reflected in the community. Other themes include deception and Agatha's agonies of conscience. Along with death go fears of death, imagined deaths, and the sudden death of Dort Holister. As noted, fear of rising water and starvation add to the catalogue of real and potential griefs.

From at least *Simon's Night*, Hassler came to be known for his sensitive, though also humorous, treatment of aging and the elderly. *The Staggerford Flood* carries on that tradition, but the first reference to aging is somewhat oblique. In the first chapter Janet Meers arrives at Agatha's house to help her write and address invitations to the anniversary brunch. Entering Agatha's house and calling her name, Janet gets no response. "It occurred to her that Agatha may be dead" (5). This common fear about the elderly will occur again, but here it constitutes a subtle introduction to the theme of aging and death.

When Agatha appears, very much alive, the reader learns of her fears that she is forgetting days and that she is mumbling. She refers to her "lazy brain" at least three times. On Friday she takes the wrong list to go shopping. When the grocery clerk, who has also heard the reports of her illness, asks, "Are you okay again now?" Agatha responds with characteristic Hasslerian irony, "Except for spells of dementia" (40). The reader also learns of her feeling "weak and exhausted," which is explained by what the reader has learned earlier (25) is Agatha's diagnosis of congestive heart failure.[4] When Fr. Healy visits Agatha on Saturday, she tells him about an unpremeditated lie to Linda Schwartzman, and Fr. Healy warns her about senior scrupulosity. Agatha counters with a quip. As Agatha's alleged ill-health becomes a grim leitmotif, her own reflections augment the theme of aging. Thinking about her parents (100-101) might make the reader wonder whether this is part of Hassler's accurately representing (however unconsciously) a habit of the elderly: to compare themselves to their parents.

On Sunday Agatha wonders about her lack of interests. "Until this winter she read two or three books each month … Now nothing seemed quite so pressing as her afternoon nap" (109). Of course part of the explanation is Agatha's congestive heart failure. Calista's telling Agatha that she hasn't read anything since graduating from high school is probably a Hasslerian exaggeration, but then Lillian's saying that she cured *her* lack of interest by reading *The National Inquirer* gives this reflection on aging a humorous and satiric conclusion (110). The aging theme also includes other characters. Early in the novel, when Agatha visits the Holisters, Dort Holister claims that her arthritis is "a hitch in my wrists now and then is all" (51). Later we learn Dort is almost too crippled by arthritis to handle her mail-sorting duties, perhaps suggesting the sometimes defensive self-deception of the elderly. A scene from Tuesday morning eerily recalls Janet in the first chapter imagining Agatha's to have collapsed. Forced to share her bed with Lillian, Agatha wakes up at dawn and calls to Lillian, who does not respond. For a moment she wonders whether Lillian might have died during the night (139). Together, these two instances reflect a typical worry by and about the elderly dying unexpectedly. These two scenes also help create a tone of apprehensiveness that Hassler maintains throughout the novel.

Another thematic thread is love and marriage, and the choice of partners. None of the younger wives in the story— Janet Meers, Linda Schwartzman, Beverly Bingham Cooper— have had successful marriages. Only Lillian Kite had remained with the same husband, Lyle, and Lillian's reflections (see below) suggest she endured much in the marriage. When, after the flood, Beverly seems ready to take up with former high school classmate, William Mulholland, the other women, including Agatha, respond with as much irony and misgiving as hope.

The husbands are, in fact, a sorry lot. Janet's Randy is successful but seldom motivated. Beverly's ex-husbands, Terry and B.W., are non-entities (though B.W. cares about Owen, who is only his step-son); Linda's ex-husband Manny was overbearing. When viewed in retrospect, the novel is really about eight women; men play at most a minor, largely comic or satiric, part. Among the male characters, Howie Holister and Randy Meers are comic-satiric characters, while French Lopat, William Mulholland, and Fr. Frank Healy are the only males who receive positive treatment.

Reflective Moments

In his conversation with Joe Plut about *The Dean's List*, Hassler noted that in his later novels he wanted to keep his characters moving; that there was less "reflection" than in many of his earlier novels. As it turns out, *The Staggerford Flood* contains almost as many passages of the main character reflecting as in the first-person narrative of *The Dean's List*. Two of the most striking are Agatha's reflections on her Grandfather McGee and her Grandfather Cunningham. Besides revealing more of Agatha's character, both contribute to the discussion of aging as they interweave humor with a tone of nostalgic recollection.

The reflection on Grandfather McGee begins on Saturday night when Agatha goes to bed early. "Lying there, she let her mind range back over the earlier years of her life, as she'd been in the habit of doing almost every day. This evening her mind was on her grandfather McGee" (87). The first thing that occurs: "She had his fear of water to thank for her house standing on high ground." It was Grandfather McGee who persuaded Agatha's father, Peter, to buy the house on River Street. The reference to water leads to a long anecdote about how Grandfather McGee came from Dublin to live in Staggerford in 1921. It is full of vivid description and shows where Agatha got the expression, "lazy brain." Her grandfather repeats his story of the ocean passage ("'Oh, the sea, the waves!'") "again and again, to the point of tiresomeness, and Agatha, in her teens, was of an age to listen. Which is to say she was more or less trapped ..." The last of her grandfather's stories that Agatha remembers before falling asleep is of her father's wild cousin, Julia. Julia, it turns out, had died in the same influenza epidemic that had taken Agatha's brother. "Agatha fell asleep and dreamed that her brother was mowing the lawn in front of their new house on River Street."

The very next day, on Sunday afternoon, her guests' discussion of men prompts Agatha to reflect on her father and her maternal grandfather Cunningham. This digression reinforces the reader's sense of Agatha's Irish heritage. Of her father, who had been an outspoken lawyer and state legislator, Agatha reflects: "[her] father had a gregarious, happy nature, and it occurred to her now to wonder why she herself had never come close to resembling her father in personality" (101). Remembering her father, she observes that "Peter McGee, for being such an outspoken man, was curiously lighthearted." She then thinks of her mother, who "was serious and silent." Agatha concludes: "I have inherited Father's outspokenness and Mother's seriousness."

It is, in fact, her mother's "strong ethical opinions" that she focuses on. These come from the influence of Grandfather Cunningham. This reflection includes an apothegm, "'God hates a mouthy woman'. By which she [Agatha's mother] almost certainly meant her father instead of God." The very next sentence reinforces the impression. "Agatha later learned from her mother's two unmarried sisters that her Grandfather Cunningham held god-like sway over the household of their childhood." As noted earlier, these reflections stress how the elderly sometimes compare themselves to their parents. They also suggest how previous generations shape the present generation in unusual but specific ways. A final bit of reflection relates to Agatha's brother Timothy, underlining the stoicism in the McGee family, as Timothy plays ball alone while his father buries the dog, Jippie, who had been the quiet Timothy's only confidant (135-136).

Language and Imagery

Language and characters' relationship to it are a sub-theme of the novel. It begins with Lillian Kite reflecting on the priest shortage and wondering whether the priests "weren't getting enough sex" (17). But she knows not to discuss it with Agatha "because Agatha shied away from all topics having to do with human reproduction." The reasons for Agatha's fastidiousness with regard to language, as we have just seen, come to light in her reflections on the past. The narrator characterizes Imogene

Kite by using clichés, saying she bought "a whole slew of flood insurance" (35). Howie Holister's not liking big words like "inundated" instead of "flooded" becomes one of the novel's running gags and a regular part of the comic texture. The narrator himself is given to some clichés, calling Sara Meers "a petite dark-haired beauty" (43), though later she turns out to be a truculent, cynical "kindred spirit" of Imogene Kite.

The single most important image in the novel is the Badbattle River in flood. Many of the most moving descriptions relate to this. From the earliest references to rain (24-25) and sandbagging (34-35), the narrator builds up a sense of the encroaching waters. Spring imagery, partially in the form of Hassler's usual references to birds, is sparingly but emphatically used. At the end of Dort Holister's burial, the narrator provides a particularly strong impression of the coming spring: "The afternoon sun, slanting through a stand of pine trees at the edge of the cemetery, was so remarkably warm that Agatha commented on it, and they all agreed that yes, it felt as if spring was here at last" (179). This unusually long sentence also signals the end of the flood narrative.

Mystery and the Grotesque

Mystery of the kind found in some of the earlier novels is in short supply in *The Staggerford Flood*. The only two mysterious events occur in a short space, and both are related to death. When the reader learns about James O'Hannon's death (73 f.), Agatha relates (in anecdote form to Fr. Healy) how she managed to get to Dublin in time for the funeral. She tells him how she was upgraded to first class and an attendant arrived with a drink that she did not order. It turns out to be a mimosa, James O'Hannon's favorite drink. Soon after this, Agatha gets a phone call saying that Dort Holister has died (79), presumably from a cerebral hemorrhage.

The one distinctly "grotesque" element in the story is

Dort's glass eye and the one "frosted" lens in her eyeglasses. Dort lost the eye to cancer. The one "bloody" event is also associated with Dort and—combined with the description of her body—adds to the macabre impression of her death. Called to Willoughby on the news that Dort has died, Agatha finds Dort "in her nightgown and robe and lying on top of her quilt with a bloody leg and her good eye half open." Agatha's subsequent behavior will soon contribute to the plot. "She [Dort] was cold to the touch. Agatha closed her eyelid and picked her glasses with the frosted lens off the bedside table." These glasses will be part of the way Agatha gets Calista to impersonate her sister.

The Catholic Dimension and the Archetypal
The Staggerford Flood classifies as a "Catholic" novel, putting it in company with all but three of Hassler's other novels, largely because Agatha's Catholicism is a significant part of the novel's plot and thematic development. The presence of Fr. Frank Healy, and his participation in what I call the conscience theme, is yet another feature that gives the novel a Catholic dimension. Actually, the closer one looks, the more thoroughly Catholic *The Staggerford Flood* is. Through the interweaving of details and running references, Hassler makes the Catholic atmosphere pervasive—despite the fact that many of the key characters show little or no interest in religion at all.

A significant religious aspect of the novel is Agatha's struggle with her conscience. When Agatha and Linda Schwartzmann talk about being single and Agatha asserts, "I've never regretted the single life," she immediately realizes, "It was the first lie of her life" (64). Awhile later it is a second lie—that the Holister sister who has died is Calista, rather than Dort—that puts Agatha in a more than ethically awkward position. She begins to realize how many people she has involved in this second lie. Besides Calista and Howard, there are the other townspeople of Willoughby, as well as the coroner and even Fr. Healy. Agatha's agonizing over these two lies makes for much of the inner tension of the story. In fact, Agatha's thinking about her lie becomes a slightly grim "running gag." One of the more curious and surprising reminders of the theme comes when Agatha responds to a comment of Lillian's about death with a seemingly unthinking, "I am heartily sorry ..."(105), suggesting that Dort's death, and her own lie to cover it up, are constantly present in her mind. Agatha later completes the "Act of Contrition" from which this phrase comes. She is still agonizing at the end of the novel. She has returned to the sacrament, but she continues to argue with Fr. Healy about the degree of her guilt, pondering whether the lie about Dort was a venial or a mortal sin (190).

It may come as a surprise for the reader, but the flood occurs during the final days of Lent.[5] Later in the week, Fr. Healy points out that Dort Holister's funeral will have to take place on Thursday or Monday, since there are no funerals during the *Triduum*[6] (160-61). Fr. Healy's "business-like" discussion of Dort's funeral reminds readers of the season, without any major reference to the end of Lent or the start of the Easter season. From an archetypal perspective, however, the bulk of the novel takes place at the end of Lent, a spring in which one death and two rather unusual resurrections occur. In the midst of water imagery that takes the form of a veritable flood, Dort Holister dies and is buried as Calista. Agatha is "reborn" as a result of her giving shelter to seven women (and getting a pacemaker), and Calista is "reborn" as Dort.

A Representative Passage

Once again, a closer look at a specific passage will highlight some of the strengths and the complex construction of *The Staggerford Flood* as well as how the author uses the details of everyday life to weave a texture of mundane mystery and transcendent comedy. The way the final chapter resolves a number of issues and answers a number of questions that the story had raised is a perfect place to examine these techniques.

Among the many things the reader learns in the final chapter, those that suggest renewal and transformation loom largest. The conclusion also includes an archetypal re-integration—if not comic apotheosis—of at least one character (Beverly), and the welcoming inclusion of another (Linda Schwartzman). The chapter opens on two minor notes, a view from the heights, and then a sign of hope. It is a year after the flood, and the narrator focuses on the seven women who receive invitations to Agatha's flood-anniversary brunch. The first is Calista Holister. Because she doesn't write letters, she is surprised to receive this one and is eager to go to the party. Then Frederick Lopat tells Calista that he will not attend the brunch. "Not invited," he says. There is a humorous exchange between Calista and Frederick over Frederick's living with Agatha so not needing an invitation, but Frederick would rather work. This minor note turns into a digressive anecdote that gives further insight into Frederick and allows the author to indulge another of his favorite "tropes."

This brief scene includes one of the more serene descriptions in the novel and one that highlights the depiction of otherwise everyday events. As the narrator enters Frederick's viewpoint and explains his preference for work—he has "become Willoughby's full-time rural mail carrier" (183)—the reader learns that Frederick loves to drive to the top of "Substation Hill," "one of the highest points in Minnesota." From this height he can look out over the countryside. "The city was eighteen miles away, but on clear days, like today, he could see the glint of the chimneys of the packing plant at the near edge of Berrington. On overcast days, he was up among the clouds."

At the end of the digressive anecdote, the narrator switches perspective, and, of course, Imogene Kite returns as the "sour apple" of the novel. The next few paragraphs in her perspective are full of spite as she first throws away her invitation, only to phone Agatha later and accept. Before she changes her mind, however, Imogene pictures "the seven women she spent those endless days and nights with" the year before. She sees some of them as uppity and unaccountably more prosperous than she. Janet Meers remains "Agatha's pet," and Imogene sniffs at the fact that Janet's daughter Sara has gotten a scholarship to college. Imogene is also puzzled that Linda Schwartzman has become so popular that she has been made a member of the library board, and hence Imogene's "overseer." Thinking of Beverly Bingham Mulholland, Imogene imagines her becoming "the first lady of Staggerford" when her new husband succeeds the retiring mayor, Thaddeus Druppers. Imogene rationalizes her change of mind about the invitation by thinking of all the gossip she might hear at the party.

The responses of Linda Schwartzman and Beverly Bingham Mulholland to their invitations present striking contrasts in tone and emotion. Linda Schwartzman looks forward to the brunch, remembering "the five [women] who hugged her last year in the Willoughby cemetery. She had seldom seen most of them since the Holister funeral, but the memory of that embrace had helped her through some very lonely days" (187). Beverly's invitation comes to her at "the Mulhollands' new townhouse near the golf course and country club, [and] provided Beverly with a diversion from her longing." This longing has to do with missing her new husband, and the next two pages describe how she deals with this longing: by writing down what she and her husband recall about former high school classmates. The high school recollections involve as much suffering as joy and include a poignant passage from the journal that begins, "*I wish time would stop.*"

When Lillian Kite opens her invitation from Agatha (while knitting at Agatha's house) and becomes excited about their planning the party, Agatha's first response is, "think of the work" (190), but in time Agatha imagines "the seven women sitting around her dining table, and she warmed to the idea [of the party], knowing that at least five of them loved her." Agatha's mind then turns to her exchanges with Fr. Healy about her lie, and when he doesn't respond to a letter she sends him, there is a hint of Providence at work.

> *Perhaps if he'd answered, Agatha might never have consented to cataract surgery or to the emplacement of a pacemaker below her collarbone. To save her sanity, and without Father Healy to spar with, she needed a distraction of some sort to keep her mind off her Big Lie.*

Like Beverly writing as "a diversion from her longing," Agatha has taken a new interest in things and is again reading not only the *Staggerford Weekly* but library books as well.

Another unresolved question that the final chapter addresses humorously is "the disagreeable period Lillian went through last year" (191). Approaching the matter slowly, Agatha recalls earlier efforts to discuss the matter. When she reminds Lillian that "this time last year, around the time of the flood, you weren't acting quite yourself," Lillian first blames Imogene. Then Agatha asks, "'But why were you taking it out on me?'" Lillian's response: "'Oh, that was different – that was an addiction problem.'" As Agatha struggles to understand this apparently incomprehensible answer, the reader may fear that another sordid detail has yet to be revealed. When Agatha is finally able to put her concern into words, she asks, "'How did you cure yourself, Lillian? You weren't in treatment.'" Lillian's answer is classic Hassler: "'No. I wasn't in treatment. The cure was Easter'" (192).

Agatha's response is pure [and naïve?] incredulity. "'Easter? You mean you prayed?'" Lillian says, "'No. I never prayed about it. See, it wasn't your normal type of addiction. I gave up *The National Inquirer* and all papers like that for Lent last year.'" As Agatha registers shock to learn that <u>she</u> had been the cause of Lillian's self-denial, Lillian goes on with her knitting as she explains. "'Yep, you talked me into it in February, and I lasted almost till Easter. I cheated a little at the end because I was suffering withdrawal symptoms.'" She closes with another classic: "'I'll never give it up again,' she added. 'Dumbest idea you ever had'" (193).

Like the many meals Hassler has orchestrated before, the brunch itself is notable for the way it handles several characters at once, and for the way it ties up further loose ends. With Imogene—who, on her arrival refuses to speak "either to upstarts or to old people"—providing tension, and Sara Meers on the alert for a "study of multiple characters" paper that she has to write for college, the brunch gets underway. Beverly expresses her happiness "to be living back in Staggerford, and how good it always makes me feel to be in Agatha's house" (194). Calling her "a second mother," Beverly thanks Agatha, and this elicits thanks from Calista, whose understated, "Oh, she's certainly changed my life" is pure Hassler. Then she continues, "'When I think of how I was before my sister died, why it's kind of a miracle.'" Of course Calista's "miracle" includes her facility with lying, to keep up the impersonation of her sister, for which Agatha, of course, feels responsible. Janet Meers adds her tribute, which includes a quick recollection of her first meeting Agatha. Lillian provides an appropriate "downer" to the brunch by telling how thirty percent of her housemates at the Sunset Senior Center have died since the flood. Imogene rushes off to return to her library duties, "disappointed that there had been so little gossip" (198), but Linda Schwartzman offers to host a get-together of the eight the following month, and Janet Meers offers to host June, and Beverly, August. "Lillian promised to entertain in the Sunset's dining room for Agatha's birthday in September."

With all the guests gone, and Agatha silent, Lillian asks, "'Are you all right, Agatha?'" The narration then shifts to Agatha's perspective.

She said she was feeling fine. Actually she'd never in her life felt better. She was looking forward to next month and seeing

this group of friends again at Linda Schwartzman's house.
She was excited to think of gathering at Janet's pretty place
on the river and at the several other venues where they would
meet between now and fall. Then she would have them here
again in October and hoped the cycle kept going. The flood
survivors had suffused today's gathering with a warmth such
as she hadn't felt since her last pajama party at the age of
twelve (199).

On one level these reflections are true to the experience of
aging, as Agatha takes pleasure in anticipating future social occasions with her friends. With this final reminder of Agatha's
childhood and its reassurance of cyclical return—a moveable
feast of upcoming ritual meals—*The Staggerford Flood* reaches
a satisfying and subtly archetypal conclusion. While *The Staggerford Flood* is not one of Hassler's most memorable novels,
its skillful construction and its treatment of aging, along with
a host of lesser themes, make it a fitting penultimate novel in
Hassler's long and successful writing career.

The New Woman[7]
Published in 2005 by Viking, *The New Woman* is Hassler's last
full-length novel and the fourth in which Agatha McGee is
the protagonist. At 214 pages, it is another one of his shortest. It is also as much a "sequel" to *The Staggerford Flood* as *The
Dean's List* was a sequel to *Rookery Blues*. *The New Woman* takes
place approximately ten years after *The Staggerford Flood*, and
within ten pages the reader meets many of the same characters
who populated the earlier novel: Beverly Bingham Mulholland,
Linda Schwartzman, grandnephew Frederick Lopat and his
girlfriend Lee Ann Raft, and the parish priest, Fr. Frank Healy.
Composed of thirty, mostly short, chapters (only two of which
disrupt temporal sequence), the novel follows Agatha's move
from her large River Street home to the Sunset Senior Apartments, a retirement facility where Agatha's friend, Lillian Kite,

had moved near the opening of *The Staggerford Flood*. But *The New Woman* is more than a novel about "senior living." It is, rather, a doubly "ironic" treatment of the elderly. In it Hassler caricatures a number of stereotypes about aging, even as he uses those stereotypes in counterpoint with a number of unusual and even bizarre incidents and situations that the elderly characters face. He uses these incidents and situations for the purposes of humor and satire, as well as to create a number of touching and thought-provoking insights. It is also a novel full of multiple transformations; most of all in the character of Agatha McGee.

The principal location, the Sunset Senior Apartments, resembles the Norman Home in Hassler's second novel, *Simon's Night*. The narrator takes the reader into the residents' apartments and the common dining room as well as visiting a number of the weekly Friday coffee hours. Late in the novel the narrator returns the novel's focus to the dining room. When Agatha moves in, there are only two male residents, Thaddeus Druppers and John Beezer. Druppers is the former mayor of Staggerford, and Beezer, a retired farmer. Druppers' fastidiousness and Beezer's boorishness make them like an elderly "odd couple." Hassler writes himself into the story in the person of Joe Rinkwitz, the sixty-something husband of Little Edna Rinkwitz, a former nurse and (like Hattie Norman in *Simon's Night*) the real manager of the Sunset Apartments. The novel presents a vignette of Joe, a stooped man who refers to "Dr. Parkinson," who causes him to fall. With his compromised posture and a soft voice, he also seems to Agatha, to have "a soft disposition" (17).

Historical references are few but sufficient to situate the opening action around 1997, with references to Congressman Paul Wellstone, and Pope John Paul II in ailing health. Near the end of the novel, Agatha acknowledges that she was born in 1910, and one character says, "It's 1998, so you're 88 years old." The seasonal focus is classic Hassler. The novel begins after Thanksgiving, and the main action concludes just before Lent the following year. The novel alludes to only one movie (*An Officer and a Gentleman* from 1982), but TV references are numerous, including *Mr. Rogers' Neighborhood, Martha Stewart, Days of Our Lives*, and *Law and Order*. All of Hassler's narrative techniques and familiar ways to create interest and tension are on display: shifting viewpoint, running gags, minor mysteries, conversations at cross purposes, a grotesque exhumation, and multiple plot twists, as well as a signature holiday meal, and, of course, more and less gentle satire on a variety of topics. As in most of his novels, the end of each chapter is punctuated with an ironic or surprising twist.

The cast of minor characters increases with each chapter, and brand new creations fill the canvas: Big Edna Brink, the Rinkwitzes, Addie Greeno, Harriet Hillyard and her son Kirk; John Beezer's son, Ernie, his daughter, Jennie, and Ernie's ex-wife Beatrice. Agatha's relationship with John Beezer is one of the more complex in the novel. With Edna Brink's help, the narrator introduces the retired farmer on page 3, describing how he "eats like an animal." Later, after suspecting him of stealing a brooch (18), Agatha finds "no guile" in him (50), which is high praise such as she has only bestowed on a few characters, the chief of whom is Lillian Kite. Later, in chapter sixteen, she sets about reforming Beezer's table manners. Kirk Hillyard is the last in a long line of Hassler "villains," a kind of "theme with variations" from earlier novels. Harriet Hillyard's fourth child, Kirk appears in the novel shortly after being released from prison where he was serving time for a drug offense. After being introduced as "sinister-looking," he displays a number of additional qualities unlikely to endear him to the reader. These include his crushing handshake and his habit of clipping his toenails onto a resident's carpet in chapter eighteen (113).

As would be expected in a novel about the elderly, *The New Woman* is full of references to death, diminishment, the loss of friends, and the need for respect. In time the story expands to include illness, suicide, drug use, and unprincipled behavior of various kinds. It is also about the capacity, or incapacity for happiness. Throughout, the narrator maintains a characteristic sensitivity to the elderly and their concerns, their particular struggles, fears, temptations, and even obsessions.

The Central Action

Agatha McGee, now eighty-seven, begins in fear, when her house "betrays her" during a power outage. She moves to the Sunset Senior Apartments, where she feels displaced and ignored. But, as happened in *The Staggerford Flood* and earlier Agatha McGee novels, in time she realizes that engagement with others and *their* needs is a tonic for her sense of worth, her happiness, and her energy. By the end of the story she is eighty-eight and speaking in the Staggerford high school auditorium, leading discussions on subjects such as moral choices (205) and changing careers (209).

Like many of the earlier novels, *The New Woman* employs a number of other "linked" plot-lines. The first finds Agatha believing her diamond brooch (a high school graduation present) has been stolen. When the possibility of theft grips the residents, Lillian Kite suggests securing everyone's valuables in an incongruously named "MX Shoebox." This humorous collection of valuables includes a pair of lottery tickets that Harriet Hillyard contributes. With Agatha's discovery of the missing brooch—it was never stolen—the plot moves, via the unexpected deaths of Lillian Kite and Thaddeus Druppers, to the exhumation plot. Before his death, Thaddeus Druppers places the MX Shoebox in Lillian's coffin. It is Kirk Hillyard who presses his mother to retrieve "a bunch of lottery tickets" buried with Lillian Kite. Kirk hopes a winning ticket will provide him with financial freedom. When he and his mother learn the tickets aren't winners, Kirk sulks. But soon John Beezer's son, Ernie, adds a soap opera element by offering to pay Kirk $250 to kidnap Ernie's daughter

Jennie from his ex-wife, Beatrice. Agatha's later interaction with Beatrice represents a particularly bizarre moment in the novel.

The Ernie Beezer plot morphs, via Frederick's former girl-friend, Lee Ann Raft, into Agatha's plan to create a support group for Frederick, who is suffering the loss of his girlfriend. All these plot lines cohere and are sustained by the relationships that form around Agatha. The chief of these is Agatha's friend-ship with Harriet Hillyard, and her growing friendship with and concern about John Beezer. The final plot-line involves Agatha's struggle to overcome her antipathy for a new resident.

The Catholic Dimension

Though not as central as it was in, say, *North of Hope*, Catholi-cism remains important in *The New Woman*. It begins in the second chapter, when Agatha says a prayer of thanks following the power outage at her house on River Street. It occurs again in chapter three when Agatha learns that the apartments' man-agement team, Edna and Joe Rinkwitz, are "probably … Polish Catholic" (17) but don't go to church.

> *Agatha winced as though slapped. She'd known others during her long life who had fallen away, but each new case caused her pain. The closer she herself came to the next life, the more of a mystery it was to her that anyone would risk eternal damnation by avoiding the holy sacrifice of the Mass.*

At the very least, Agatha's Catholic consciousness is on display, and it is passages like this that make *The New Woman*, despite its emphasis on plot, one of the more reflective—and subtly religious—of Hassler's late novels.

Thaddeus Druppers' death in chapter eleven allows the nar-rator, through the characters, to examine the Church's view of suicide. Agatha's continued reliance on Fr. Healy for moral guidance also assures the reader that the emphasis on Catholi-cism and Catholic values remains strong. In fact, Agatha's need for "moral guidance" in the penultimate chapter will be the subject of this chapter's last analysis, when Agatha visits Fr. Healy, ostensibly to talk about her next "support group" topic. But this encounter becomes, instead, a revelation of her changed attitude toward Corrine Bingham, and a kind of "miracle cure" (206).

Forms of Humor

Much of the early humor focuses on the habits of the elderly. Big Edna eats her own and John Beezer's pieces of pie (19). In a brief scene that borders on the bizarre, Lillian Kite visits Agatha's apartment, where she borrows toothpaste by scraping it off the wall where Little Edna Rinkwitz had used it to patch nail holes (34). Some of the humor occurs in digressive fragments, such as when, as she recoils at the idea of visiting an Indian casino, Agatha tries to recall where her image of "gambling" came from. She "decided it must have been a composite of movie scenes she'd watched on TV over the years. (She hadn't attended a movie theater since 1982, when Debra Winger, naked as a jaybird in *An Officer and a Gentleman*, crawled into bed with Richard Gere)."

When Agatha capitulates and joins the group going to Blue Sky Casino, her response to this turn of events becomes the novel's second running gag: "*What am I doing here?*" Then the exaggerative descriptions add subtly to the humor as Agatha notes a "ten- or fifteen-acre parking lot" and the "mammoth building." Commenting on the parking lot "with a thousand yellow lines painted on it," Agatha's seat partner on the bus, Thaddeus Druppers, adds a final touch of exaggeration. "He sighed like a man who's just been granted a glimpse of paradise and said, 'All that tar!'" At the casino, Lillian takes home the $5 worth of quarters that the casino gives to seniors as an "incentive" to gamble. Chapter 8 introduces a series of conversations taking place at the same time that makes for a standard form of Hassler humor. In this conversation, two characters' use of clichés is a sure sign of the author's ironic tone and satiric intent.

The final conversation thread initiates a satiric look at "liberal" educational ideas, as Agatha learns about the methods that Harriet Hillyard's daughter Laurie employs. With her students having no assigned seats and some students sitting on window sills, Laurie explains, using various liberal educational clichés: "It's so they don't grow up feeling restricted, so they can be unfettered and think for themselves" (45). A bit later she proclaims, "Childhood is a time for freedom." Agatha calls it "the return of the Dark Ages." The dramatic punch line comes at the end of chapter twenty-one, when Agatha visits Laurie's classroom in Bartlett and experiences the pandemonium first hand (142-144).

The MX Shoebox

Agatha's reflections on an out-of-date *Newsweek* article, about the testing of the MX missile-system, lead to an uncanny climax in chapter four, which is a lead-in to the humorous solution to the residents' fear of theft. Hassler's familiar, exaggerative imagination is on full display as Agatha considers the idea of the missile being carried on a train and thinks "*How novel*" (23).[8]

> *She imagined the MX missile carried round the country, across the South, up the East Coast and then west through the upper tier of states, including Minnesota. She pictured it chugging through Staggerford some night, the missile no doubt concealed in a boxcar with a false roof so that no one, except the crew of the train, knew what the deadly cargo was.*

Chapter five begins with a characteristically short sentence: "The shoebox was Lillian's idea" (24). Explaining that Agatha had told Lillian about the MX and her dream of a train carrying her brooch around the country, the narrator observes Lillian elaborating on this idea. "They would put their valuables in the shoebox and move it from room to room ... so that the thief would never know where to find it." In this way Agatha's uncanny dream becomes the stimulus for the bizarre solution to the residents' worries about theft.

But it will be Big Edna Brink who names it, "Watching her [Big Edna] write *MX Shoebox* on the pad, Agatha resented the way Big Edna Brink had taken over Lillian's project, but at the same time she felt that Big Edna's officiousness and enthusiasm proved her to be as trustworthy as Lillian said she was" (26). Ultimately, six Sunset residents put "valuables" in the shoebox, the most important of which is the "bunch of old lottery tickets" that Harriet Hillyard includes (33). When, in a moment of panic at Lillian Kite's funeral, Thaddeus Druppers puts the shoebox in her coffin, it sets the stage for one of the most bizarre episodes in all of Hassler's fiction.

The Exhumation

When, in chapter eleven, Big Edna asks whether Agatha wants Lillian's casket dug up to retrieve the shoebox, Agatha says "no." "She rather liked the thought of her two mementos in Lillian's keeping. There was something fitting about gifts from the two men in her life remaining for eternity with her oldest friend" (69). This reflection verges on the sentimental, but Agatha's next comment is an understated counterbalance. "'Besides,' she said, 'I know where they are and I won't lose them. Did I ever tell you I found my diamond brooch?.'" As chapter twelve develops the exhumation episode, and Harriet Hillyard admits that it is her son Kirk who is urging her to get the lottery tickets back, the potential of a "sordid" intergenerational theme emerges; older parents being bullied by their younger, unprincipled children.

The run-up to the exhumation is attended by numerous omens. First, there is the anecdote of the burial Mrs. Schmitt-bauer, the front ropes of whose coffin break, sending the coffin into the grave head-first. The gravediggers don't bother to right the coffin but fill in the grave with the coffin positioned as it is. Then a large stone breaks Junior Thompson's leg as he is about to reach Lillian's coffin (102). Finally, as the day for the exhumation arrives, a two-foot snowfall further complicates events.

Though the exhumation itself (chapter seventeen) is a kind of climax to the MX Shoebox plot, it is also an anti-climax. With four TV stations present, Mayor Mulholland descends into the grave and hands the shoebox to John Beezer, who has it snatched from him by Big Edna Brink. The opening of the box, which occurs in the backseat of the Mayor's car, is, like violence in classical drama, merely reported. As Agatha faces forward (not wanting to see the look of avarice on Kirk Hillyard's face), she only hears as the billfold is opened and Kirk Hillyard says, "'Dammit, dammit, Goddammit!" (110). In another classic ending, the final paragraph of chapter seventeen finds Agatha watching a TV news report in which the actual lottery winner comes forward on the very last day of the "sixty day grace period," with the winning ticket and his lawyer. "'I got a whole bunch of relations who'll try to get their hands on this money, and me and my lawyer took quite a little while to figure out how to keep it to myself'."

The Last Hardscrabble Girl

Like a number of the other chapters, chapter nineteen begins abruptly, with Kirk Hillyard dropping Ernie's daughter, Jennie, at Agatha's apartment door. He has obviously "kidnapped" Jennie, according to the plan.

> I'll call the police immediately, Agatha told herself. I won't be arrested as part of this hellish plot. But looking at the girl, she saw that her face was streaked with tears and her nose was running (117).

Though Agatha's reaction may seem somewhat exaggerated, and the description of Jennie, "who is about five," verges on the sentimental, in the next page and a half the reader becomes acquainted with Agatha McGee's last "hardscrabble girl." Hassler's deft handling of intergenerational exchanges is also on display.

They moved into the kitchenette and sat at the table. With Jennie munching on a Hydrox, Agatha asked if she went to school.

The girl answered weakly, "Kindygarden."

"I see, and what school do you go to?"

"The one by the post office."

"In Bartlett?"

After a moment's thought, the girl nodded (118).

Agatha's empathy enables her to identify with the softly crying little girl. "'I know exactly what you're feeling,' Agatha told her. 'Two months ago when I first moved in here, I wanted to cry myself.'" This confession, to a child who would scarcely understand, represents a rare degree of honesty and openness. As Jennie drinks milk and eats cookies, Agatha assimilates Jennie's experience to her own. "'Displacement is a terrible thing. That's what you're feeling right now, displaced.'" With a bit of irony directed at his protagonist, the narrator dramatizes Agatha's genuine care for others.

But to insure that the scene not become sentimental, the narrator shifts the focus as Agatha tries to occupy the child, who is prone to crying. Agatha shows Jennie her jewelry box. A coral necklace seems to satisfy the child and "She went over to Agatha's dressing table and admired herself in the mirror" (119). But when Jennie goes into the living room and says, "'Mr. Rogers is on'," Agatha seeks to exert her characteristic "guidance" for the new hardscrabble girl. "'Oh, we don't watch TV during the daytime.'" But Jennie "wept and screamed so loud" that Agatha quickly turns on the show. As Jennie sucks her thumb and fidgets with the coral necklace, Agatha "loved Mister Rogers instantly, particularly his polite, soft-spoken manner with children." Agatha's empathy makes her open to new experiences, even when suggested by a child.

Enter Corrine Bingham

A final narrative episode begins with a support group for Frederick Lopat. The reader learns little about why his live-in girlfriend, Lee Ann Raft, leaves him for the divorcée, Ernie Beezer, but Agatha tries to get Frederick to talk about his depression, even sharing her own experience of it when she first came to Sunset. He says little, but the reader gets a glimpse of Frederick's grief when he sits down in front of a TV talk show to which he pays no attention. The narrator slips into the veteran's perspective as he recalls a girl he met in a bar while he was a soldier in Vietnam. She "was taking him home with her. He was so happy he could hardly contain himself." But the girl ran out ahead of him and was blown up by "a grenade that came sailing in from out of nowhere" (155). With the loss of Lee Ann, Frederick feels the same sense of loss and grief that he had in Vietnam. Frederick takes Agatha to a Parkinson's support group. She is looking for other possible members for the "mental health support group" (158) she intends to form for Frederick. An "old woman wrapped in a black, wooly shawl" shows interest.

When, at the beginning of chapter twenty-four, the Monday night support group convenes for the first time in the dining room of Sunset Senior Apartments, "the heavy woman in the black shawl" (161) is there. When, in order to give other members a chance to talk, Agatha stops Mrs. Severson's expression of grief over the recent death of her husband, Agatha points to the woman in the black shawl, and the reader gets a first detailed description. "This woman, seen up close, was a mess. Her hair was unclean and unkempt, lying plastered over her ears and forehead. Her eyes were bloodshot. She spoke in a measured, toneless voice ..." The woman reveals that she had spent thirty-five years in a mental institution in St. Peter, Minnesota. When, a bit later, Agatha has the group draw pictures of their families, the woman in the shawl objects. "I did this pitcher so many times in the hospital that I'm sick and tired of it" (164).

With her "heavy threatening gaze" and then a "small smile playing across her lips," the woman with the shawl becomes a figure of mystery. A bit later Agatha is asking herself: *Who is that woman? ... and why does she intimidate me so?*

The revelation comes when Frederick later reveals the heavy woman's identity: Corrine Bingham, the mother of Beverly, and the person who had killed Miles Pruitt at the end of *Staggerford*. The exact reason for Corrine Bingham's release from St. Peter isn't made clear. Before the end of the chapter, however, Agatha is on the phone with a local judge and former student, asking how and why Corrine Bingham was released from the asylum. The judge conjectures parole, or a "budget shortfall." Agatha slams down the phone then reflects on her behavior: "she couldn't seem to control the emotion—the anger—caused by Mrs. Bingham being back in circulation."

In chapter twenty-five, Agatha's "detached" response to John Beezer breaking an heirloom eggcup prepares for her visit to Fr. Frank Healy. When John offers to pay for the eggcup, Agatha says, "'There was a time in my life when that eggcup meant a great deal to me but not anymore'" (172). Like her response to the *Newsweek* article several chapters earlier, this statement signals another stage of aging. The next sentence is an important moment of reflection. "For several minutes, getting ready to visit the parish house, she puzzled over this statement, wondering why it was true." Even in the midst of the inner turmoil she feels when she is around Mrs. Bingham, Agatha is capable of recognizing a significant change in herself. If she had to put a name to it, she herself would probably not use a current term like "relinquishment."

She tells Fr. Healy she is visiting about "'a moral problem ... I find myself—could it be?—hating someone.'" She briefly explains her encounters with Corrine Bingham and asks for advice. Frank Healy, who admits, "'I have had no experience with hatred'" (173), urges her to "'perform some act of kindness toward Mrs. Bingham, and let me know what comes of it, if anything.'" As Agatha prepares for the Monday night discussion of "experiences with death," she recalls Fr. Healy's having minimized her anger and defiance against God after Lillian's death. He had said, "'Don't worry about it, Miss McGee. God is big. God can take it.'" Agatha starts the next Monday's support group meeting by sharing her exchange with Fr. Healy. "Her account of her own reaction to death took only fifteen minutes. She concluded with Father Healy's advice to her concerning her anger at God. 'He said to me, "Relax, Miss McGee. God is big. God can take it." Well, I have pondered those words long and hard, and I don't know what to make of them. I mean, suppose he's right? I would truly love to think that it makes no difference to God how mad I get at funerals'" (178).

After Bernice Falk and Nadine Oppegard speak about their responses to death, another former student, Sylvia White Hoffman, begins to speak, "when Mrs. Bingham blurted out, 'How much longer do we have to listen to this crap? My ass is gettin' mighty tired'" (179). Agatha's response is telling. "Agatha suddenly felt so exhausted that she couldn't utter a word of reprimand." To explain to herself her exhaustion, Agatha considers the "three quarters of an hour" she has been on her feet, and a theory she had "that a good class always fed energy into the teacher, while a difficult class took energy away." Agatha feels better once Corrine Bingham has left the room. Then the stories of women's experiences of death continue. Chapter twenty-six ends with Agatha calling John Beezer, and Corrine Bingham answering it. Agatha hangs up, thinking she has gotten the wrong number (185). At the start of chapter twenty-seven Agatha learns that Corrine Bingham is John's sister.

When, in chapter twenty-seven, Fr. Healy calls Agatha to ask how her encounter with Mrs. Bingham went, Agatha admits, "'Not well at all, Father. She left early and I didn't get a chance to do her a kindness'" (187). When Agatha admits that "'the Lord only knows what I'll do for her,'" Fr. Healy again says, "'Relax, Miss McGee. Sooner or later the opportunity will present itself, and you'll know.'" Agatha's opportunity to do a kindness comes sooner than she could have thought. When John Beezer brings his sister to Agatha's apartment, it is to ask Agatha to give his sister the same kind of lessons in proper speaking that she had been giving him. "Agatha would remember this conversation for the rest of her days. She thought it marked a turning point in her life. She knew she could not turn down this request. This was what Father Healy had spoken of. He'd said the opportunity to do a kindness to Mrs. Bingham would present itself, and Agatha had promised to seize it" (193-94).

Even as Agatha begins her lessons with Corrine Bingham, she experiences the same "hateful, angry scowl" and "forbidding look" (195). Then Judge Caferty calls to tell Agatha that Mrs. Bingham "was not a danger to herself or the public anymore. 'She's nearly eighty years old and going blind.'" Agatha cannot believe this news. "'Going blind?' said Agatha. 'She's no more blind than I am.'" But later, in the lunch line at Sunset, Agatha corrects Mrs. Bingham and notices, instead of the angry scowl, "a thoughtful look on her face."

Over the course of the next days, Agatha's relationship with Corrine Bingham is transformed. "Agatha discovered Mrs. Bingham to be an even quicker study than her brother." Agatha overhears Corrine telling Big Edna about the 1984 blizzard when their father died, and Agatha realizes "she was behaving like her fellow residents. *At this rate*, thought Agatha, *perhaps I won't have anything to fear from Mrs. Bingham come next Monday evening*" (198). Agatha notices the improvements in posture, language, and her polite responses over coffee (199). Then, one evening, when the Beezer men come to Agatha's apartment to pick up Jennie (who had asked to watch cartoons in Agatha's apartment), Agatha asks about Corrine's scowl. "'Yep, it takes some getting used to all right,' said Ernie" (200). Then John

Beezer explained that "it was his sister's habit of trying to see people she was talking to. 'She's dang near totally blind, you know, and squintin' like that's the only way she can make out who it is'" (200). This mundane resolution to a potentially uncanny glance is a classic Hassler technique to balance the everyday and the mysterious.

Some Archetypal Reflections

Once again, in *The New Woman*, as in a number of earlier novels, the archetypal comes swaddled in the mundane. Agatha's reaction to Corrine Bingham and her angry scowl takes on the proportions of an almost demonic possession. It is a mixture of hatred and fear. In the presence of Corrine Bingham, Agatha feels a strange, almost mysterious exhaustion come over her. The scowl continues to haunt Agatha. When she offers to give Mrs. Bingham lessons in proper speech, and when she learns that the woman's scowl is a way for the woman to compensate for her failing eyesight, hatred melts away and is transformed into pity.

Chapter twenty-nine—the shortest in the novel—brings the Agatha-Corrine Bingham plot to a climax and a close. Wanting his advice on the topic (moral choices), and to invite him to the next support group meeting, Agatha visits Fr. Healy again. In the course of their conversation he asks, "'By the way, how are you coming with your nemesis,[9] the woman from prison?'" Sounding like the former teacher, she says, "'I may be gaining the upper hand. It's too soon to tell, of course, but her behavior seems to be improving.'" To Fr. Healy's, "'Ah, and your hatred of her?'" Agatha's response is almost offhanded. "Agatha searched her heart for hatred and found not a trace of it remaining. She shrugged and said, "'I must be cured.'" This statement suggests that it was *she* who had been "ill," or even possessed by her hatred. Agatha's response also suggests that she remains somewhat unconscious of what has just happened. "'The woman still causes a strong reaction in me, Father, but it doesn't feel like hatred. It feels more like pity'" (206). Agatha's experience is not unlike what Jungian psychologists and the critical anthropologist and literary critic, René Girard, have argued. One's hate and fear often represent an ignorance of one's own feelings, a blindness to one's own shadow, making every encounter an almost debilitating encounter with one's own darker self.

The denouement of the Agatha-Corrine plot is also a resolution of the theme of happiness. Asking whether he has "any other experiments" for her, Agatha prepares to leave Fr. Healy's rectory and receives this response: "'No, but thank you very kindly,' he answered, not understanding her facetiousness and then added, 'But you can come and see me more often.'" This is the moment for yet another almost transformative revelation; this time one that Agatha herself makes. "*Why, this man really is fond of me,* she thought as she allowed him to give her a brief hug at the door. She was shocked to hear herself say aloud, 'I'm lucky to have lived so long.' What she meant was that she was overcome with a degree of happiness such as she hadn't felt for many years" (206). Reviewing what had happened in the previous twelve weeks (of the novel), she concludes: "For a moment she felt something close to ecstasy. In other words, she felt like a new woman."

Conclusion

The last chapter of *The New Woman*—taking place in early December, ten months after chapter twenty-nine—ties together a few loose ends and confirms the sense that Agatha McGee has acclimated well to her new home, and her new role in the community. This last chapter, most of which is told from Frederick Lopat's viewpoint, begins on the night of another "town hall" style meeting. The reader learns that Corrine Bingham has died of a heart attack and that the next meeting of what was once Frederick's "support group" is now a weekly event, taking place in the Staggerford High School gym. The reader also learns that the weekly meeting "fuels her engine." Through Frederick, the narrator identifies some of the former students and retirees in attendance. At the end of the hour and a half, Bernice Dodson proposes the topic "lifelong friends" for the next meeting. On the drive home, Frederick and Agatha discuss her age and the energy the meetings require of her. He asks if she has considered giving them up. "'I get far too much out of them ever to give them up, Frederick. Besides, they're better than sleeping pills. They wear me out so that I get a good night's sleep'" (213). Compared to some of the other novels, this subtle sense of Agatha's rejuvenation in the final chapter of *The New Woman* nevertheless underlines Andrew Greeley's conclusion that Hassler's novels often leave his characters "not perfectly happy, but happy enough to sustain [them] into old age" (Greeley, "The Last Catholic Novelist," 23-24).

The Staggerford Murders[10]

It is early in the 2000s; Hassler's health continues to deteriorate, but he continues to write. He tries his hand at drama, adapting an early short story, "Yesterday's Garbage," enlarging it with additional comic and satiric characters, complicating the plot and introducing familiar themes, like greed and child molestation, and calling it *The Staggerford Murders*. Then he turns the play into a novella, publishing it with *The Life and Death of Nancy Clancy's Nephew*, another adaptation of an early short story. The two novellas are "linked" in only the most superficial and tenuous ways.

Throughout the process of transforming the play into the novella, Hassler continues to try out new techniques. One of the cleverest probably derives from the dramatic version; it is the idea of presenting the narrative through the voices of five different characters who had major parts in the play. Each first-person narrator has a chapter or two or three to tell a part of the story from *his* point of view. To liken this technique to

William Faulkner's *The Sound and the Fury* only points up the caricature, and the satire involved. At one hundred and one pages, this is not a novel, let alone a major one. And there is nothing like the lyricism, passion, and seriousness that Faulkner mustered in that early "experiment." Hassler is just "having his cake and eating it too." He has frequently moved the narrative viewpoint from character to character in order to achieve the maximum effect. Here, the narrator is able to enter all five viewpoints, in sixteen short chapters, developing the unique flavor of each character as he comments on the other characters. Each chapter moves the plot along as the individual narrator adds digressive anecdotes and apparently random details of everyday life in small-town Minnesota. Meanwhile, Hassler takes every opportunity along the way for humor and satire. He makes the principal narrator of the short story, re-tired Finnish garbage collector and widower, Dusty Luuya, older, sicker, and even more absent-minded than he was in "Yesterday's Garbage," but with the same moral obtuseness. He then develops a minor character, Grover, into a principal narrator, who might be a stand-in for the author himself.

While by genre *TSM* is a kind of melodramatic murder mystery, thematically it is heterogeneous, to say the least. With two of the chief narrators being elderly men, old age is an important "background" theme. Though touched on only briefly, the accusation that the original murder victim, Edward W. (Needy) Nichols, was molesting his daughter, Penny Jean, is a shadowy, dark element in the story and, in fact, one of the "motives" for his wife, Blanche Nichols, wanting to mur-der her husband. Her second husband, George Bauer, and his greed for the Nichols' property, along with implied desire for Blanche, adds a further dark motivation for Blanche's murder and much of the subsequent action. Then, of course, the in-troduction of Ollie Luuya, the former derelict, now itinerant fundamentalist preacher, and his made-up quotations from the strangest canon of Scripture imaginable, adds an element of religious satire to the mix.

Hassler lets the first three characters—Grover, Ollie and Dusty—tell their stories as though they are all together in the lobby of Staggerford's rundown Ransford Hotel. Thereafter, alternating narrators move the action out of the hotel in a more conventional narrative manner. By the end Grover has become the principal narrator, and it is Grover's voice that the reader hears in the concluding chapter.

Among a number of less important changes from the short story, Hassler switches the murder from July 4th to the Saturday before the Eve of Christmas. The scene is much the same as in another early short story, "The Willowby Indian." It is the town's Christmas Eve Saturday matinee for children. Hassler also changes the names of the murdered couple in the short story from Grosneth to Nichols and adds Susie Nesbitt as an off-again, on-again love-interest for Ollie. "The main cog over at the Chamber of Commerce office" (18), Susie is a prickly character with whom Ollie Luuya has a fraught relationship. She is introduced in the second chapter where Ollie says he "kicked her out" of his church because she was so bossy. The reader also learns more about her when Ollie details her and Ollie's Catholic grade school background.

One character who plays an important part in "Yesterday's Garbage" is relegated to a less than minor role in *TSM*. That is Dusty's late wife, Caledonia Wolsey. "Cal'donie," as Dusty refers to her, is one of the two chief characters in the short story. Her hoarding and her deductive skills uncover the first clues to the murder that is central to *TSM*. In chapter three, Dusty provides a vignette of "Cal'donie." A final minor character, old Mrs. Heffington, is only referred to a few times, but it is her interest in Grover that precipitates his return to Florida, alone, at the end of the story.

Murder Mystery Clues

Hassler has always been good at dropping hints and providing clues to whatever secrets or mysteries his novels contain. In this parody of a melodramatic murder mystery, that skill is on display. In the first few pages Grover notices a letter from Penny Jean Nichols in the *Staggerford Weekly*, seeking information about her mother, who disappeared nine years earlier. A page or two later, in the story of Dusty coming to the Ransford, Grover tells how Dusty only brought along his easy chair and "a great big rock—he calls it a keepsake" (8). The rock turns out to have been part of Blanche Nichols' murder. Three pages later, as Grover talks about Edward W. Nichols' murder ("shot in the chest, a twenty-two-caliber bullet right through the heart"), Dusty interrupts with, "I got me a rat gun that's a twenty-two revolver. Me and Cal'donie used to go out to the dump on summer nights and shoot rats" (11). Dusty's rat gun turns out to have been the murder weapon, disposed of in the Nichols' garbage, which Dusty scavenged.

There are even "false clues" and "false deductions." Grover speculates that Nichols' "'was a gangland murder. Nichols was into porn'" (12). Grover deduces this from the "pictures of naked people" Nichols brought to work, and the size of the house he built. "'Where does the executive secretary of the Staggerford Chamber of Commerce get the money for a spread like that?'" Grover asks. Dusty's various "non-sequiturs" are only apparently false "clues." At one point he claims, "'Old man Nichols, his wife's dead, too, you know.'" Grover tries to "ignore him when he talks nonsense." But a few moments later Ollie tells Dusty "'we don't really know what happened to Mrs. Nichols,'" to which Dusty responds, "'The flower lady over on Hillcrest? Oh, she's dead all right. Deader'n a doornail. I kilt her'" (14).

The Basic Plot, with Back-Story

Other details of the murder come out in the first four chapters. Mrs. Nichols shot her husband outside the Staggerford Theater,

in order to protect their daughter, Penny Jean, who was being molested. George Bauer gave Blanche the gun to do it and
helped her rehearse the deed. When Ned is dead, George marries Blanche. On one of his garbage collection days, Dusty, with
the information Caledonia had gleaned from their garbage, tells
Mrs. Nichols he knows about the murder. She pokes him with
a broom and breaks his ribs. Dusty punches her, and—in his
telling—she falls down dead. But then, when he returns, he sees
George Bauer with a rock as he "dropped it on her head" (38).

The Old Age Theme

As noted, old age is an important background to *The Staggerford Murders*. The novella opens with Grover, the eighty-one
year old desk clerk of the Ransford Hotel, commenting on his
long-time tenant, Dusty. "I can tell it's one of those mornings
when Dusty's at loose ends and he's going to spend the day attached to me like a bloodsucker" (3). Old age dependency becomes an issue. Then Grover says, "I can kill three hours easy on
the *Weekly*" suggesting the boredom that can occur in old age.
The reader learns that Grover is indeed an old man, celebrating
his eighty-first birthday (9), and this precipitates an argument
about Dusty's age. Dusty doesn't recall how old he is, but he
has been retired from garbage collecting for some years. When
Grover tells Dusty to look at his driver's license, Dusty says he
lost it (another symptom of old age). Dusty's falling asleep in the
lobby is another sign of old age, and here it is also a sign of the
heart disease that will become a factor in the plot. Dusty's "little
heart attack," and his taking "nitro" to control his "angie pecca-
doris" (23) is a short-lived running gag that presages what Grover calls a "granddaddy of a heart attack" (41) that later sends
Dusty to the hospital.

In the short (one-page) chapter four, Grover notes the arrival of George Bauer, "a great, big, white-haired guy wearing a
ten-gallon hat on his head and a sneer on his lips" (33). At this

point the novel moves into the realm of melodrama. Bauer is a caricature but the reader, expecting merely hyperbole and bluster, will get something of a surprise two chapters later.

In the fifth chapter, Dusty, in the presence of George Bauer, tells the story of Blanche Nichols' murder, including Bauer's part in it. Then, the sixth chapter moves the action seamlessly along but adds complexity as Grover states, "Those are the last words out of Dusty's mouth, because the next minute he's having himself a granddaddy of a heart attack" (41). With Dusty's heart attack, Hassler turns the story in the direction of a satiric-comic sit-com or TV soap opera. In Bauer's chapter seven, as he works on Penny Jean, he provides further exposition about the circumstances of the murder. Here Bauer himself transcends sentimentality and becomes a true villain by shocking Penny Jean when he bluntly reveals, "Your mother's buried in the city dump" (49), having learned this from Dusty in Chapter Six.

Dusty's final appearance as narrator occurs in chapter eight and is a zany contrast. The whole chapter in the hospital ("'I've watched enough *E.R* to know a hospital when I see one'") is an elaborate digression as Dusty—perhaps mentally impaired — describes what he calls an "Assumption" in Crusty's diner (51-52).[11] As reported by Dusty, Hap Conlon's being lifted up has to be taken at least somewhat seriously. But this is one of Hassler's gifts: to make the improbable seem plausible, in the context of the everyday world. The switch to Ollie's perspective in chapter nine makes possible further digressions as the reader learns more about Ollie's past. He goes to see Susie and concocts his idea to baptize Dusty in the hospital.

A chapter in Grover's viewpoint (chapter ten) is slapstick, with a trip to church for a blessing of the car they are driving (and all its contents), then on to the hospital (69) to baptize Dusty, where the humor becomes a (somewhat grim) TV sit-com, with Ollie trying to read the rite while Grover holds the book. The farce continues until Dusty loses his oxygen tube and "flat-lines." Then the scene grows soap-opera grim as George Bauer comes in to smother the already deceased Dusty, who was the only witness to Bauer's murdering Blanche Nichols.

The remaining short chapters by Ollie (11), Grover (12), Henry Jr. (13), Grover (14), Ollie again (15), and finally Grover (16) take thirty pages, but the chief action is already over. In chapter 14 Grover is in Coral Gables, Florida, and this is really the start of the denouement. Ollie's final appearance in the short chapter fifteen moves him and Grover back to Minnesota in the spring for the third trial of George Bauer. There the story introduces a bit of courtroom drama, and the reader learns that Ollie will stay in Minnesota.

Because the prosecutor has no evidence to prove that George Bauer killed Blanche Nichols, the Staggerford part of the story ends with George Bauer's being found guilty in civil court of defrauding Penny Jean. But she only gets the Nichols home and $5,000. Among the mundane—and humorous—details are the fact that Penny Jean's husband, Sandy Sanderson, needs to get back to the ice cream store where he works in Fresno, California, and Bauer's wife Margie (44) is too busy with her bowling team to come to her husband's trial. All of this is, of course, standard Hassler satiric humor.

Grover begins chapter 16 with signature abruptness, "Guilty, Your Honor" (94). After reporting the jury's verdict and the consequences for George Bauer, Grover hits the road, hitch-hiking back to Coral Gables, to avoid the clutches of Widow Heffington. Herman Schroeder, a garrulous retired car salesman (100), picks him up near the Florida line, and Schroeder's digressive stories of mother and wife lead into the understated and slightly off-center conclusion. Schroeder, who Grover decides is looking for "somebody to tell his troubles to" (97), buys a condo in the complex where Grover lives with his sister, Grace (87). Schroeder's stories of his Navy father, a Greyhound trip across country, and his wife's death (more religious satire) are vintage

Hassler digressions. The novella ends with Grover "tuning out" Schroeder when Schroeder's stories are not interesting, calling Schroeder a new "Dusty."

Imagery and Humor

Unlike Hassler's novels, *The Staggerford Murders* contains little natural description. Even the change of seasons is at most briefly noted. Characters use some familiar clichés like "blow his stack" (10) and "blowing his cork" (14). Grover's laconic, if sometimes clichéd humor benefits from *TSM* having started out as a stage play. An early interaction between Grover and Dusty, over Grover's eighty-first birthday, is right out of vaudeville or a stand-up comedy routine.

Ollie Luuya's name is an onomatopoetic, almost meta-fictional parody, and his supposed quotations from Scripture constitute a running gag. Early in the first chapter, Grover records Ollie's response to an argument between himself and Dusty. Ollie says, "'*Straighten up and fly right, sayeth the Lord, and beat thy anger into plowshares* – chapter one, Paul's letter to the Carpathians'" (10). A little later, in connection with Dusty defaming the deceased Ned Nichols, Ollie responds with "'And the dead you will always have with you, sayeth the Lord,' Paul's letter to the Theologians, chapter eighteen'" (13). The snappy end of the first chapter finds Ollie responding to Dusty's criticism. "His ears turn red; but he holds himself in by quoting the Bible. 'Avoid storm and strife,' he says. 'Treat thy neighbor as thou wouldst be treated thyself. Geronimo, chapter three'" (15).

Fundamentalism and Religious Satire

Such religious satire has long been part of Hassler's writing. From *Staggerford*, with Agatha McGee's pre-Vatican II Catholicism, to the "liberal" Catholicism of Bishop Baker and Sister Judith Juba, Hassler has never been shy about being critical of his own denomination. That focus continues in *TSM*. Hassler uses an anecdote about May Day to characterize Susie Nesbitt's stubbornness, but it also has a satirical punch line. Ollie tells how Susie threw a tantrum when Sister Angeline did not choose her as "Queen of the May" at St. Isidore's Junior High, selecting instead one Mary Catherine Corcoran. Ollie's explanation of the May Day ritual has some edge to it.

> *May Day was the highlight of the year for Sister Angeline. You can read about May Day in books, and how it got started as a fertility ritual. It makes you think, doesn't it, how the church took it over and went the other direction with it. I mean, virginity instead of fertility. Honoring the statue of Mary instead of dancing around some phallic-looking maypole (19).*

But, as if that comment is not enough, Ollie adds a further anecdotal punch line. "I guess it was Mary Catherine Corcoran's peerless grade-point average that made her queen. I wondered, too, if it would have made a difference had Sister Angeline known that Mary Catherine had been letting boys diddle her in the grove of trees behind the blacksmith's shop since the sixth grade" (19). There is a certain poetic rightness to a satiric line that ends with a supposedly virginal "Queen of the May" also representing something like a fertility goddess.

Following this gentle satire on Catholicism, *The Staggerford Murders* then makes fundamentalism its target. Ollie Luuya's humorous quoting of imagined scripture passages is a running gag. It is also probably a hold-over from the dramatic version, when, one can imagine, it brought many laughs. But the religious satire may cut more than one way, depending on how one looks at it. Ollie was raised a Catholic.

> *In those days we were brought up with a heavy dose of church, and it sticks to you like Velcro. I guess quite a few of my classmates stayed Catholic, while I found another way. But aren't we all brothers and sisters under the skin? Amen, I say to you,*

Lutherans and Hottentots shall lie down together like lambs in the peaceable kingdom. Paul's letter to the Romanians, chapter twelve (20).

From "In those day…" with its echo of the Gospels, this passage obviously satirizes the loss of faith or a change of denomination. But the wildly imaginative garbling of Scripture makes the whole passage extravagantly hyperbolic and verging on nasty parody. With the exception of the digressive "Assumption" story in chapter eight, for the rest of the story the religious satire is generally subdued, though still present, until Hassler "winds down" the story of Grover heading back to Florida alone. Grover reports that Ollie is staying in Minnesota because, as a preacher, he doesn't like "the style of worship" in the South, where people are always interrupting the speaker.

Conclusion

The Staggerford Murders moves from melodrama to farce, with a fair dose of TV sitcom and soap opera thrown in. Like the play from which it was adapted, it is almost sheer entertainment, for the reader and—we assume—the author. If there is any poignancy, it is in the portrayal of old age, Dusty's nostalgic recollection of Caledonia, and Grover's replacing one annoying companion with another. Compared to the second novella in the collection, *The Staggerford Murders* is the comic balance to a sadder and more serious exploration of old age, depression, loyalty, and betrayal, with a touching final revelation that is completely absent from *The Staggerford Murders*.

The Life and Death of Nancy Clancy's Nephew[12]

In his writings about rural Minnesota life, Hassler has depicted the occasional farmer. Sometimes, as in *North of Hope*, they are brother farmers, men worn out and often broken from working the land alone or nearly alone. In strong contrast to the relatively loquacious Agatha McGee, they are generally taciturn

271

or manifest at best a dry, laconic sense of humor. As such they resemble the parody of Scandinavian Minnesota farmers that Garrison Keillor popularized on this radio show, *A Prairie Home Companion*.

The second novella contained in the volume titled *The Staggerford Murders* is *The Life and Death of Nancy Clancy's Nephew*, the story of such a farmer. One could hardly imagine a stronger contrast to the volume's title piece in narrative strategy, focus, theme, or tone. Whereas *TSM* is a satiric farce presented from the perspectives of five different characters, *Life and Death* employs a conventional, somewhat distant but empathetic third-person narrator most often in the perspective of an eighty-two year old farmer. The theme is aging and diminishment, and the tone is, by turns, satiric, elegiac, solemn, agonizingly poignant, and as such a thoughtful and thought-provoking tale of aging. One could argue that the narrator encourages a "reverent" attitude toward W.D. and his world, an openness to mystery—with an arguably visionary ending.

Like *The Staggerford Murders. The Life and Death of Nancy Clancy's Nephew* began as a short story, "Nancy Clancy's Nephew," published in *The North American Review* and later in the collection, *Rufus at the Door and Other Stories*. Comparing the short story with the novella, the first thing a reader will notice is that the short story (sixteen pages long) is the basis for the final, twenty-four page, sixth chapter of the novella. To use an artistic analogy (such as the author himself might approve), Hassler has taken a focused and detailed sketch of old age, the protagonist's climactic visit to his aunt Nancy Clancy, and turned it into a complex portrait, deepened and shadowed with nuance and chiaroscuro. Or, like one of Hassler's own landscape paintings of fields and a few isolated farms, the story introduces isolated characters who feel and reveal little about their inner lives. The isolation of the characters and the starkness of the portrayal can suggest the bleakness of rural Minnesota life.

For the novella, Hassler changes the protagonist's name from George Post (who is seventy-five) to W.D. Nestor (who, by the end, is eighty-two). In the short story, little mention is made of George Post's wife, and there is no reference to a son. It is George's daughter who cares for her father, and she is married to a Mr. Mullens, who is a traveling salesman, not a farmer. It is Mrs. Mullens who agrees to drive her father to town to visit Aunt Nancy Clancy, leaving him with Nancy Clancy while she goes shopping.

The chief additions that make the novella the complex story it is are the sections, largely flashbacks, concerning W.D. Nestor's brother, Albert, W.D.'s wife, Lucille, and W.D.'s relationship with a young "latch-key kid" named Kevin Luuya, as well as the story of W.D.'s son, Sonny, who left home as a teenager and was never heard from again. Hassler drops a key digression from the short story and, instead, expands the story of a little boy whom Kevin and W.D. meet outside Nancy Clancy's apartment. This episode includes a potentially symbolic event with the little boy's kite. For the final, climactic chapter of the novella, Hassler also augments the short story with W.D.'s recollections of Lucille, his own brief confusion of Kevin Luuya with Sonny (when he introduces Kevin to Nancy Clancy), and a careful rearrangement of the final two pages.

At first, W.D. Nestor might seem indistinguishable from the host of Midwest farmers who have appeared in Hassler's novels and stories. It is a complex, subtly ironic, but moving story of a man who grows old without having come to a sense of self-understanding commensurate with his age. While sympathetically told, it is also without doubt one of the sharpest critiques Hassler has applied to any character in his fiction. *The Life and Death of Nancy Clancy's Nephew* is the portrait of an emotionally and spiritually crippled old man who experiences one moment of deeply felt humanity before he dies.

The challenge for a writer whose work, for decades, embodied the Roethkean principle that "things throw light on things" is to maintain that perspective as he seeks to depict an individual life and a community whose chief attributes are disconnection, alienation, and isolation. The characters in this work have few relations, in both senses of the word: few near family members and few lasting ties to others in the community. Nevertheless, Hassler's careful depiction of W.D. Nestor emerges as key to the story's overall empathic sensibility. In the portrait of W.D. this empathy is not readily apparent but is rather something caught, as if out of the corner of one's eye. Unlike many of Hassler's other characters, who are attentive observers of the world and their own lives, W.D. becomes increasingly insensitive to much that occurs around him, including his own diminishments and limitations. It is, rather, the narrator who "attends to" things, even as W.D. sees less and less – both literally and figuratively.[13] Except for the now familiar Hasslerian flashbacks, the narrator seldom ventures far beneath the surface of W.D.'s mind. The reader's view of W.D.'s inner life is, therefore, oblique, fragmented, and conjectural. The effect is a flat, unreflective portrayal that gives a somber sense of rural life around the fictional town of Bartlett, Minnesota, somewhere along the South Dakota border. Our "sense of the whole" and how "things throw light on things" is only there obliquely, by negation or implication, until the last few pages of the story.

It is primarily through W.D.'s memories—spare, specific flashbacks, but muted, bleak, and just slightly out of focus (or cloaked in darkness and snow)—that Hassler is able to depict the pervading sense of W.D.'s disconnection, loss, and sadness. The novella's putative title character provides an example of this. Until the last chapter, Nancy Clancy is just a distant relative, referred to only twice. Though Nancy is said to keep track of "half a dozen branches of the family (141)," these few early references merely serve to underline the actual aloofness and disconnectedness of the family's relationships.[14] As far as W.D. goes, the title's placing him last—and not even naming him—indicates a "suppression" of the character that the story embodies and that the narrator strives to overcome.

Near the opening of the final chapter (which was the substance of the short story) Hassler includes a passage that—for one familiar with the author's life—reads like a painter's signature in the corner of his work.

> *Without help, W.D. shuffled through a puddle of melting ice near the back door, moving each foot an inch at a time and leaning heavily on his rubber-tipped cane. Halfway through the puddle he stopped to survey the distance he had come and, turning, he nearly lost his balance. (177)*

Well along in the course of the supranuclear palsy that would take his life, the author describes a man who moves slowly and whose balance is precarious at best. This is just one of the many details that make *The Life and Death of Nancy Clancy's Nephew* a poignant portrayal of old age, diminishment, and its attendant woes.

The novella's only references to religion—Protestant and evangelical—are incidental and satiric. The one explicit reference to religion comes when W.D. elopes with Lucille Schuler (an orphan and another of Hassler's "hardscrabble girls"). They drive together to Abernathy, South Dakota, where they are married by Joe Smiddick, a school friend of W.D.'s, who has become a minister and now the pastor of the Abernathy Gospel Chapel. The Reverend Smiddick is one of Hassler's most gently humorous vignettes of a clergyman, but, gentle as it is, the satiric perspective does not present a very positive view of rural Christianity in the late twentieth century. Yet there is a truth in the portrait of the pastor ("Around here I'm known as the Little Preacher"), and an element of empathy for a young man trying to find meaning in his own life as he helps others to find it in theirs.

The introduction of the "Little Preacher" might recall to

some readers, by ironic contrast, Rev. John James, the congrega-
tional minister in Marilynne Robinson's *Gilead, Home*, and *Lila*.
Gentle humor on Smiddick bringing the village church "back
from the dead" keeps Hassler's depiction light; no harsh satire.
When the reader learns that W.D. Nestor's son, Sonny, had left
home, never to return, and that W.D. grieved for him, this recalls Jack Boughton, the prodigal son of Rev. John James's friend
and fellow minister, Robert Boughton. The fact that *Gilead* and
The Life and Death of Nancy Clancy's Nephew appeared in the
same year, 2004, precludes the possibility of direct influence,
but the presence of similar motifs should bid the reader and
critic pause to consider the archetypal nature of the relationships and the themes.

W.D. is a stoical, undemonstrative individual, and with
good reason. He has had a difficult life, and the reader learns
of the difficulties only indirectly, through the flashbacks. He
grew up on a farm, one of two sons. When W.D. was nineteen and his brother Albert was twenty-one, Albert was shot to
death one hunting season by a hunter who was never found.
At first Albert's mother thinks that W.D. killed him, and for a
brief time fears that he may shoot her too. W.D. does not cry
over his brother's death: "He shed no tears that day or at any
time afterward—not until the final weeks of his life, over sixty years later" (114). This utter emotional repression, born of
tragedy, determines the story's tone and gives it a strangeness
bordering on the grotesque. Even when Sonny runs away as a
teenager, and W.D. loses his wife to Alzheimer's, his response
remains impassive.

When he is seventy-two (the point at which the story begins), W.D.'s farm has shrunk to a turkey lot run by his daughter
Viola and her husband Kermit Kilbride and leased to the local
poultry processor. One of the more subtle, but also more obvious, examples of Hassler's insight into the minds of older adults
is the way he suggests W.T. Nestor's anger and lack of charity.

Neither Viola nor W.D. has much forbearance or kindness in the treatment of each other. When W.D. comes in from running, he wipes his feet, but Viola still orders him: "Wipe your feet." He says "I did." But she returns: "There's droppings in your cuffs." Later, when she serves him prunes without pits, he complains, "'What happened to these?'... She tells him he can't eat the pits. 'I never ate the pits when they weren't pitted.'" At the end he says of the whole bowl, "'Throw 'em out. They took out the flavor with the pits'" (124). This is a willful, even petulant self-deprivation, because things aren't the way he's used to them. A few pages later, at the end of an abortive run on the country road, W.D. is sitting out a shower under a bridge. "It occurred to him that, like himself, the world was very old and set in its ways" (126).

The one routine to which W.D. clings is his mile-a-day jog around the turkey yard.[15] He began the habit years before, after he and his wife had watched a newsreel clip together about the Finnish runner, Paavo Nurmi. At the start of one day's run, W.D. passes the sick-turkey pen. The narrator's careful and attentive recounting of W.D.'s observations and memories is almost clinical in detail. As W.D. passes by the pen, he notes that one of the sick turkeys[16] staggers over as if to peck him but then stops and hangs its head. Immediately, a memory of his wife, Lucille, surfaces: "He kept a picture of Lucille taped to the wall in his bedroom ... It showed Lucille sitting up in bed and staring emptily straight ahead—her typical Alzheimer's look ... Her head hung forward, it seemed, in exhaustion" (116-117). At the end of this description—certainly one, as Gerard Manley Hopkins would put it, "counter, original, strange"—the narrator records: "Sometimes in his dreams, since Lucille died, life was a mile and he could not run" (118). W.D's whole relation to his wife is filled with just such a painful and unexpressed sense of loss. Chapter three is a long flashback in which W.D. recalls his elopement. It is a minimalist celebration of Lucille and their marriage; its culmination is W.D.'s realization; "Lucille turned out to be exactly the woman he thought she was, quiet, pliable, unassuming, and innocent ..." (147), an elegiac tone that evokes pathos as the reader remembers the earlier image of Lucille's having ended her life with Alzheimer's.

A single positive turning point in the story is W.D.'s meeting with Kevin Luuya, whom W.D. meets for the first time when the boy is about ten years old and W.D. is seventy-four. Coming into Bartlett to run on the high school track, W.D. watches a Little League baseball game and observes Kevin, the weakest member of the team.[17] The son of a minister who is too wrapped up in his ministry to pay attention to his son, Kevin turns up again later in the fall when W.D. visits the library to watch videos, as he and Lucille had often done together. A latchkey child, Kevin is alone in the library, spending time after school before returning to his empty home. W.D. invites Kevin to watch videos with him so that, as with Lucille, he has someone to whom he can explain or comment on them. Thus begins the unlikely friendship of an aging man and a young boy, both lonely and without family support, attention, or affection.

Over the next eight years W.D. and Kevin watch videos and play pool together every week, and W.D. is surprised at how fond he becomes of the boy. The narrator notes, "The boy was on his mind day and night the way Lucille used to be." When, at the age of eighteen, Kevin joins the army, W.D. misses him and sends several postcards. Kevin writes a few letters back, but "after that he wrote nothing" (173). This characteristically flat, uninflected narrative report conveys a deep sense of loneliness and implies an even deeper sense of loss. It also helps explain Kevin's seemingly callous behavior when W.D. dies. Yet such reportage does not leave the reader with an impression of either disgust or pain. Instead, however quiet and laconic, the attentive narrative voice makes even such sadness luminous. The simply reported fact that "the boy was on his mind" is a brief revelation of what lies deeper in W.D.'s heart than even he might realize.

On the last day of his life—a fact to which the narrator alerts us—W.D. gets a sudden urge to visit his Aunt Nancy Clancy. It is March, just before the start of spring, but the reader doesn't learn that immediately, because W.D. has lost track of months as well as days. W.D. is now eighty-two years old, Kevin has returned from the army, and is caring for W.D. while Viola and Kermit winter in Florida. As the narrator briefly takes the young man's perspective, Kevin notes how rapidly W.D. is failing. As he helps W.D. into his winter coat, Kevin empathetically recalls how his parents "used to complain of the trouble it was to dress him to go out" (176). On the ride to town, W.D. thinks about his son, and this awakens a memory of the last day that he, Lucille, and Viola had seen Sonny. Arriving at the apartment where Nancy lives, Kevin and W.D. encounter a small boy bundled up for winter—just as W.D. is. With Kevin's earlier recollection of being bundled up as a child, this parallel is not lost on the reader. Kevin takes notice because "he [the little boy] spoke so clearly for his size. He stood no higher than W.D.'s cane" (183). The small boy is amazed to hear that the person W.D. and Kevin are visiting is one hundred years old. There is something almost uncanny in the appearance of this dwarf-sized human at this juncture in the story.

As Kevin and W.D. begin to climb the stairs in the building, which has no elevator, the narrator notes, "Kevin, following W.D., watched his old friend pause with both feet on each step, like a pilgrim approaching a shrine" (183). Then the narrator returns to W.D.'s perspective. "Halfway up the second flight W.D. felt giddy. A fountain seemed to be rising up his spine and bubbling in his brain … He felt as though he had outdistanced some vital part of himself—his lungs, his soul—and he was waiting for it to catch up" (183). When Nancy answers the door, W.D. mistakenly introduces Kevin as Sonny. Nancy invites them in, and Nancy and her nephew start to reminisce.

They argue gently over things in their past that they remember differently, and a tone of pathos grows. One recollection causes W.D. to laugh silently, "but [the laugh] grew until it shook him like a convulsion and caused tears to spring into his eyes. Kevin had never seen W.D. laugh before" (187). The pathos rises as W.D's mixture of laughter and tears causes the old man to wet his pants.

After tea, Aunt Nancy brings out a photograph album. W.D. misreads the pictures but won't admit that his vision is failing. Almost imperceptibly, the tone moves from pathos to uncanniness. The narrator reports, "They spent a long time absorbed in the album, speaking low and sighing, like sleepers mumbling in a dream" (191). Kevin, growing bored, looks out the living room window. The tone becomes even more uncanny as Kevin observes the little boy they had met earlier, looking at a kite caught in a tree. To relieve his boredom, Kevin goes downstairs and helps untangle the kite from the tree. Meanwhile, Nancy and W.D. continue to look at the photo album. A question posed by Nancy about Sonny brings back thoughts that had occupied W.D. on the trip to town. W.D. recalls that from the time Sonny was eleven they could not sign up for the annual father-son dinner at church because Sonny refused to go. At the memory, W.D. tries to hide the tears that begin once more to overflow his eyes. Once again the narrator's detailed but empathetic account implies more about regret and remorse than had he tried to put the feelings into words.

Outside, Kevin tries to help the little boy fly his kite, and their conversation is a study in miscommunication. It seems clear that the little boy is where Kevin was eight or ten years before; left on his own by a father who builds him a kite but is not around to help him fly it. After two attempts, Kevin manages to get the kite into the air, and then the level of uncanniness rises again as the narrator explains how odd the kite appears, heavy rather than fragile, "as though something earthbound had taken flight." Suddenly the boy shouts for Kevin to bring it down, informing him, incongruously only now, that his father had told him not to fly the kite because its string was too weak and would break. Kevin tries to bring the kite down, but it "spun in the sky and the string snapped. The boy was crying aloud" (194).

In this continued series of discrete impressions from which the reader must construct the whole, the narrator recounts how Kevin, turning back to the apartment, sees W.D. lying in a snow bank. As he tries to help the old man, he hears what he thinks is the ringing of a bell but it is, he realizes, Nancy in the apartment window, beating W.D.'s pipe on a brass bowl. "'He's dead. I know he's dead,'" she said. "'Looking at old pictures up here, he cried like a baby. And when he left, I came to the window to tell him he forgot his pipe, and I saw him fall.'" Kevin looks up past Nancy's window, sees a star in the sky and realizes that it is dark. After a further, brief exchange with Nancy Clancy, Kevin, who is shivering with cold, takes W.D.'s cane out of a snow bank and lays it next to the old man. When Nancy drops an afghan to cover W.D., Kevin instead wraps it around himself and then gets in his car.

For a moment, the story jumps back, and the narrator is now with the little boy, as he too hears the "bell." He goes to investigate and sees an old lady shouting from her window and an old man lying in the snow. The improbable and strange then become almost grotesque in a way reminiscent of Flannery O'Connor's work. The boy tries to raise W.D.'s arm, "but the old man, scowling, seemed determined to stay where he was" (197). From his car, Kevin calls to the boy to come and get in so they can look for his kite.

The flat, almost external account of the final events in W.D. Nestor's life do little to create a sense of hope, redemption, or forgiveness. Regret, heartache, and incomprehension seem the burden of the tale. Yet something in the selection of details as well as the style and focus of the story lends not just a sense of mystery but also a sense of enduring value unacknowledged by the characters. W.D.'s life has obviously not been a happy one. It has been a series of continual losses and surrender; loss of a brother, a son, a wife, a farm, his own powers, and those things he has come to appreciate, too late and perhaps too little. Ultimately it is gradual surrender to the forces of life that attack us all. Yet despite the narrator's implicit and explicit criticism of W.D. along with that of his relatives and the community in the alienated and alienating world of rural Minnesota, *The Life and Death of Nancy Clancy's Nephew* pays respectful attention to and affirms the essential mystery of human life. It does so as it acknowledges suffering and those moments of clarity and focus when startling images break through our consciousness. A kite broken free and whipping in the wind, the sudden appearance of a single star or a mysterious child, a banging pipe that sounds like a tolling bell; these are hardly unambiguous signs of hope, let alone harbingers of meaning and salvation. Yet these distinct images, like those in Roethke's poem, "The Small," bear witness to a sense of grace and presence in this world. And, in a way, the possibility of grace and redemption suffuses the scene of W.D.'s death through the evoking of such images.

Abandoned at the moment of his death by his only friend, while just one woman tolls a "bell," W.D. Nestor is a fitting tragic protagonist, not unlike the bereft, tragic protagonists in other Hassler novels. Like Miles Pruitt, for instance, W.D. Nestor experienced much of his life as "a ransom of cholers." But in each work the narrator's voice has, like Roethke in his poem, sought to show how "things throw light on things." Even in the midst of satiric criticism, the reader can find strangely consoling the narrator's perspective on these characters' fates, coming to view these often anguished lives with the same attentive, caring gaze that the narrator has lavished on them.

For some readers, it might prove worthwhile to consider *The Life and Death* as patterned on, or at least a commentary on

Flannery O'Connor's final short story, "Judgment Day." Like O'Connor's protagonist, Tanner, Nestor, too, feels he has to "get back" to an earlier connection in his life—in this case to Nancy Clancy—before he dies. His climb to her apartment is an ambiguously revelatory climb, as opposed to Tanner's "fall" into revelation.[18] More subdued than O'Connor's story, *The Life and Death* is still a cautionary tale about how a narrowing of one's emotional and spiritual arteries can lead to impoverishment of soul and outlook. W.D.'s moment of revelation, the second time in his life that he laughs and cries, is accompanied by ambiguous images and uncanny omens that suggest to the reader if not redemption at least a late but welcome moment of grace and peace. Of course the final two pages of the novella, as W.D. lies dead beneath Nancy Clancy's window, are harshly anti-climactic. In the end, the young man whom he had befriended leaves W.D. uncovered and abandoned as he drives off with the little boy whom he himself had befriended moments before. Kevin's final comment is a classic Hassler indictment. "He felt terrible. He knew now why he disliked old people. He hated the way they died" (198). Even Flannery O'Connor at her most satiric and brutal does not end her short stories in this way.

Conclusion:
Hassler's Significance

A s an only child, Hassler remembers a childhood luminous with his parents' love. He has recorded memories of that love in *Good People*, but perhaps the most vivid statement is the often-quoted passage from *Grand Opening*, referring to Brendan Foster, the seventh-grader who is a stand-in for Hassler himself. "His parents were linked by a love as direct and mute as a beam of light, and very few of Brendan's joys equaled that of coming between them and feeling himself pierced by that beam" (14). Hassler's sensitivity to children, their fears, their joys, and their dreams forms a rich background for the adult narratives. Frequently, too, as in *Grand Opening* itself, the interactions of youth and age, in this case Brendan and his Grandfather McMahon, make for an intergenerational dimension that enriches and deepens the larger narrative. With the examples of a grandfather and a maiden aunt to provide details, Hassler, from very early, showed a sensitivity to the elderly, understanding their fears, their ideals, and their stubbornness. Beginning in his earliest story, "Smalleye's Last Hunt," he patiently observes and records the habits and foibles of over a dozen memorable senior characters in almost as many novels. Perhaps it is this sensitivity to the elderly that attunes him to the dangers of loneliness, depression, and, its best antidote, the security and comfort of friends.

Unlike Flannery O'Connor, who studied at the prestigious

Iowa Writers' Workshop and then lived and worked for a time at Yaddo, the famed artists' community at Saratoga Springs, New York, or J. F. Powers, who broke into the East Coast literary scene with short stories in *The New Yorker*, Hassler learned to write in the high school and college classrooms where he taught, read, and wrote. But he also learned his craft from carefully and attentively observing his students and the small Minnesota towns from which they came. As noted in the biography chapter, Hassler had a "proclivity for patient watchfulness." His journals are rich in the detailed perceptions as well as the kind of anecdotes and images that would later become part of his books. As he imitated the sentences of John Cheever and the plots of William Trevor, while admiring the poetry of Theodore Roethke, Richard Hugo, and later Ted Kooser, he developed a lean and readable style, distinct in its ability to make the everyday world luminous and memorable.

As he began writing in the 1970s, he looked back to the 50s and early 60s as well as more recent decades. Focusing on the cities of central Minnesota, he almost inadvertently became a witness of significant changes in rural America, and the chronicler of the stresses that would wrack small-town America in the 80s, 90s, and beyond. Alcohol and drug addiction; sex abuse and dysfunctional families; relations with other races (in Hassler's case, Native Americans), all formed the texture of his greatest novels.

Starting with the "undistinguished poet" who reads "potty poetry" to a grade school class in *Staggerford*, Hassler, with a brand of Irish humor rich in grotesquerie and slapstick, satirizes with accuracy and humor the changing culture and many of the habits, customs, and social mores that had constituted what cohesiveness those rural communities possessed. Readers raised on the exaggerative satire and over-the top, no holds barred comedy of late-night television may find Hassler's brand of humor and satire somewhat tame. But the discerning reader will also see in some of his novels' situations the seeds of the more outrageous gags and send-ups popular in recent years. That reader will also find outlandish, unbelievable, and improbable-but-possible characters, situations, and plot contrivances enough to satisfy. In fact, it would be useful to compare Hassler's brand of novelistic comedy with one of the contemporary practitioners of such humor, Richard Russo. Russo praised Hassler's style, but the reader can find affinities between Russo's treatment of character in, for instance, *Nobody's Fool*, and Hassler's comedy throughout his career.

As has been noted, Hassler's novels frequently incorporate fragmented aspects of the hero's journey. The overall patterns of the novels often describe a circuitous path from chaos to order and reconciliation, rejuvenation, or reintegration into community. The different ways that he handles characters, develops themes, and introduces images restore a sense of order and peace into the chaotic world created by betrayal, illness, misunderstanding, and selfishness. Love discovered, first love with all its passion, love realized, enduring love, even illicit love, and moments of intimacy highlight early novels like *Simon's Night* and *The Love Hunter*, as well as later novels like *North of Hope* and *Rookery Blues*. Throughout it all, seasonal celebrations, festal meals, quiet conversations, quiet midnight meetings, and tranquil scenes from the heights reassure and "console" the reader who enters his narratives. Amid these more and less mundane events and comic episodes, and not a few melodramatic situations, his novels almost explode on occasion with suspense, surprise, and mystery. Some of his novels contain moments of such high prophetic eloquence as to create a sense of mystery that borders on the transcendent. Other novels build suspense and burst the bubble of apprehension with hilarious surprise, or, conversely, with shock and disbelief.

Reviewers and critics have praised Hassler for his straightforward, trustworthy approach to storytelling. The "unreliable narrator" is not a feature of Hassler's fiction. For readers of Don

Delillo or David Foster Wallace, the lack of postmodern fictional pyrotechnics may seem unfashionable. But viewed from the longer perspective of American fiction in the twentieth and twenty-first centuries, Hassler demonstrates a number of fruitful innovations within that tradition. His condensed time-frames, multiple plot-lines, creative use of flashback, point of view, interpolated anecdotes, letters, and journals show a relish for narrative novelty that should be considered an important contribution to the American novelistic tradition. After all, neither Flannery O'Connor nor J. F. Powers—nor one of Hassler's own models, John Cheever—were particularly innovative in narrative technique.

Hassler's final significance rests on the rich variety of everyday details and the variety of contrasts that his novels create. Mundane and mystical, comic and tragic; it is how, amid this diversity that Hassler makes "things throw light on things," turning mere contrast into insight and illumination. For these reasons, each of his novels bears reading and rereading, opening up a wealth of new insights to the reader prepared to receive them.

This admittedly sometimes long-winded survey of Jon Hassler's life and work only touches on many of the riches that await the reader who takes the time to enter Hassler's imagined Minnesota world. The "cuttings" on the figurative editing floor could probably make another book. Also largely untouched are the riches to be found in Hassler's journals and papers, which are housed at Saint John's University, Mankato State University, and the Hassler Library at Central Lakes Community College in Brainerd, Minnesota. The two published journals (*My Staggerford Journal* and *My Simon's Night Journal*) are samples of that richness. It remains, however, for younger scholars and adventurers to launch out into those largely uncharted waters, perhaps bringing back to the rest of us additional treasures of insight and illumination.

Endnotes

Introduction

1   This book will not deal with stage adaptations, except in passing, nor will it deal with the two books of non-fiction, *Good People* and *Stories Teachers Tell*.

2   He uses caricature sparingly, sometimes – as great authors do— turning a caricature into a fully-drawn character.

Chapter 1 - Biography

1   In a number of the paragraphs that follow, I am indebted for biographical information and quotations to Katherine Bailey, Susan Barbieri, Anne Cormier, Colin Covert, Rebecca Hill, Peg Meier, Debbie Musser, and Dick Dowd of *The Critic*, all of whose work can be found in the bibliography at the end of the book.

2   *Good People*, (Chicago: Loyola Press, 2001), p. 14. Hereafter cited in the text as (*GP*, page).

3   *Why I Am Still A Catholic*, edited by Kevin and Marilyn Ryan NY: Riverhead Books, 1998, p. 1.

4   Anne M. Cormier, "The Wit, Wisdom and Wonder of Writer Jon Hassler," *St. Anthony Messenger* November, 1998, pp. 16-21, p, 16. Hereafter cited in the text as (Wit, page).

5   *My Staggerford Journal* (New York: Ballantine, 1999), p. 3. Hereafter cited in the text as (*MSJ*, page).

6   *Why I Am Still A Catholic*, 4-5.

7   *Ibid.*

8   When Hassler published a revised version of this story in *Good People*, he changed the title of the Timmy Musser section to "A Nine-Year-Old Terrorist."

9   "The Last Generation of Readers?" Convocation speech, St. John's University, September 5, 1995,(published in *St. John's Magazine*, pp. 6-7), p. 6.

10 Joseph Plut, *Conversations with Jon Hassler* (Minneapolis: Nodin Press, 2010), p 10. Hereafter cited in the text as (*C*, page).

11 It was reprinted as "The Passion of Agatha McGee" in *McCall's*, July, 1977, 132; 174-75.

12 Joseph Plut's interview, "Jon Hassler: *Staggerford* Revisited," *Lake Country Journal* 6.1 (January-February, 2002, pp. 39-41), p. 39. Hereafter cited in the text as (*LCJM*, 2002, page).

13 "The Catholic Novels of Jon Hassler," Vol 163 No. 15 (November 17, 1990, pp. 366-67; 382. Greeley also wrote an appreciative piece commemorating Hassler's passing: "The Last Catholic Novelist: The grace-filled fiction of Jon Hassler" (*America* 199.no. 14, Whole No. 4833, November 8, 2008, pp. 21-24.

Chapter 2 - Hassler's Growth as a Writer

1 Cynthia Ozick, "Last But Not Least," *New York Times Book Review*, May 20, 2018, pp. 1 & 28.

2 See "Surrounded by Birches" in chapter seven of *Good People* for further recollections of his time at the cabin.

3 "Jon Hassler: Catholic Realist," *Renascence* 47.1 (Fall, 1994), 59-70

4 "Tender Mercies," *First Things* (August-September, 1994), 60-62.

5 "On the Novels of Jon Hassler," *South Dakota Review* 32.1 (1994), 47-87.

6 The late Andrew Greeley also did a survey evaluation, "The Catholic Novels of Jon Hassler," *America* 363.15 (November 17, 1990). But like Truesdale, he makes the occasional factual error, saying, for instance, that *Grand Opening* "returns to the Staggerford of 1945" (367).

7 Among the thinkers who have discussed an Incarnational view of the world should be included Pierre Teilhard de Chardin, David Tracy, and the late Fr. Andrew Greeley. All of these thinkers would ascribe to the truth of Gerard Manley Hopkins' (poetic) statement: "The world is charged with the grandeur of God."

8 "Hope on Ice: The Felicitous Fiction of Jon Hassler" (*Crisis*, 19, no. 5, May, 2001).

9 See particularly her comments in various essays of *When I Was Young I Read Books* (New York: Farrar, Straus and Giroux, 2012).

It also applies to Mary Relindes Ellis, author of *The Turtle Warrior* and *Bohemian Flats*.

10　Paraphrasing William Carlos Williams as he, Donoghue, speaks about J.F. Powers " ("The Storyteller," "Bookend," *New York Times Book Review,* March 26, 2000, p. 35).

11　Joyce Carol Oates criticized *Staggerford* for "devolving into a series of unexceptional comic scenes reminiscent of television" (*C*, 21). "Four Novels," *New York Times Book Review,* July 24, 1977.

12　Dick Dowd, "Intrerview with Jon Hassler," *The Critic* 49.4 (1995), 18-28.

13　One of the most famous studies of the hero's journey is T. S. Eliot's referencing Jessie L. Weston's *From Ritual to Romance* in his notes to *The Waste Land.*

14　"In fact, it is Hassler's use of archetypal themes like hope and redemption, as well as his explicit treatment of Catholicism, that has attracted the attention of Catholic critics like Andrew Greeley," Joe Towalski, "Conversation with a Catholic Novelist," *Catholic Digest* August, 1998, pp. 6-13 (p 8).

15　The term comes from "numen," a term which Jung and Neumann use to describe the more than natural and material.

16　Ed Block, "A Conversation with Jon Hassler," *Image* No. 19 Spring, 1998, pp. 41-58), p. 58.

17　In his poem, "Pied Beauty." It is not unusual that Hopkins has been seen as an early "ecological" poet. Hassler's love of the "local" includes the "local" details of rural Minnesota: its birds, its trees, its small towns, its local customs, however twisted, "denatured," or debased they sometimes are, by economics, forgetfulness, carelessness, and greed.

18　As will be noted in later chapters, I base much of what I say about Hassler and Native Americans on the reports of Rev. James Notebaart, who, for over twenty-five years, ministered to Native Americans through The Office of Indian Ministry, and as pastor of a Native American congregation in Minneapolis, Minnesota.

19　The late Andrew Greeley noted approvingly that "Hassler's world is the same as that of Louise Erdrich – northern Minnesota and the Native American reservations that dot that part of the state" (*America*, November, 1990).

Chapter 3 - The Short Stories and *Four Miles to Pinecone*

1   Both were published in the well-known journal, *Prairie Schooner* (Summer, 1972 and Winter, 1974). A footnote to "Willowby's Indian" also refers to Hassler having, by 1974, published in *Sunday Clothes, Four Quarters, North American Review,* and *South Dakota Review.*

2   "Willowby's Indian" even includes explicit reference to the American Indian Movement (AIM) and one of its better-known leaders, Russell Means.

3   Jon Tevlin reviewed *Keepsakes* for the *Minneapolis Star Tribune* on November 7, 1999.

4   Hassler's friend, Joseph Plut, interviewed the author about both of these collections. This chapter refers to these unpublished interviews; the first (about *Keepsakes*) conducted on April 3, 2003, the second (about *Rufus at the Door and Other Stories*) on April 10, 2003.

5   To Debbie Musser in *The Catholic Spirit* (June 22, 2006), Hassler said, "Ever since I was a child, I've enjoyed watching priests. They're all different, and I find them absolutely fascinating." www.thecatholicspirit.com/archives.php?article=5556).

6   In an interview with Dick Dowd for *The Critic*, Hassler told of "this older priest, a doddering old man, who made me an altar boy . . . I would work for him. I cut the grass around the rectory . . .and he would pay me. He would open his checkbook and, every Saturday, he would ask me the same question: 'What's your name?' (27).

7   The moment of "recognition" or "epiphany" became a key feature of the short story form, at least since the Guy de Maupassant, O'Henry, or James Joyce's *Dubliners.*

8   In the interview, Plut compares "The Life and Death of Delano Klein" to Edgar Lee Masters in his *Spoon River Anthology* – "pared down diction, matter-of-fact reporting, somewhat bleak outcome." Hassler admits to having seen Woody Allen's *Zelig* and Peter Sellers in *Being There* about the time he wrote the story.

9   "Willowby" is a different spelling that is used in an early draft of *Staggerford*. Readers familiar with Hassler's fiction will also recognize a number of names – Romberg and Crowninshield, for instance – that occur not only in *Grand Opening* but other Hassler novels as well.

10 *McCall's* published "The Passion of Agatha McGee," "The Holy War" (based on his daughter's experience of confirmation in Brainerd) and "Midnight Visit" (Janet Raft's giving birth, which became the beginning of *A Green Journey*). According to Hassler in the interview, this title refers to "the Chicago Seven" at the1968 Democratic convention.

11 Accepted for publication in September, 1976, within ten days of *Staggerford* having been accepted (*C*, 5).

12 With mystery and one seemingly good-hearted villain, it might remind some readers of the work of Robert Louis Stevenson.

13 Tom's asking the detective whether he and Mouse will ever be friends again adds a touch of pathos to the story of the boys' relationship.

Chapter 4 - Early Successes

1 One of the first of many parties Hassler includes in his novels, this Halloween Party is a veritable Saturnalia.

2 *Simon's Night & My Simon's Night Journal* (Minneapolis: Nodin Press, 2013), p. 271.

3 Fr. James Notebaart says that Native Americans would call Miss Frost an "apple": red on the outside but white on the inside.

4 As noted, I rely for the veracity of my conclusions on conversations about *Jemmy* with Fr. James Notebaart.

5 Somewhat melodramatic here, as Hassler can be at moments of high emotion. Hearing a subdued echo of Oscar Wilde's *The Picture of Dorian Gray* would not be inappropriate for anyone remembering Hassler's Irish background and his years of teaching high school and college English.

6 See Joseph Plut's insightful comments on the novel's beginnings (*C*, 27-28). Page numbers in parentheses refer to the hardbound copy of *Simon's Night*.

7 *Locus amoenus* is a technical literary term for an earthly paradise or a place of comfort and repose.

8 Page numbers in parentheses refer to the hardbound copy of *The Love Hunter*.

9 A curiosity: the title Ginsberg suggested -- but which Hassler and his agent thought "lame" -- was actually the title of a song

in "Bookends," a very successful album by Simon and Garfunkel, released about the same time as the novel was written. The song, "Old Friends," includes a line ("Old friends, sat on a park bench like bookends") recalling the line in *The Love Hunter*: "Like flowers, like old men on park benches, Chris's natural inclination was toward the sunlight, away from the dark . . ." (73).

10 Hassler says that the DeNiro movie had nothing in common with the themes of *The Love Hunter*. But, interestingly enough, the movie and the novel do share a number of themes, and even an unusually similar scene. The movie begins as a hunting trip with friends, after which there is betrayal, and a friend's death. Early in the film there is a drunken argument which one character ends by discharging a rifle.

11 As Olympus Mall was a kind of journey into the underworld, the two days at Blackie's camp constitute a similar kind of comic "hell." Joseph Plut and Hassler touch on this similarity (*C*, 79).

12 One of the first comes as they drive north and Chris notices "blocks of cloud" (24). Acrylic paintings, Renoir (49) and Van Dyck and Goya at the Institute of Arts in Minneapolis (221,222) also have important parts in the story.

Chapter 5 - Maturity

1 Hereafter, quotations from the hardcover copy of *Grand Opening* will be given in parentheses (page).

2 Anton Chekhov (1860-1904) was a Russian doctor, playwright, and short story writer, much of whose work was both elegiac and tragic.

3 Hereafter, quotations from the hardback edition of *North of Hope* will appear in parentheses (page).

4 Hassler uses this spelling. It is also more commonly spelled "Ojibwe."

5 Reviewing the novel – and Hassler's career – for *America*, the late Andrew Greeley said "a fascinating mystery story, a compelling suspense novel and a poignant love story" (367). "The Catholic Novels of Jon Hassler, *America* 363.15, November 17, 1990.

6 William Jayne, in the *Washington D.C. Times* (October 22, 1990). See *C*. 166-67.

7   Which contrasts with its "vast kitchen" (167).

8   Hereafter, quotations from the hardback version of *A Green Journey* will appear in parentheses (page).

9   Earlier the reader had seen Agatha "enjoying the play of the hot breeze through her sky-blue blouse, through her blue-rinsed hair" (44), suggesting that the repetition of the cliché "let your hair down" is – at least unconsciously – by design.

10 The theme of satisfaction with, or reconciliation to life will surface again – somewhat surprisingly – with reference to Randy Meers, suggesting a further similarity between the two.

11 This is one of two significant scenes involving gulls, and the novel's key demonstration of Hassler's continued fascination with birds.

12 This is a further elaboration of the principles that Otis Chapman articulates in *Jemmy*. They are also, arguably, part of Hassler's theory of art.

13 The stones seeming "lighter in weight than the gray, not so earthbound" (276) is a rather heavy-handed hint of what is to come, but most readers would probably not catch it on first reading.

14 With this third repetition, the "high notes" comment reveals itself as one more running gag.

15 Hereafter, quotations from the hardbound edition of *Dear James* will be indicated by parentheses (page).

16 After the audience, as Agatha and James are standing, talking about the pope, a white pigeon "walked stumpily over to him and stood now, unmoving, beside his right foot" (310). On the next page "The white pigeon at James's feet cleared its throat and cooed" (311). Their walk back to the piazza, before they discuss the audience, was accompanied by "birds outnumbering the people, flocks of gray and white pigeons moving in slow circles over the sun-warmed stones and exchanging utterances made up of long vowels, 'Due to doom' the birds seemed to be saying."

17 For Hassler, who, as an English teacher must have taught the poems of W. B. Yeats at some time in his career, Agatha's calming Bobby by the sea has echoes of Yeats's Cuchulain, Aengus, and Michael Robartes' poems.

Chapter 6 - Back to Campus

1   Hereafter, quotations from the hardbound edition of *Rookery Blues* are indicated in parentheses (page).

2   Though a "rookery" is a dwelling for "rooks," a species of crow, the title contributes nothing more than its associations to the novel's bird imagery.

3   Given Hassler's experience running an outdoor movie theater during several summers, perhaps a comparison with filmic techniques would be more appropriate.

4   Here Hassler again takes the "long view," as he had done in a number of earlier novels, like *Staggerford*, *The Love Hunter*, and *A Green Journey*.

5   Hereafter, quotations from the hardbound edition of *The Dean's List* are indicated in parentheses (page).

6   The title is a pun on the academic honor and a list of tasks that Leland Edwards keeps jotting down.

7   "Graves of Academe," *Washington Post*, June 1, 1997.

8   The dedication, to Dean Robert L. Spaeth, acknowledges Hassler's appreciation for his dean at St. John's. See "Sacred Places," chapter six of *Good People* for a portrait of Bob Spaeth (pp. 78-81).

9   Hassler's "creation" of a nationally famous and beloved. though hard to get along with poet (modeled on Robert Frost *C*, 240) – along with his reputation -- whose poetry everyone knows and is able to recite, is one of the signal achievements of the book.

10   The poet's name is an interesting shortening of the title of John Cheever's last novel, *Falconer*, which Hassler had read (see *Simon's Night Journal*) and – after initially *not* liking – said he enjoyed. While Cheever's title refers to a prison, in which the protagonist is confined, the name itself – and the avian associations – might have appealed to Hassler. They certainly add resonance to the poet and his reputation.

11   The actual poems are ones that Hassler himself wrote – and published in a chapbook, *The Red Oak* -- years before.

12   Described as "the ancient Roman festival of Saturn in December, which was a period of general merrymaking and was the predecessor of Christmas," and an occasion of wild revelry.

13   One could argue that such a poem – which would be the ancient form of "epithalamion," or wedding celebration – is a further archetypal feature to end the novel.

Chapter 7 - The Final Years

1   Hereafter, quotations from the hardbound edition of *The Staggerford Flood* are indicated in parentheses (page).

2   "Yesterday's Garbage," found in *Keepsakes* (1999).

3   "Nancy Clancy's Nephew," found in *Rufus at the Door and Other Stories*.

4   The introduction of "congestive heart failure" comes at the same time that Lillian's "testiness" is broached for the first time, showing how carefully these various hints are planned.

5   The reader doesn't learn this until the narrator identifies Sunday as Palm Sunday (93).

6   The *Triduum*, Latin for "three days," refers to the final, most solemn days before Easter.

7   Hereafter, quotations from the hardback edition of *The New Woman* are indicated in parentheses (page).

8   She doesn't read further to learn that the train would only travel on a circular track in some western desert. In light of more recent events with North Dakota's Bakken oil trains, this uncanny moment has peculiarly contemporary resonances.

9   Hassler used this term on a few occasions to refer to a character's enemies. "Nemesis" is an allusion to the Greek goddess of retribution.

10   Hereafter, quotations from the paperback edition of *The Staggerford Murders* are indicated by parentheses (page).

11   This digressive anecdote also belongs to the "tall tale" genre, or the genre of "miracles" such as are reported in newspapers like *The National Inquirer* (which Hassler had satirized, most recently, in *The Staggerford Flood*).

12   Hereafter, quotations from *The Life and Death of Nancy Clancy's Nephew*, in the paperback edition of *The Staggerford Murders* are indicated in parentheses (page).

13   W.D.'s weakening eyesight (which is implied in the first

paragraph of the short story) is a motif that assumes increased prominence as the novella proceeds.

14 A symbolic reading of the story (such as one might apply to a story by Flannery O'Connor) would emphasize Nancy Clancy's literal "aloofness" looking down from her third floor window in the final pages of the novella.

15 There are just enough repetitions of W.D.'s efforts to continue running in order to emphasize the senior's need for 1) routine, 2) something that is meaningful, and 3) a reminder that he is still capable.

16 Hassler's familiar use of birds as suggestive images is here in evidence.

17 W.D. habitually refers to Kevin by the name he saw printed across the back of his baseball jersey: an advertisement for "Charlie's Shoes." Like other readers seldom hearing W. D.'s given name, the narrator's referring to Kevin as "Charlie's Shoes" is another diminishment of character.

18 Another similarity to O'Connor: like O.E. Parker (in the story, "Parker's Back"), Hassler's W.D. Nestor suffers the diminution of himself by being referred to by his initials only.

BIBLIOGRAPHY

Barbieri, Susan M. "Good People," review of Hassler's *Good People*, *Minnesota Monthly*, August, 2001, pp. 54-57.

Bailey, Katherine. "Jon Hassler," PW Interviews, *Publishers Weekly* May 17, 1993, (pp. 52-53).

Bakhtin, Mikhail. *The Dialogic Imagination: Four Essays*. Austin, TX: U of T P (1982).

Balthasar, Hans Urs von. *The Grain of Wheat* (San Francisco: Ignatius Press, 1995.

Block, Ed. "A Conversation with Jon Hassler," *Image* No. 19 Spring, 1998, pp. 41-58.

————. "A Grace-Filled Light: The Transformational World of Jon Hassler," *America* Vol. 213 No. 6 Whole No 5099 (September 14, 2015), pp. 30-32.

————. "'A Ransom of Cholers': Catastrophe, Consolation, and Catholicism in Jon Hassler's *Staggerford, North of Hope*, and 'The Life and Death of Nancy Clancy's Nephew,'" chapter Seven in *Between Human and Divine: The Catholic Vision in Contemporary Literature*, edited by Mary Reichardt,. Catholic University of America Press (2010), pp. 119-135.

————. Review of *Rookery Blues*, by Jon Hassler, *Milwaukee Journal-Sentinel*, Sunday, August 6, 1995, p. E6.

Bly, Robert. Interview by Keith Thompson in *New Age Journal*, May, 1982.

————. *Iron John: A Book About Men*. Reading, MA: Addiston-Wesley, 1990.

Chardin, Pierre Teihlard de. *The Phenomenon of* Man. London: Collins, 1959.

————. *The Divine Milieu*. New York: Harper, 1960.

Cheever, John. "The Swimmer," "Goodbye My Brother," "The Fourth Alarm," in *Collected Stories and Other Writings*. New York: Library of America 188.

———. *Falconer*. New York: Knopf, 1977.

Covert Colin. *Minneapolis Star-Tribune*, Thursday, August 3, 1995, pp. E-1 and E-8).

Cormier, Anne, M. "The Wit, Wisdom and Wonder of Writer Jon Hassler," *St. Anthony Messenger* November, 1998, pp. 16-21.

Donoghue, Denis. "The Storyteller," "Bookend," *New York Times Book Review,* March 26, 2000, p. 35.

Delillo, Don. *Zero K.* New York: Scribner, 2016.

Dowd, Dick, Intrerview with Jon Hassler, *The Critic* 49.4 (1995), 18-28.

Eliade, Mircea. *The Sacred and the Profane*. New York: Harcourt, Brace, Jovanovich, 1959)

———. *The Myth of the Eternal Return* (1949; English Translation, New York: Pantheon, 1954.

Eliot. T. S. *The Waste Land* (1922).

Ellis, Mary Relindes. *The Turtle Warrior*. New York: Viking, 2005.

———. *The Bohemian Flats*. Minneapolis, MN: U of M P, 2014.

Englert, Jim. *A Badbattle Bibliography*. Mankato, MN: Mutual Aid Books, 2015.

Friel, Brian. *Dancing at Lughnasa*. First produced, 1990. London: Faber and Faber, 1998.

———. *Faith Healer.* First produced, 1979. London: Faber and Faber, 1981.

———. *Molly Sweeney*. New York: Penguin, 1994.

———. *Philadelphia, Here I Come!* (1964). New York: Farrar, Straus, and Giroux, 1965.

Frye, Northrop. *Anatomy of Criticism*. Princeton: Princeton U P, 1957.

Girard, René. *Deceit, Desire & the Novel*. Baltimore: Johns Hopkins U P, 1961.

———. *The Scapegoat*. Baltimore: Johns Hopkins U P, 1982.

———. *Violence and the Sacred*. Baltimore: Johns Hopkins U P, 1972.

Greeley, Andrew. "The Catholic Novels of Andrew Greeley," Vol 163 No. 15 (November 17, 1990, pp. 366-67; 382.

———. "The Last Catholic Novelist: The grace-filled fiction of Jon Hassler" (*America* 199.no. 14, Whole No. 4833, November 8, 2008, pp. 21-24.

Hassler, Jon (dates and publishers indicate first edition publication)

_____. *Staggerford*. New York: Random House, 1977.

_____. *Four Miles to Pinceone* (young adult). Random, Fawcett 1977.

_____. *Simon's Night*. New York: Atheneum, 1979.

_____. *Jemmy* (young adult). New York: Fawcett Ballantine, 1980.

_____. *The Love Hunter*. New York: William Morrow, 1981.

_____. *A Green Journey*. New York: William Morrow, 1985.

_____. *Grand Opening*. New York: William Morrow, 1987,

_____. *North of Hope*. New York: Ballantine, 1990.

_____. *Dear James*. New York: Ballantine, 1993.

_____. *Rookery Blues*. New York: Ballantine, 1995.

_____. *The Dean's List*. New York: Ballantine, 1997.

_____. *My Staggerford Journal*. New York: Ballantine, 1999.

_____. *Underground Christmas*. Afton, MN: Afton Historical Press, 1999.

_____. *Keepsakes*. MN: Afton Historical Press, 1999.

_____. *Rufus at the Door and Other Stories*. MN: Afton Historical Press, 2000.

_____. *Good People*. Chicago: Loyola Press, 2001.

_____. *The Staggerford Flood*. New York: Viking Penguin, 2002.

_____. *The Staggerford Murders*. New York: Viking Plume, 2004.

_____. *The New Woman*. New York: Viking Penguin, 2005

Articles and Interviews

———. "Agatha McGee, John Milton, and I," *South Dakota Quarterly* 33:3-4 (Fall-Winter, 1995), pp. 176-177.

———. "Remembering Churches" in *Why I Am Still A Catholic*, edited by Kevin and Marilyn Ryan NY: Riverhead Books, 1998.

———. "The Last Generation of Readers?" Convocation speech, St. John's University, September 5, 1995,(published in *St. John's Magazine*, pp. 6-7).

———. "Of Colleges, Characters, & Courage: An Interview with Jon Hassler," by Joseph Plut, *Lake Country Journal* March-April, 1997), pp. 34-38.

Short Stories

———. "The Undistinguished Poet," *South Dakota Review,*1972.

———. "Smalleye's Last Hunt," *Prairie Schooner* 1972.

———. "Willowby's Indian," *Prairie Schooner* 1974.

———. "Chase" was published in *Milkweed Chronicle* then referred to as published in *Loonfeather* (Fall, 1979) as "Portrait of the Novelist as a Young Man."

———. "Rufus at the Door," *Stiller's Pond* (An anthology of Midwestern writing).

———. "Anniversary," *Redbook*, July, 1978.

———. "The Passion of Agatha McGee," "The Holy War" and "Midnight Visit," *McCall's* (Jim Englert's *Badbattle Bibliography* lists the dates of 1978 and 1979, but with question marks).

———. "Christmas in Omaha," *Image*, 11 (Fall, 1995), 15-34.

Two interviews on PBS KTCA "Almanac," on *Dear James* (April 18, 1993) and *The Dean's List* (June 6, 1997) and a production of *The Staggerford Murders* on WCCO's "Dimension," March 8, 1999.

Master's Thesis: "Moral Choice in the Novels of Ernest Hemingway. Fargo, N.D. U of N D,1961.

Hays, Charlotte. "Hope on Ice: The Felicitous Fiction of Jon Hassler" (*Crisis*, 19, no. 5, May, 2001).

Hemingway, Ernest. "The Short, Happy Life of Francis Macomber," in *The Complete Short Stories of Ernest Hemingway*. New York: Scribner's, 1987.

Hill, Rebecca. "Remembering Jon Hassler," *Minnesota Monthly*, May 114, 2008, http://www.minnestamonthly.com/June-2008/Remembering-Hassler/.

Hopkins, Gerard Manley. "God's Grandeur," in *Gerard Manley Hopkins: The Oxford Authors*, edited by Catherine Phillips. New York: Oxford U P, 1986, p. 128.

Hynes, Joseph. "Midwestern Loneliness," *Commonweal*, Vol. 122, No. 19, November 3, 1995.

Jayne, William. Review of *North of Hope, Washington D.C. Times* (October 22, 1990).

Jung, Carl Gustav. *Memories, Dreams, and Reflections*. (1962) English Translation; New York: Pantheon 1963.

Lange, Dan. (DVD interview of Jon Hassler, in the author's possession).

Loyola, Ignatius of. *The Spiritual Exercises*. Translation and Contemporary Reading David L. Fleming, S.J. St. Louis, MO: Instistute of Jesuit Resources, 1978.

The Love She Sought, a made-for-television adaptation of *A Green Journey*, available on Netflix.

Low, Anthony. "Jon Hassler: Catholic Realist," *Renascence* 47.1 (Fall, 1994), 59-70.

McDermott, Alice. "A Conversation with Alice McDermott," *Image* no. 52, Winter 2007, pp. 61-72.

———. "The Lunatic in the Pew," *Boston College Magazine* (Summer, 2003) http://bcm.bc.edu/issues/summer_2003/ft_natural.html

MWS "'Carry Thee Whither Thou Wouldst Not'," *Christianity and the Arts* August-November, 1996.

Meier, Peg. "The Will To Write," *Minneapolis Star Tribune*, Sunday, June 5, 2005, Variety Section, page E1, continuing on page E6.

Musser, Debbie. "Faith, hope, redemption are themes in Jon Hassler's novels," *The Catholic Spirit* (June 22, 2006) http://www.thecatholicspirit.com/archives.php?article=5556

The National Catholic Reporter is quoted as calling *AGJ* "a novel of personal discovery and transformation" (*C*, 105).

Neumann, Eric. *The Great Mother*. New York: Pantheon, 1955.

———. *Art and the Creative Unconscious*. 1949; rpt; Princeton, NJ: Princeton U P, 1959.

———. *The Origins and History of Consciousness*. 1949; rpt; New York: Pantheon, 1954.

New York Times Obituary, March 28, 2008.

Oates, Joyce Carol. Review of *Staggerford*. "Four Novels," *New York Times Book Review* July 24, 1977. www.nytimes.com/1977/07/24/archives/four-novels-novels.html

O'Connor, Flannery. "A Good Man Is Hard To Find," "Good Country People" "The Lame Shall Enter First," "Parker's Back," "Displaced Person," "Judgment Day," in *Collected Works*. New York: Library of America, 1988.

Ozick, Cynthia. "Last But Not Least," *New York Times Book Review*, May 20, 2018, pp. 1 & 28.

Percy, Walker. 1989 Jefferson Lecture in the Humanities, entitled "The Fateful Rift: The San Andreas Fault in the Modern Mind."

Plut, Joseph. *Conversations with Jon Hassler* (Minneapolis: Nodin Press, 2010).

———. "Jon Hassler: *Staggerford* Revisited," *Lake Country Journal* 6.1 (January-February, 2002, pp. 39-41.

———. Hassler, Jon. *Simon's Night, Including Jon Hassler's "My Simon's Night Journal,"* edited and annotated by Joseph Plut (Minneapolis, Nodin Press, 2013).

Postlethwaite, Diana. "Graves of Academe," *Washington Post*, June 1, 1997.

Powers, J. F. "Lions, Harts, and Leaping Does" in *The Stories of J. F. Powers.* Introduction by Denis Donoghue. New York: New York Review of Books, 2000.

———. *Morte d'Urban.* New York: Doubleday, (1962).

———. *Wheat That Springeth Green.* New York: Alfred A. Knopf, 1988.

Propp, Vladimir. *The Morphology of the Folktale.* Austin: U of T P, 1968.

Robinson, Marilynne. *When I Was Young I Read Books.* New York: Farrar, Straus and Giroux, 2012).

———. *Absence of Mind,* New Haven, CT: Yale U P, 2010.

Roethke, Theodore. "The Small" in *The Collected Verse of Theodore Roethke: Words for the Wind.* Bloomington, IN, Indiana U P, 1961; rpt. 1966, p. 178.

Scott, A. O. Review of Marilynne Robinson's *Home. New York Times Book Review*, Sunday, September 21, 2008, p. 16.

Sheffer, Roger. Review of *Rookery Blues* and music (*C*, 211)

Shelby, Don. Reviewed *The Staggerford Murders* briefly on his *Dimension Report*, on WCCO Television, Minneapolis, March 3, 1999.

Shepard, Sam. *Buried Child.* New York: Knopf/Doubleday, 1978.

Stegner, Wallace. *Wolf Willow: A History, A Story and A Memory of the Last Plains Frontier.* New York: Viking, 1962.

Sutter, Bart, Review of *The Love Hunter. Minneapolis Star-Tribune*, June 28, 1981.

Tevlin, Jon. Review of *Keepsakes, Minneapolis Star Tribune* on November 7, 1999.

Towalski, Joe. "Conversation with a Catholic Novelist," *Catholic Digest* August, 1998, pp. 6-13.

Tracy, David. *The Analogical Imagination: Christian Theology and the Culture of Pluralism.* New York: Crossroad, 1981.

Trevor, William. *The Children of Dynmouth.* New York: Penguin, 1982.

Truesdale, C. W. "On the Novels of Jon Hassler," *South Dakota Review* 32..1 (1994), 47-87.

Twain, Mark. *Autobiographical Writings*, New York : Penguin Books, 2012. See also

———. *Autobiography of Mark Twain*, Berkeley: University of California Press, 2010-2015.

Wallace. David Foster. "Mr. Squishy," in *Oblivion*.

Weston, Jesse. *From Ritual to Romance*. 1920 rpt. Courier Corporation, 1997.

Williams, Sarah T. "Obituary," *Minneapolis Star Tribune*, March 20, 2008.

Zaleski, Phillip. "Tender Mercies," *First Things* (August-September, 1994), 60-62.

INDEX